Sharehouse Confidential

Sharehouse Confidential

◆

Sex and the Single Life Inside an Epicurean Beach House

a memoir

John Blesso

Silk City Press
New York

Sharehouse Confidential
Sex and the Single Life Inside an Epicurean Beach House

ISBN: 978-0-9654452-3-8

Author photo by Todd Chalfant

Printed in the United States of America

For my mother, my father, and my brothers

I returned,
and saw under the sun,
that the race is not to the swift,
nor the battle to the strong,
neither yet bread to the wise,
nor yet riches to men of understanding,
nor yet favor to men of skill;
but time and chance
happeneth to them all.
—*Ecclesiastes 9:11*

Life is what happens when you are busy making other plans.
—*John Lennon*

Contents

Acknowledgment

Since certain so-called memoirists have recently pissed all over our thriving genre, blurring the lines between poetic license and outright horseshit, I wish to state, categorically, that this memoir, and all events depicted in it (with the sole exception of a violent act perpetrated against a senior citizen) are true. Television icons will never couch-grill me under the glare of klieg lights and a studio audience as to whether or not I actually ditched the corporate world in New York City to purchase, renovate, and manage a beach sharehouse. I shall not be pressed as to whether or not the people depicted in these pages actually participated in the array of sexual and bacchanalian exploits retold here.

This story unfolds during the summer of 2005, when more than sixty people (not including guests) stayed at the Chance beach house. In an effort to be less sadistic than Gabriel Garcia Marquez, this book contains far fewer characters, many of which are composites. Several names, physical descriptions, occupations, and other identifiers have been changed to protect the very, very guilty. Additionally, some events and details from other seasons have been incorporated, while some incidents have been compressed into a single weekend to further streamline the narrative.

I'd like to thank all past and present members of the Chance beach house, as well as the town of Kismet.

Introduction

It is the Fourth of July, 2005, and I have already broken Rule Number One.

Bystanders clad in bikinis and swim trunks crowd the railing of my house's second-story deck overlooking the federal preserve between Pine and Seabay Walks in Kismet, the westernmost town on Fire Island, a thirty-two-mile barrier island—most of it undeveloped—that lies south of Long Island, west of the Hamptons. Instead of looking out at the deer flitting through the overgrown brush, or at the cardinals lighting off from misty treetops, people are staring down below. I approach the railing and peer over their shoulders, glancing down upon the bodies crammed into the jacuzzi.

All of the women are topless.

It is 6:30 p.m.

Like most Americans, we are commemorating that proud day in our nation's history when a band of ragtag peasant farmers—eighteenth-century shitkickers, really—told the vast British Empire to go fuck itself. There is a serious level of commemoration happening at my house. Cruising on adrenaline, I contemplate leaping over the railing. It is a fifteen-foot drop to the jacuzzi, but in my frenzied state I imagine that the bobbing breasts might break my fall.

I turn and face a petite Asian woman staring hard at what remains of the whole pig I had roasted earlier that day. Fifty-five pounds of oink picked clean in less than an hour by my housemates and random drop-ins who transformed our pig roast into a raging, impromptu party. All that remains is the spine and the head. I cut a path around her, not wanting to deal with yet another outraged vegetarian.

"Hey!" She hooks my arm. "Did you cook this pig?"

I'm through apologizing to the herbivores drinking for free at my house. "Yes. I cracked open its rib cage with my bare hands."

"Cool," she says. "Would you mind if I broke open the head?"

I search her deadpan expression for any trace of irony or sarcasm, but she is serious.

"Not at all," I say. "Be my guest."

"Do you have any tools?"

"I've got tools." I wonder if she belongs to a sharehouse. (Members in a beach sharehouse purchase a set number of weekends during which they commune with a pool of people from their demographic who, more often than not, are single.) Any woman who in the middle of an unhinged party decides that she wants to dissect the head of a pig, well, that's the kind of woman I want in my sharehouse.

"I'll be right back," I say, stepping inside. I file through the crowd toward the stairs. One of my house members calls out to me, looking for the juicer and triple sec.

"The juicer is up on that shelf next to the ice cream maker!" I shout over the blaring music. "There's more triple sec beneath the wet bar!"

Someone else wants paper towels. I point out the holder still bearing the end of a roll. This person, however, needs an entire roll. I don't want to know why; I just point out the reserve supply on the overhead shelf that runs the length of my kitchen, a command center fully loaded with all manner of cooking equipment, some of it commercial grade. I'm still trying to make it downstairs, but a throng of people I don't know is pushing up the stairwell, their heads swiveling and straining with that classic look of need: they need drinks; they need food; they need to find out who is single, or, more importantly, who is available.

Beneath the stairwell, my tools are in disarray from my ongoing renovations, a project that began the previous March. It's like Bob Vila on acid. Suddenly, I remember the scene in my hot tub. No stranger to obsessive-compulsiveness, I bolt outside and down the ramp to the jacuzzi. People above cheer as I lean back over the corner of the tub. Digital cameras flash as one of the women pulls me down and further in, my head mashing up against something soft. When I power out of the tub, the back of my Bermuda shorts is soaked. This is when I see that some of the women aren't just topless; they are nude.

Back inside, I sift through my tools, grabbing a hammer and an old screwdriver with a fat, blunted tip. My cordless power tools lie in a pile, and I grab the drill and the sawzall, my absolute favorite tool. Shaped like a submachine gun, it is loaded with eight inches of wild, reciprocating blade that will rough-cut anything in its path. I snap a battery into its housing, imagining—as I always do—that I'm jamming a clip into an Uzi. Clutching it over my head, I charge upstairs while squeezing the trigger, the juiced motor buzzing and chugging with life.

Out on the deck, the Asian woman is still staring at the pig's head. I rouse her with another depression of the sawzall trigger.

"Hmm," she says. "Do you maybe have something less powerful?"

I place my power tools on the table and hand over the hammer and the screwdriver. She sets to work as Jeffrey, our resident stoner, steps in front of me.

"Dude," he says, "something is totally wrong with the keg."

This he tells me as though we have suddenly become trapped in a coal mine, although Jeffrey regularly freaks over the slightest wrinkle in his partying sail. I head back inside, crossing my living room to the kitchen, where the kegerator resides opposite our large dining table. I open the door and see that the CO_2 gauge had dropped off to zero. I crank it up to four and close the door.

"Rock on, dude," I call out. Engrossed by the stream of beer now pouring into his cup, Jeffrey doesn't hear me mimicking him. Taking in the sight of this full-on fiesta, I consider how I am personally responsible for this chaos, how I ran myself ragged during the previous two years to create this. It is something of a joke that I, ultimately, am the most responsible person here. Still, it's so much better than the previous July 4, when a round of industrial-strength pot cookies led to a number of reckless fire incidents that forced me into the scolding role of high school principal. This, right now, is the good kind of crazy, the kind that generates scientific experiments within twenty feet of group nudity.

Wanting to check the progress of the Asian woman, I begin trekking back across my living room, where people are dancing on the large square coffee table that I fashioned out of the boards from my old deck. They are all gyrating to that Usher song, "Yeah!" I find the high-pitched intro to the song so grating. How can my housemates, people I've hand-selected, possibly find those screeching tones aurally pleasing? Is it them or is it me? It doesn't matter because that intro drives me postal. I decide, on the spot, that "Yeah!" will be added to the growing list of tracks banned from further play in the house.

Out on the deck, the Asian woman is surrounded by a gaggle of partiers gaping at the pig's skull pulled back like petals, exposing the curves and twists of its brain. Next to them, a woman in a jean skirt raises her cocktail glass and shoots me a sly look. She is Rule Number One, the house member whom I—the owner and manager of Chance, "Fire Island's Premier Epicurean Sharehouse Experience"—have gotten to know in the biblical sense.

Before my first season, I had decided that I simply couldn't hook up with any of the SHMILFs. (Share House Member I'd Like To...) It's that whole not shitting-where-you-eat thing. Still, it required a Herculean effort to keep my mitts off the many SHMILFs in my house. That I was unofficially off-limits (amid rampant hookups) seemed only to heighten the curiosity that a couple of the women began to have about me, the Master of the House. These are women with whom I race around the sharp turns of Flirtation Pass, where the smallest extra tap on the accelerator could send me veering off into the crash land of drunken, casual sex that I fear will destabilize the dynamic that exists among the pool of New York City singles with whom I share my seven-bedroom beach house for the summer.

There's Natasha, a six-foot choreographer with an amazing rack and a set of delicate legs that rise up to my chest, a woman who at the breakfast table that morning described the high-tech features of her vibrator, trumpeting the device as though bragging about the accessories in a brand-new Lexus. There is Tracy, who with her pulled-back hair and thick glasses has this whole sexy-librarian thing working for her big time—only she is an honest-to-goodness librarian. There are other SHMILFs. Many others. Ultimately, however, it was Rule Number One who broke me down during a nighttime stroll on the beach. She is still flashing that coy grin, making me an offer that I can't refuse, and suddenly it dawns on me that upstairs—an open-floor kitchen, dining room, living room, and deck—is where all the action is. No one is downstairs. I narrow my eyes at her and then make for the stairs, hearing the chorus of two, possibly three cocktail glasses crashing against the kitchen floor.

Downstairs in my room, I check my reflection in the full-length mirror. I am shirtless, wearing only Crocs and a pair of soaking-wet Bermuda shorts.

This is my work uniform.

I wonder for the six-thousandth time if I shouldn't be doing something else, if I shouldn't go back to school or put my talents to work at something more important than facilitating a playground for sixty people to get their grooves on. Then I remember that I am my own boss. After twelve years of working underpaid, under-appreciated jobs, I am finally, thankfully, my own boss. I remind myself that I was never cut out for the classroom or the office, and that Bermuda shorts and Crocs beat Business Casual any day.

"Are you checking yourself out again?"

I hadn't heard Rule Number One slip into my room. Still grinning, she closes the door and locks it. I grab at her like an animal, hiking up her jean skirt and kissing her wildly as she eggs me on. I pull off her top and we crash down on my bed. I can still hear and feel the thump of the music that I know will drown out the noise that Rule Number One and I, for once, will be free to make in my own house.

kis-met *n.* fate; destiny.

Memorial Day

Deep-Fried Turkey

It was Sunday, Memorial Day weekend, 2005. The sun falling behind the Fire Island Lighthouse lit up the weathered cedar shingles and unpainted siding of the boxy houses stretching across Kismet, bathing them in a pink glow. Out on the deck, I handed Maggie a glass of chardonnay and a fire extinguisher—everything she'd need to guard the tall pot of canola oil perched over the 40,000 BTU flame of my jet burner. In the kitchen, I injected a twenty-seven-pound turkey with a syringe loaded with a deep-fry speedball: Worcestershire sauce, sherry, and Dijon mustard. Then I smacked it with a dry rub and carried it out to the deck, relieving my helper.

Maggie, a smart, progressive, thirty-two-year-old focused on her career and in love with the cultural life of New York City, dreamed of being in a relationship that might lead to marriage and kids. Despite being quite attractive, women like Maggie regularly lose out to women with a lot less going for them, women for whom their appearance is their best (and often only) asset. Of all the Chance house members, I most rooted for Maggie to develop a relationship as a result of coming to Kismet, hoping that her experience might live up to the name of the town and give meaning to the name of the house.

The house's logo consists of a reversed Chance square from Monopoly, a theme that sprang from my desire to name the seven bedrooms, something that saves a house manager a lot of time, since a room can be referred to by its name instead of explaining its location ad infinitum. The house's larger, corner rooms were named after the corners of the board—Go, Just Visiting, Free Parking, and Jail—while the two middle rooms are Short Line and Pennsylvania Railroad, after their corresponding positions. The low-ceilinged loft became Baltic. (Whenever someone pitched the tent on the deck, that became Mediterranean.) Monopoly, however, was just an excuse to call the house "Chance." An unspoken truth about singles' sharehouses is that most people join them, first and foremost, as a means of spouse hunting. No one EVER talks about this. Meanwhile, New York City, per capita, has more single-person households than any other American city. (Much to my parents' chagrin, I am one of them.) Despite its size, New York, statistically, is the loneliest city in America. Still, most City singles will sooner admit to peeing in the shower than state what is true for an overwhelming majority of them: More than anything else, they would like to meet someone. So I was trying to tap people's sense of fate, offering the house as a benediction—maybe even for myself—planting the idea that joining Chance would be similar to landing on that square in Monopoly, where picking up one of those pink-orange cards can ultimately change your fortune.

Once the thermometer in the canola oil read 350 degrees, I impaled the turkey vertically on its holder and fished out a work glove from my tool bucket. House members crowded around and digital cameras flashed as I hoisted the turkey up and lowered it, inch by inch, into the spitting and bubbling oil. The sun had gone down and the chilly air filed people back inside. There were twenty-three people staying at the house. During nonholiday weekends we had twenty-one—seventeen house members and four guests. (Guest fees paid down our weekly four-figure food and booze bill.) Twenty-three was a lot of people, but they were all sharing the sandbox so it felt like less. Most of them were new house members and it was their first time meeting one another, the collective excitement turning flirtier with each popped cork.

I tapped myself a Killian's from the kegerator and hunkered down with the fire extinguisher, studying the flames licking up the sides of the blackened pot. A chorus of catcalls rife with sexual energy rang out from the living room. Staring at the fire, I lapsed into a familiar reverie where I am not the owner and manager of the Chance beach house but just another house member flirting with abandon, not having to worry about the all-important goal of successful sharehouse management: maintaining a high level of returnees.

Vanessa, a new house member, stepped out onto the deck, pinching a glass of wine. In her first e-mail to me, Vanessa described herself and included a long list of outdoorsy sports and activities, none of which piqued my interest until I noticed one of her hobbies: Homebrew. I sat up in my chair. Here is a woman, I thought, who *makes her own beer*. I had recruited enough chefs to start my own cooking channel, but no one made beer; I decided right then that I wanted beer to be brewed at Chance. Vanessa's candidacy was further elevated by the fact that she was a woman. I had never—*never-ever-ever*—heard of a woman involved in homebrew. When considering new people, I'm drawn to those who perform jobs or engage in hobbies that buck stereotypes—it flags them as having minds of their own, of being the kind of people who give free rein to their curiosity. And to have that hobby be homebrew? Unless Vanessa turned out to be a barking psychopath, I knew I would offer her a spot. When we finally met, she ended up checking out in the extreme. She had a warm disposition and she knew how to play nice. (When evaluating potential shares, there is nothing more important than gauging their ability to share the sandbox.) She had an awful lot of questions, though, and I answered them all, trying not to seem overeager when I offered her a spot. Aside from her obvious qualifications, Vanessa was also a total SHMILF. Big time. A mane of platinum blond curls cascaded over her shoulders, and she had one of those sexy, asymmetrical Ellen Barkin mouths, her upper lip seeming to curl with a mind of its own.

"So." She pulled a chair next to me and sat down. "We need to talk about making beer."

"What's involved?"

She began detailing the processes, but I soon got lost in all that chemistry.

"...since you have a spare CO_2 tank," she said, "we could make a small keg instead of bottling it. Do you think I could convince you to buy a pony keg?"

Staring at that wild curl of her lip, I might well have agreed to buy an actual pony.

"Let's do it," I said.

She promised to bring her equipment out to the house for our first batch.

"I can't believe you do this," she said.

"What?"

"This house. This." She gestured at the ocean and the federal preserve. "And this." She pointed at the turkey frying. "All of the cooking. The kitchen's amazing and I guess I'm just really excited to cook and to hang out and make beer."

"I'm pretty excited, too."

"So is Maggie your girlfriend?"

"No." I laughed. "A lot of people ask us that, but we're just friends."

She finished her wine. "So do you have a girlfriend?"

"Nope. What about you? Do you have a girlfriend?"

She laughed. "How come you're not married yet?"

"Because it would make this house less fun," I said, somewhat shocked by the reflexiveness of my answer, wondering if owning and running a singles' share-house contributed to my rather long stretch sans serious girlfriend.

"What about you?" I asked Vanessa. "How come you're not married yet?"

"Fuck if I know." She stood and motioned with her empty glass before sashaying back toward the screen door. Catching me staring, she shot a flirty glance before stepping back into the house.

"Hey, guy?" It was my little voice. *"Remember Rule Number One."*

"Yeah, yeah, yeah," I mumbled. "Don't hook up with anyone in the house."

I pulled back the leg of my Bermuda shorts, exposing a patch of poison ivy that had spread across my knee. My house is lined with a moat of the stuff beneath the walkways and I come in contact with it whenever I crawl beneath the house. This was a bad patch and the heat of the flame felt heavenly against it. I slid closer, bending my knee until it was six inches from the flame.

"John, what are you thinking?"

It was Tracy, the sexy librarian, extracting a cigarette.

"I was thinking that of all the SHMILFs in the house, I would most like to have sex with you."

I didn't say this. And it took me a minute to realize she was referring to my knee. I had slid within an inch or two of the flame, singeing off all of my knee hair and covering my poison ivy with a first-degree burn that felt fabulous.

"Poison EYE-vay-ey-yay-yay," I sang. "I've got a bad spot and it feels good next to the flame."

"Isn't it hot?" She lit a cigarette.

I could still hear the song in my head: *You can look but you better not touch*...My eyes coasted up to the stream of smoke passing between her lips.

"It's pretty hot."

"John, you're burning yourself." She pointed at my knee.

"I'll be fine," I said. "So how does one go about becoming a librarian?"

"You have to get a Master's in Library Science."

"What kinds of classes do you take?"

"They start us out with Shooshing 101." She rested her forearms on the deck railing, looking out over the federal preserve. We continued to chat as she stood there, smoking.

"Do you need anything?" She stubbed out her cigarette.

I thought for a minute. There were so many things I needed. Too many things.

"No thanks," I said. "I'm good."

"Okay. See you inside."

I watched her walk back to the screen door.

"Need I remind you?"

"Nope," I muttered in response to my little voice, sliding my knee a touch closer to the flame.

A few minutes later, Troy marched out onto the deck pressing a BlackBerry to his ear, gesticulating as he yapped his way through yet another pedantic work conversation. He worked for some ad agency and that BlackBerry had been glued to his face all day long. Sadly, there were an awful lot of Troys out there. Millions of young, overworked New Yorkers on the verge of having their lives slip out from under them. They molested their scant leisure time with a vengeful regimen of bad television, celebrity obsession, and hard-core partying, attacking any trace of self-reflection as though it were an insurgent rebellion, something to be crushed with a workweek that the CrackBerry extended to nights and weekends.

I had been part of the workforce in New York City all through the economic boom of the nineties, a time when Americans edged out the Japanese to become the planet's reigning workaholics (with New Yorkers leading the pack among Americans). By the summer of 2000, the Joneses, at least in Manhattan, were on the juice. This was right after the NASDAQ tagged 5,000 and the rat race had become an extreme sport. The Joneses were sprinting faster than coked-up Kenyans, and my contemporaries were breaking their legs in a desperate effort to keep up. I couldn't take it anymore. So I convinced the magazine conglomerate for which I was doing a mediocre job as an associate editor to lay me off.

I just never caught that workaholic fever, something I credit to the three years that I spent in France during my early twenties. You see, France is one of those snooty "European" countries that forbids its workers to put in more than thirty-five hours a week; even more despicable, all French people are forced to take five weeks of paid vacation. Despite the inherent cruelties of the French system, I grew to appreciate the pace and quality of their lives. In both Normandy and Paris, many French people (renowned for their snobby rudeness) invited and welcomed me into their homes. These families regularly ate dinner together and, aside from the amazing food, I liked the way that they talked and what they talked about. I liked watching kids formulate and advance concise arguments—their more pleasant and effective take on public-speaking classes. More than anything, I cherished their ample free time. Unlike fewer and fewer Americans, the French had the time to fully engage life, liberty, and...well, you get the picture.

In addition to ruining my prospects as a member of the American workforce, the French further brainwashed me with *la vie quotidienne*—an appreciation of the slower, modest pleasures of everyday life. While having anything positive to say about the French these days goes over about as well as admiring the leadership qualities of Adolf Hitler, the French taught me how to eat, drink, cook, converse, and relax. I learned that it wasn't necessary to destroy myself during my leisure time—the way I had during my first two years of college. I learned that gastronomy is an art and a science, that eating—like sex—is a fundamental human activity that calls for creativity and is best when drawn out over longer stretches. Despite America's renewed interest in food, we still eat and drink the way sixteen-year-olds screw—pants twisted around ankles in a fumbling rush to the finish. Unfortunately, most Americans just don't have the time. Especially in the City.

I love New York City and doubt I could ever live anywhere else, although Manhattan is about the most inhuman place I've ever known. A lot of this has to do with density—a couple million people crammed into twenty square miles. "Personal space" is big in Manhattan. People learn to tune everyone else out (which partly explains why the City is such a terrible place to meet someone). When I first moved into my condo in West Harlem, little old black ladies would chat me up in the elevator. At first this seemed strange, until I'd find myself on the elevator with other younger, white people, both of us staring at the walls and counting the ticks until we could get out of one another's personal space. Why didn't we exchange a simple pleasantry? Had we expended our quota at the office? What was wrong with us?

With Chance, I wanted to create an environment where my overworked friends could step out of the breakneck pace of the City; I wanted a lush, plentiful haven where they could truly unwind and collect themselves; I wanted to share with them the voluptuous beach lifestyle I had first experienced at Cannes, Monte Carlo, and other towns on the French Riviera where meals went on for hours, where sex was something to do between meals, and where no one was talking about interest rates.

When first attempting to recruit house members, I billed Chance as an "epicurean" house. It wasn't long before someone asked me what "epicurean" meant, and I realized that I wasn't exactly sure. I had guessed, from usage, that an epicure was someone who prioritized eating, drinking, and sex. Still, I realized that if I was going to use this word, I should know exactly what it meant. So I asked the Internet. The word stemmed from Epicurus, an ancient Greek philosopher who believed the pursuit of sensual pleasure to be the highest good—especially through good food, drink, and comfort—and that a life free from anxiety and open to the enjoyment of other pleasures was deemed equal to that of the gods.

Of course, Greek philosophers were a dime a dozen back then, and Athens produced marquee thinkers far more popular than Epicurus—household names like Plato, Aristotle, and Socrates. The more I read about Epicurus, however, the more I couldn't fathom why he didn't exist in their league. I found his philosophy so much more appealing, especially his notion that we could all live in perpetual bliss, our enduring optimism and serenity reinforced by the continual, drawn-out experience of modest pleasures.

Why, I wondered, didn't all ancient Athenians sign on to the epicurean life?

Why don't New Yorkers sign up for the epicurean life today?

Epicurus believed that what prevented people from enjoying this good life was an anxiety that stemmed from fear of death and punishment. Once we eliminated this anxiety—and the irrational desires it creates—we would experience true freedom. This would naturally lead to our pursuit of all physical and mental pleasures, creating a peace of mind that results from regularly expecting and achieving gratification.

It was what I read next, however, that blew my mind. Many philosophers had their own schools in Athens: Plato had the Academy; Aristotle had the Lyceum. Epicurus, however, wanted to escape the hustle and bustle of the city, so he bought a house outside of the city. He shared his house—and its lush garden—with those in search of a respite from the stress of city life, all of them practicing his hedonistic philosophy, gathering and communing in this utopian natural setting, creating his school that came to be known as "The Garden."

Holy fuck! Epicurus was a sharehouse manager...

Aside from our preference for airy, comfortable footwear, that gastronomic Greek and I turned out to share quite a bit more in common.

My goal with Chance was the same as was his with The Garden: Take people out of the crazy life of the City and give them the time and space to reflect and relax. Since Fire Island banned cars during the high season, it was the perfect antidote to the sensory overload of Manhattan. When I further considered Epicurus's belief that irrational fear of death was the primary cause of anxiety, everything began to click. After 9/11, our government had hooked us to an IV of fear—a slow, persistent drip that left us more afraid than ever, scaring the crap out of us with talk of impending mushroom clouds and color-coded terror alerts. During the years after the attacks, Americans were also made to work longer hours while job security and faith in our institutions crumbled. Stuck under this boot of fear, we were being slowly—almost imperceptibly—squeezed, too scared to notice that our coffers were being looted by a band of bloodthirsty billionaires, hollowing out our country for their own sick, exclusive orgy.

After learning about Epicurus, Chance started to feel less like an investment and more like a mission; luring people out of the vicious circle of work-fear-consumption-oblivion with the epicurean life began to feel less like a way to cover costs and more like a calling. And if all of my efforts could just change one person, well, then those efforts would absolutely be fucking futile. (*One person?* Are you kidding?) Anyway, I wasn't trying to transform anyone. Rather, it felt like appealing to swing voters—people who, with the right approach, could be coaxed off the fence over to the epicurean side. So a good number of Chance house members merged elements of the epicurean life with the default of racing toward oblivion, whereby a multicourse sit-down dinner is followed by three tequilas, two bong hits, and the mad pursuit of a hookup. Which is fine. Sometimes I'm still up for a bit of oblivion myself, and when I am, I know which house members to approach. Still, some of them had become so entrenched in their workweeks that no number of lush weekends would ever help them appreciate the present moment. People like CrackBerry Troy, who turned out to be a middlebrow jackass in spades.

During his first night at the house, Troy tipped his hand as one of those guys who needs to get ripped before loosening up enough to engage in the mating ritual. Indeed, my little voice had piped up when I first met Troy, only he wasn't screaming trouble; my little voice had sized up Troy as "minimally acceptable." In March, however, "minimally acceptable" was not something to walk away from. It's tough to find good guys. I could fill Chance three times over with great women, but really, there just doesn't exist in New York City a reservoir of cosmopolitan straight men who are cultivated yet rugged, jocular yet considerate, and whom the sexy, urbane women in my house might want to date. So I offered Troy a spot.

I hit my low point on the male-recruiting front back in May 2004, two weeks before the beginning of my first season. Still short half a dozen men, I began offering discounts as well as finder's fees euphemized as "Testicular Location Rewards" to house members who managed to produce a suitable guy. Still desperate for decent guys, I set out on foot in Central Park like some kind of debauched Mormon missionary. I figured Sheep's Meadow would be a good filter, in that any guy who was spending a sunny day outside playing a sport instead of watching one on TV would be a good prospect. I walked past scores of Frisbee flingers and bike riders, judging them—in many instances—by their sunglasses. Most of the guys I approached wore hard, skeptical expressions—the kind of face I would present to anyone attempting to sell me something in the commercial-free temple that is Central Park. (Note to Straight Men: If you think it's tough to approach women in bars, try picking up other guys. To describe men as less communicative would be like describing Saddam Hussein as grumpy.) Women were so much easier to recruit. When women e-mailed me about the house, they regularly described themselves in a few declarative sentences. They asked thoughtful questions and volunteered their age, occupation, and what they were looking for; they included a phone number. Nine out of ten men do none of this. Here is the near-exact text of an e-mail I've received from more than a hundred guys:

hey your house looks cool, would love to hear more

If I got an e-mail like that from a woman, I would delete it without hesitation. My website includes lots of photos and content that give a good feel for the house's unique vibe. You want to hear more about the house, guy? How about this: I'm the gatekeeper of two dozen single, hot women and if you can manage to properly mind your p's & q's, they'll be staring at you like you're the Christmas ham.

I usually responded to the vague e-mails of men by explaining that the women in the house were overwhelmingly cute, single, and fun, while I fished for a phone number. On the whole, however, men really, really suck. We *really* do. Not only do I now empathize with every smart, cultured, single woman in New York City, I feel terrible for the way that I've acted toward every such woman who has crossed my romantic path. If you happen to be one of these women, please let me tell you that I am sorry for being an uncommunicative asshole prone to mixed messages. I would also like to apologize on behalf of the rest of my inferior sex. You are higher beings and you deserve better. (That you've also been saddled with menstruation, the pain of childbirth, and cannot pee standing up only proves that God can sometimes be a real douche.)

People who work in advertising know that adult males below the age of thirty-five are the hardest demographic to reach. Having learned this the hard way in 2004, I focused the bulk of my 2005 recruiting energy on my lesser gender, responding to e-mails from men immediately, trying to get them on the phone. If they seemed like good prospects and my next meet-up was days away, I'd try to arrange a meeting ASAP. Another strike against men is that we're shitty planners. Women start thinking about their summer plans in March, while men don't start thinking about their summer plans until May. If you run a beach house, this is maddening because Memorial Day is only a few weeks away and you're still five figures from your profit margin.

Aside from men being difficult, there are many more women than men interested in the beach. It's like chocolate—the beach does something for women that men just don't understand. So if you're one of those straight, single guys who perpetually laments the sausage-fest ratio of so many New York City bars (where you and your friends ritually fight over the one woman who doesn't look like Luca Brasi) and you wonder where all the single women are hiding, I can tell you: They are in beach houses, many of which have favorable ratios.

Despite the temptation to kick back and fill the house with cool women, I wanted an even ratio. Luckily, my disproportionate efforts paid off; by early May, I had no more spots left for men. Amazingly, I still had two spots left for women. So of course I now regretted having offered CrackBerry Troy a spot. Still, a long time ago my father told me that no matter where you go, there's always gonna be at least one asshole, and you're gonna have to deal with him. It's really quite true. So I just chalked up Troy in that inevitable slot.

I really couldn't complain. With a majority of house members returning from my first season in 2004, I only had to recruit half as many people in my established, newly renovated house, and I was able to be more selective in 2005. Among the crackerjack new house members was Rufus. Only twenty-three, my little voice warned me that Rufus—who fell well below my target age range of twenty-eight to thirty-eight—was just too damn young. Still, he was a scrappy journalist who worked the graveyard shift at Fox News. I joshed him about writing right-wing propaganda for Team Bush, and he responded that if I had any friends at the *New York Times*, he would love to meet them. He spoke five languages, and I found his intellectual exuberance irresistible. After offering him a spot, he was one of the first house members to sign up to cook a Saturday night dinner—sushi, no less. He was gregarious and offbeat, and he kept the blender running with batch after batch of fruity cocktails. The women in the house loved this. It also contributed to a solid level of drunkenness by mid-afternoon that Sunday.

"Hey, John?" Rufus called out to me from the wet bar, clapping his hands together. "Do you have any margarita mix?"

I walked over and put an arm around his shoulders, thinking, you sweet, sweet child.

"Go grab a half-dozen limes," I said, plugging in the juicer and grabbing a shaker. He squeezed the limes and I taught him how to make an authentic margarita with tequila, triple sec, and fresh lime juice strained of pulp. A lot of people have never had a real margarita; they've only ever drunk fauxgaritas—those sugary-sweet concoctions pummeled with sour mix. A fauxgarita is to a margarita what Wonder Bread is to a baguette. I served Rufus a real margarita straight-up in a chilled cocktail glass rimmed with salt.

"That's really good." His face lit up with the look of a boy who had just learned how to play with his penis. "That's really fucking good." He took another sip and then shook me down for the proportions, repeating them under his breath as he grabbed the tequila.

"Who wants a margarita?" he called out. There were takers. People were burning off the wild energy that came with the excitement of getting to know one another, of finding themselves in a free-flow, heady environment, of trying to decide just whom they found the most attractive. I am more than partly responsible for sexually charging the atmosphere. On the house website, in a section entitled "Belief & Technique for Epicurean Sharehouse Management" (a combined parody of Jack Kerouac's *Belief & Technique for Modern Prose* and the Dr. Bronner's Soap label), I extolled the benefits of "Horizontal Refreshment," which I jokingly promised as a reward for all selfless participation. Still, most of them knew better than to hook up in-house during their first weekend. No one was more wary of this than me, and my ball-breaking little voice was determined that I would once again make it through the summer without breaking Rule Number One.

During the '04 season, I ended up cooking about two-thirds of the

Saturday night dinners. This year, I wanted other house members to step up and figured that a sherry-infused deep-fried turkey would let them know that I wasn't fucking around. They were already proving to be serious about food, though. Earlier that afternoon, what began with Rufus trash-talking someone else's guacamole recipe bloomed into a spirited difference of opinion about the relationship between cilantro and lime juice, a debate that would be settled with what came to be known as the "guac-off." Surreptitious trips to the Kismet Market were followed by covert slicing and dicing. The whole house judged the recipes and in the end, Rufus lost. Still...trash-talking about cooking? This was going very well. This was moving a step closer to the brash, epicurean mix of high- and lowbrow that I had envisioned at the outset.

After just an hour in the oil, I pulled out the turkey and placed it on a silver platter to carve. (A deep-fried turkey may well be healthier than an oven-roasted turkey, as much of the fat cooks away, leaving the skin wonderfully crisp and sealing in all the juices. And regardless of fat content, it absolutely tastes better. The wings are particularly good...) We devoured the turkey along with Cajun-spiced sweet potato fries and a spinach salad. Then Risa, a food writer, along with my younger brother Matt, a real-estate developer, began deep-frying Oreos, which we ate for dessert paired with flutes of prosecco. Most of the house was now solidly impaired, their wild energy spiked by this massive infusion of sugar. During my years working as a nanny in both New York and Paris, I learned to fear and respect sugar. We know full well what it does to kids, and really, it's no different with adults, except that adults are larger, stronger, and can hire personal-injury lawyers. Sugar bursts nudge drunken people into that realm of Doing Really Crazy Shit, so once drunk people get jacked on sugar, I will do anything in my power to corral them to the bars. (I'd rather fight the sugar...*over there*, so that I don't have to fight it at home.) It was still too early, though, and the after-dinner dance party was just getting cranked up. Maggie began dancing with Matt, while over on the couches, a sloppy drunk CrackBerry Troy slid closer to Tracy, who rolled her eyes and inched away. Nearby, Rufus was gesturing wildly at Nancy, a woman who had joined the house under rather peculiar circumstances.

My renovations the previous winter took longer than expected. Trying to keep costs down, I did whatever work I could do myself. Two weeks before the start of the season, however, my downstairs bathroom was not tiled, nor had I installed the new sinks and vanities, nor reconnected the toilets. I had already sublet my West Harlem condo and moved out to the beach for the summer. Meanwhile, I still had to fill my last two women's spots. After posting a new ad on Craig's List, Nancy e-mailed me, exclaiming that she loved the website and wanted to join the house.

I never allowed anyone to join without first meeting them, preferably when other house members were present, to help ensure that they know how to play nice. I e-mailed her back, letting her know when I was next coming to the City. The following day, however, my brand-new on-demand tankless water heater went on the fritz. A number of teeth-grinding phone calls to the manufacturer attempting to troubleshoot it failed. My shares would be showing up in ten days, and not only were my bathrooms not finished, I now no longer had hot water. People would be willing to sleep on straw mattresses before subjecting themselves to arctic showers in May. But how was I going to line up both a plumber and an electrician during the run-up to Memorial Day?

Luckily, I've studied various forms of eastern meditation and yoga. Never had this vital practice, which had frequently helped calm and order my mind, been more fucking useless. This was not a time for oms; this was not a time for alternate-nostril breathing. People had paid eighteen hundred bucks to come out to my beach house, and suddenly I didn't have hot water. This was a time to freak the fuck out.

Having long believed that there are few problems in this world that can't be cured with five ounces of gin, I approached the wet bar, chilled a cocktail glass, and shook myself a glacial martini. I leaned over for a sip, evacuating enough gin to make room for seven olives, so as not to be drinking on an empty stomach. It was a sunny, crisp day, and I carried my martini out to the deck, forcing myself to sit and watch the rolling waves, drawing a series of deep breaths as I drank. After chomping my last olive, I punched up Dave Lambie, my electrician. Dave is super-friendly, and I explained my predicament, telling him that I knew how busy he was and then more or less pleading with him to please, please help me. Dave graciously told me that he would make time to wire a traditional tank heater, only we'd have to find a plumber. He promised to ask around and gave me some names to call.

At the time, I didn't know any plumbers in Kismet the way I knew Dave, so here is the conversation that I imagined having:

Me: "I'd like you to install a hot water heater in my house this week."

Plumber: "I'm booked straight through July 4. I can make time for you after that."

Me: "How much would it cost for you to make time this week?"

Plumber: "This week? That's gonna cost ya, because somebody's gonna be upset. I can do it for ten grand."

Me (scooping half a jar of Vaseline into my ass crack): "That would be great."

I had my list of plumbers and was about to start cold calling when I checked my e-mail and received a message back from Nancy, who told me that she wasn't free when I was going to be in the City, but that she definitely wanted in. I knew right then that I would never have time to meet up with her (plus I still had another spot to fill). So I replied that it would be great to have her join the house. Later that afternoon, we spoke on the phone and a knot settled in my stomach. I am a terribly prejudiced person, and one of the many groups against whom I am prejudiced include women who constantly uptalk. You know who they are. They speak that retarded Valley Girl idiom, inflecting every declarative sentence into a question: "I live in Murray *Hill*? I went to *Har*vard? I work in *sales*?" Uptalking. They speak as though they're apologizing for everything they've done, as though accomplishment were a disease, that annoying lilt casting doubt on utterances that normal people plainly state as fact. Hearing that persistent lack of authority spilling from the mouths of women, a startling number of whom do in fact have Ivy League diplomas, it's hard not to think that, forty years after Betty Friedan, the Women's Movement had begun to backslide. However it came about didn't matter, because that sing-songy insecurity drove me apeshit and fuck it if—

"*Hel*-LO?" My little voice again. "*You don't have hot water. HOT. FUCKING. WATER!*"

Since every single one of my calls to plumbers was met with an answering machine, I swallowed hard and scheduled Nancy. The following day produced my first correspondence with Tracy. While her grammatically correct complete sentences sounded like a birdsong after Nancy, you never know how someone is going to stack up until you meet them. Still, given my predicament, I scheduled Tracy and closed out my recruiting season for 2005.

Luckily, Dave Lambie pleaded my case to a local plumber named Mark Gilmore, and amazingly, four days later, I had a fully operational hot water heater. Anyway, those were the circumstances under which Uptalking Nancy, a woman whom I had never met, joined Chance. As I mentioned ninety-seven paragraphs ago, Nancy was talking to Rufus, who was gesturing wildly, drink in hand. Nancy hadn't become caught up in the wild energy that had taken hold of everyone else. Earlier that afternoon, she got off on the wrong foot after stubbing out a cigarette in one of the planters hanging off the deck railing. Maggie had pined for those planters like a six-year-old campaigning for a puppy. I finally caved and told her that I would buy all of the stuff so long as she took care of them. Maggie put a lot of thought into the proper selection of perennials and herbs, so she was pretty pee-owed to discover Nancy twisting a lit cigarette into something that she had conceived and nurtured. I approached the wet bar and eavesdropped on Nancy's conversation with Rufus. She was giving him an earful of boilerplate left-wing grief because he worked for Fox News.

"Well," Rufus asked her, "what do you do?"

"I'm a financial analyst?" Nancy responded, flipping her straight blond hair.

"Ohhhh," Rufus said. "So you're not exactly saving the whales then, are you?"

Nancy's eyes popped and I skulked away, suppressing a fit of laughter.

The collective sugar rush now peaking, Chris, a freelance writer, began juggling fruit in the kitchen. Matt rushed in and joined him. Like Vanessa, Chris was another candidate whose incredible strength on paper held up in person. Unlike most men, Chris actually described himself and provided full contact information. After receiving his initial e-mail on a Saturday afternoon, I gave him a call. He happened to be in Central Park (at Sheep's Meadow, in fact), and so I delivered a white lie: I told him that I was just about to head out for a bike ride—maybe I could ride over to the Meadow and we could talk? He agreed and I pedaled like a madman south through the Park until I found him. After a brief conversation, I offered him a spot. Since he worked from home, the unlimited midweek access (and our WiFi) was of particular interest to him. Having already put in a fair amount of midweek time, Chris had proven to be considerate and a good conversationalist. My impulsive speed-ride down to Central Park had not been a waste of time.

Rufus joined Matt and Chris juggling fruit, while a half-dozen dancers crowded onto the coffee table beneath a cloud of pot smoke.

"Hey, John?" It was Natasha.

"What's that, pussycat?"

"Ooh," she said, embracing me. "I *like* when you call me that. It's de-*li*-cious."

Despite pressing up against Natasha, a dyed-in-the-wool SHMILF, my little voice kept quiet. Even though she flirted with abandon, she kept her pursuits, to the best of my knowledge, outside of the house.

"What do you need, pussycat?"

"I don't need *any*thing." She squeezed me and then hopped up on the coffee table, while Mandy, a tall, brown-haired vixen hopped down from the table and grabbed one of the hula hoops from behind the couch. The hula hoops were an impulse buy during a housewares run in Kmart. I think they cost a buck-twenty-nine apiece. Of the hundreds of thousands of dollars spent creating Chance, I doubt I got more bang for my buck from anything. (In fact, I can think of a few times when someone actually got banged as a result of those three bucks.) The hula hoop transported Mandy back to the uninhibited play of her childhood in a regression that was pretty damn sexy for the rest of us. Mandy worked in finance, and when we first met back in '04, my little voice questioned whether she might be too buttoned up for the house. This is pretty funny to think back upon, because the straight-laced, corporate exterior that she presented to her bank couldn't be any more different than the character that came out to play once she sucked down a couple of cocktails. While at times she just oozed sexiness, she had never become a SHMILF. (Maybe I found her near double-life too jarring...) But watching her now, writhing inside the hula hoop, I could hear my little voice, for the first time, clearing his throat.

With juggling and hula-hooping flanking either side of the dance party, the upstairs felt like a circus. I've always thought of the circus as a metaphor for the ideal world—a place where people's peculiarities are strengths and where everyone contributes through their quirks. So when Matt set down the fruit and began juggling spatulas like pins, I zoomed over to the wet bar and soon had three lemons cutting through the air, synching up my tosses with the booming bass line. Dancers in the living room began to gravitate toward the jugglers on one side and Mandy on the other, forming an archipelago of shaking booties. Rufus upped the volume on the music and then stood at the top of the stairs with a playing card wedged between his fingers. With a flick of his wrist, he made it disappear. With another flick, the card reappeared in his hand. Magic works even better when your audience is stupefied, and Vanessa kept asking him do it over and over. I liked that Rufus was brazenly showing off. Too many party atmospheres degenerate into a replay of the same old script—the sloppy advancement of the mating ritual. So whenever anyone says or does anything novel, I am for it. Watching Rufus, I felt lucky to have this magical, intellectual desperado in the mix.

Meanwhile, CrackBerry Troy was slurring and starting to paw at Tracy. Someone cranked the music even louder, and Rufus set back to work at the blender. Mandy added a second hoop, while Matt graduated up to two ladles and a whisk. Amid the whir of the blender and the industrial groove pumping from the speakers, Grace, a new house member, sat in a chair near the stairs, straining in the dim light to read the *New Yorker*.

I was dumbfounded. It was the partying equivalent of attempting to meditate in the middle of Grand Central. I then remembered the ways in which Grace had begun to reveal herself as difficult after I had offered her a spot: leaving me with her drink tab; twice changing an appointment for payment; printing up her own formal receipt for me to sign. Nothing grievous, but a clear pattern. I lumped her with Troy—just another buzzkill who managed to slip under the wire, further proof of the Frank Blesso Doctrine of Asshole Inevitability.

Thankfully, Matt lowered the music and announced that we were heading to the bars. Troy roared like a lineman; Grace informed me that she was going to bed.

In Kismet, there are only two bar/restaurants: The Kismet Inn and The Out. (Most towns on Fire Island relegate all commercial activity to the bay side where the ferries pull in, leaving the ocean blocks residential.) While I first thought it a downside that Kismet was served by only two bars, I later considered this limited choice a blessing, an antidote to the 500 channels of crap offered up on our satellite TV. If you were to total the ass-scratching time I've spent standing around on Manhattan street corners with my friends trying to decide upon our next bar, I could have learned to speak Urdu by now. Having only two bars (and having them right next to one another) eliminated the deadlock of endlessly choosing. The Inn or The Out. What's it gonna be? When you can't find your friends at one bar, no need to pull out the cell phone, just cross the walk and find them at the other one.

We stopped first at The Inn, a large, L-shaped hall adorned with sundry items related to sports, seafaring, and gun ownership. Directly opposite the bar is a mounted fish next to a faded, wooden sign displaying the American flag beneath the word "LIBERTY." The Inn is run by the Cole family, an extended clan with eclectic tastes. While they frequently booked blues-rock bands during the weekends, they also presented Dixieland jazz every Tuesday and a modern jazz quartet every Thursday. They never charged a cover. And Ashley, the oldest son, had assembled the kind of jukebox you'd want if you were stranded on a desert isle. Most great bars have a clientele that cannot be pigeonholed, and The Inn is no exception. I've spent many a night seated at the long bar with septuagenarians sipping vodka on one side of me and twenty-one-year-olds throwing back lemondrop shooters on the other. Ultimately, what most great bars have in common is that they are places of community, places where people can go by themselves and be sure to bump into friends—kindred spirits with whom they can share stories or recount their days while getting totally faced.

After a round at The Inn, we filed over to The Out, where, following the dinner hour, the tables were cleared for an all-out dance party throwdown. As The Out regularly accommodated bachelorette parties and other such groups that were only in Kismet for a single night, many of those people wanted to hear the same songs—namely eighties music and the disco canon. None of my house members complained about the music at The Out more than Natasha, who wanted all hip-hop all the time. Once, she described going to The Out as being stuck in the movie *Groundhog Day*. Indeed, if you were to spend the evening at The Out, you could bet vital organs on the probability that you will hear "Stayin' Alive." Our national security could be staked on the certainty that you will hear "Jessie's Girl." And once Rick Springfield has graced the deck, well, "Come On, Eileen" can't be that far off. More than the repetitive song list, however, Natasha deplored the DJ's knack for trashing a groove by then playing a groaner like "Knock Three Times." (Some of these track selections were so drenched in irony that if that DJ were to move to Berlin, Germans would hail him as some kind of genius—maybe the auditory equivalent of David Hasselhoff.) As I was a prepubescent during the dawn of MTV, I still like early eighties music, but once a song has been used to sell dish soap, it kind of ruins it for me. The disco songs have been featured in so many commercials that they became crisp for me a long time ago. So after enduring "Play That Funky Music" for the eight millionth time in my life, I was getting ready to slip away when I spotted Johnny Thunder making his way to the dance floor.

Johnny Thunder (not to be confused with the late, great, proto-punk glam rocker Johnny Thunders) was a waiter at The Inn, and everyone in Kismet knew him, although his local fame had nothing to do with excellent service. Johnny Thunder was a dancing machine. Tonight, he was sporting a Kangol, shades, and a windbreaker over a gold chain, grooving to the beat while seamlessly nipping from a bottle of Heineken, two flashy young ladies in his tow. The bass line intro to "White Lines" filled the hot, thick air, and Johnny set down his Heineken. People stepped back as he started to pop and lock in the middle of the dance floor. My brother Matt stepped out and challenged Johnny to a duel. Johnny knew the rules and dropped back as all 200 pounds of my brother hit the floor, legs and arms kicking in a circle, culminating with a backspin. He came to a stop and rocked back on his shoulders, springing up to his feet and flashing a white real-estate developer's version of a gang sign.

Matt backed away and Johnny took his turn. It was hard to say who won—Matt was a better breakdancer, but Johnny Thunder was an all-sport athlete who could pick up any kind of ball and have game. Besides, Saturday night was what Johnny Thunder did. (If he and Matt were to instead duel over the purchase of a condemned four-family brownstone, renovate it, and then sell off the pieces as luxury condos, I'd give Matt the edge.) With the exception of falling into casual sex with a pair of Swedish/Latina au pairs, watching Johnny Thunder was about the most fun I was likely to have at The Out. He was one of those rare guys who truly made his own rules, slowing down for a second to acknowledge his irony before hitting the gas and leaving it all in the dust, having fun in a way that was absolutely his own.

"White Lines" came to an end and Natasha groaned when the DJ cued up "Sugar, Sugar." (I could almost hear the Germans typing.) Arms went limp and the dance floor slowed to a bounce. I was going to leave without saying good-bye, lest one of my house members tried to strong-arm me to stay. They were soldiering on through "Sugar, Sugar," their wild ride of the new at its peak, so in that moment they were feeling more gratitude toward me, the linchpin, than they would ever probably feel. They wanted me to party with them, but I was living out there for the summer and just couldn't roll like that every night. I was about to slip away when I caught sight of CrackBerry Troy, his eyes glazed over as he lumbered from foot to foot independent of any tempo that ever existed, grabbing Tracy's wrist to dance. I sidled up to my brother and asked him to keep an eye on Troy. Matt nodded knowingly. Tracy slipped away from Troy, and I flashed on just giving him his money back, shuddering at the thought of doing any more recruiting. Studying his drunken, teetering frame, I thought that this is what eighteen hundred bucks looks like.

I left The Out and headed home, walking past my large, red house on the ocean block of Pine Walk and continuing toward the beach, remembering one of the tenets from "Belief & Technique for Epicurean Sharehouse Management":

"Never go straight from bar to house but stop at beach."

Near the dune crossing, a young buck, his antlers covered with fuzz, had gotten into the trash. As I got closer, he stopped eating and stared at me. There is no shortage of deer on Fire Island and most of them are not wary of humans. As soon as I passed, he resumed feeding, getting his groove on like the rest of us.

The beach was deserted. A lot people don't go to the beach at night, other than for horizontal refreshment when they lack a private room. While nighttime beach-going is underrated, I hardly wished that I happened upon a crowd there, any more than I wished that Kismet and Fire Island weren't underrated as well. I sat on the sand staring at the oncoming waves until I felt like going home.

Back at the house, I brushed my teeth and then grabbed my iPod. In an hour or so, a horde of house members would return for the next phase of the evening: the jacuzzi. Drunk people are loud enough, but when you strip them down and put them in a hot tub, which for some reason magnifies their voices, they can be really loud. Even though my house is a hundred feet from the surf, and my bedroom is the best positioned to hear the ocean, I scrolled through my iPod for the fifty-minute track of ocean sounds, putting it on a loop repeat. I have a special pair of sound-blocking headphones and if a screaming orgy were to break out in the hot tub, I wouldn't hear it. And thus wouldn't be tempted to become a part of the action.

*   *   *

The next morning I was up before anyone. I usually am. I like the quiet early morning as it breaks up the raucousness of the weekend. Upstairs, I pressed a button on the cappuccino machine and the grinder began to whir. Thirty seconds later, a dark, rich espresso with a creamy, golden head was dispensed into my cup. I frothed some milk and spooned out the mousse, topping it with a sprinkle of cinnamon. This is as good as coffee gets, and it is the way that I want everything in the house: top-notch and served in the best way possible. In spite of regular breakage, I stock the house with stemware from a restaurant-supply store because serious diners shouldn't have to drink wine from a plastic cup; because a martini can only be properly served in a chilled cocktail glass; because a *digestif* should always be poured into a snifter. So it goes with our flutes for prosecco and the eighteen-ounce glasses for the draught beer tapped from the kegerator. This was part of how I was trying to slow everyone down, offering bits of elegance as a bulwark against our jihadi-like worship of speed and convenience. Sometimes I felt like a cowboy leading a large, charging herd; while I couldn't turn them on a dime, I tried whenever possible to nudge them a few degrees in the epicurean direction.

I drank my coffee out on the deck, watching the long slow roll of the sea. Afterward, I biked over to the Kismet Market to fetch the newspapers and get a total for our tab. Back at home, I opened up my spreadsheet and began doing the expenses for the weekend. We set a house record, having spent more than $1,300 on food and booze. Our guest fees covered a good chunk of this, however, and the balance divided up among shares—including Matt and me—cost each house member $31.

I clicked on another worksheet that contained a row for each house member's contact info. (This will become my record of whom I'll invite back in 2006.) I scrolled down to Troy, selected his row and painted it red. I then did the same with Grace's row. While it sucked to have to count them out, it was still only two people. At this time the year before—when I had had to recruit the whole house—I had already painted more than a dozen rows red. So to have only two people not working out was nothing to complain about.

As I stepped out of my room, the smell of bacon drew me upstairs. I posted up the weekend sheet along with all receipts and surveyed the action. Risa was overseeing the production of strawberry pancakes, while Natasha was loading the dishwasher. I carried a plate of pancakes and bacon out to the deck and sat down next to Tracy.

"Was everything okay last night?"

"Absolutely," she said. "Thank you for asking."

CrackBerry Troy had already cruised out. Then Uptalking Nancy left after breakfast to put in a few hours at the office. A lot of house members didn't make it past mid-afternoon before catching ferries back to Bay Shore, where they would pick up the train to Penn Station. I suspected that the energy level would die down a bit now that a good portion of them had gotten to meet one another. At least I hoped it would.

The following day, I received an e-mail from Nancy stating that the house was not what she had expected, specifically citing the number of people sharing rooms and the wait she claimed to have experienced for the bathrooms. She requested that I drop her down to four weekends.

I e-mailed her back, explaining that I did not offer quarter-shares. (Even though I could charge a lot more per weekend, quarter-shares didn't spend enough time at the house to feel as though they had a stake in contributing to the community we were building.) I had spent much of March and April telling perfectly good candidates that I just didn't offer quarter-shares. (Most houses offer quarter-and half-shares based on an A and B weekend series, while I created third-shares with an A, B, and C weekend series of six weekends each.) I tried to assure Uptalking Nancy that the house was a bit crowded due to the holiday weekend, and that the first weekends were always high energy, but I could tell that she had already fixed her coordinates. After getting caught stubbing out her smoke in Maggie's flower box, her situation hardly improved once Rufus lit her up as a limousine liberal. Of course, she mentioned none of this in her e-mail, shying away from specifics while continuing to insist that the house was not what she had expected. (I could even hear the uptalking in her e-mail.) Nancy wouldn't be coming back to the house until June 18, and I tried to convince her to wait until then, that if the house still didn't meet her expectations, she would have plenty of time to sell Labor Day. Still, she remained adamant.

"Screw your rules! Let her sell off her whole fucking share!"

My little voice couldn't have been more right. Many of the new people—having only signed up for third-shares—had e-mailed asking if they could buy additional weekends. So I sent an e-mail to all of the women not scheduled for Labor Day and offered up Uptalking Nancy's spot. Mandy snatched it up before day's end.

I opened up my spreadsheet and clicked on the tab with everyone's contact info. After selecting Nancy's row, I clicked on the little paint-can button, coloring it red.

Smoked Salmon Tartines

Homophobia cost me a quarter of a million dollars.

I'll explain why in a bit, but let's first back up to the summer of 1992. I was twenty-one and had just completed my junior year "studying" abroad in Normandy. During my travels that summer, I bummed around the French Riviera. After a long night of clubbing with some students in Cannes, we tiptoed into one of their parents' houses and raided the refrigerator, nicking a bottle of Veuve Cliquot, a mound of smoked salmon, and a lemon. I dropped into a bakery for a *baguette de campagne* fresh from the oven. We crashed out on the beach and broke apart the warm, crusty baguette, stuffing it with salmon and squeezing the lemon over it, drinking Champagne as the sun came up.

After breakfast, one of the girls untied her sarong and spread it out on the sand. She pulled off her top and, clad only in her panties, lay back on the sarong and folded her top into a blinder that she draped across her eyes. I tore off another hunk of baguette and stuffed it with salmon, giving the lemon another squeeze. (With the sole addition of capers, this is how I still eat smoked salmon. I don't need cream cheese, for whenever I bite into a smoked salmon tartine, I am already tasting the creamy breasts of topless French nineteen-year-olds.) Eyeing the houses up on the hill toward Monte Carlo, I wondered if—by the distant age of twenty-six—I might be able to score an advance large enough to buy such a house.

Eight years later, with literary stardom nowhere in sight, I followed up a five-year stint as the managing editor of the Authors Guild *Bulletin* with an associate editorship at a glossy trade magazine for the salary of $46,000 a year. While hardly a fortune for a Manhattanite, after five years of nonprofit wages at the Authors Guild, forty-six was dancing-in-the-streets money. It was my first meaningful disposable income, and in short order I bought a motorcycle and joined a sharehouse in Southampton. Situated north of Route 27, the house's property lay adjacent to a horse farm. My housemates were a heady, eclectic bunch, and we would barbecue and drink and eat, watching the horses galloping across the field as the sun went down. I spent as much time there as I could. During overcast days I'd downshift along winding roads, crisscrossing both forks of Long Island on my Honda Shadow in search of some downscale hamlet where I might find a modest house where I could cover costs by sharing it out. Unfortunately, the dotcom bubble was still stretching its irrationally exuberant seams, and houses in the Hamptons were already ridiculously priced. The numbers weren't realistic—even for a guy earning the kingly salary of $46,000.

Like a majority of New Yorkers, I dismissed Fire Island as gay. (Fire Island is comprised of seventeen different communities, only two of which—Fire Island Pines and Cherry Grove—cater to predominantly gay crowds.) Writing off all thirty-two miles of that barrier island as Tom Cruise Central easily cost me a quarter-mil, as prices in 2000 were half what they were when I finally bought my house in 2004. But, as they say, better four years and $250,000 worth of additional debt later than never.

In addition to the enduring misconception that All Of Fire Island Is Gay, I had to overcome another marketing challenge: For many New Yorkers, the word "sharehouse" is an epithet, and I used to be one of those people. My first sharehouse experience was as a guest at a house in Quogue, a town on the western edge of the Hamptons. Arriving on a Saturday afternoon, I had to weave around a parking lot clogging the driveway. (This was one of the many Hamptons houses in which the only way to access the beach is to drive, and beach passes are either limited to a certain number per house or are prohibitively expensive.) I walked into a large living room packed with bodies, the couches settled by four or five comatose guys. In front of them, a lower tier of guys sat cross-legged before an outlandishly large TV broadcasting baseball. Dark, puffy bags hung beneath their eyes, and they barked at the action in front of the remnants of deli sandwiches and half-drained liters of Mountain Dew. Near the breezeway, a gaggle of women huddled in front of a large mirror, gossiping as they applied makeup. Passing by one of the bedrooms, I stuck my head inside. In addition to two sets of bunk beds, a number of cots were set up to accommodate seven or eight people in the one room. Five people were passed out. Everyone had packed into van taxis at midnight to go to the bars, returning at 5 a.m., when, I suppose, it hardly mattered if there were 100 people sharing a room. I wandered out back where a couple dozen people lounged around the pool, clutching bottles of Zima and cans of Coors Light. Two women were arguing over a hookup, the uptalking flying fast and furious:

"*OHMYGOD!* I can't believe that you like [head shake] *DID* that?!"

No one seemed to hear or notice their conversation, as though it was just part of the house's white noise.

Inside and out, the house was just jam-packed with people, many of them unconscious, as though some kind of bloodless massacre had taken place. When I met the guy who ran the house, I exclaimed that the place must really fill up once everyone returned from the beach.

"Actually," he said. "This is pretty much everyone. We don't really go to the beach."

I was aghast. Why pay all that money and go all the way out there to sit around a pool? I could do that in Hackensack. Of course they all went there for the same reason that anyone joins a sharehouse. It was no different from some half-empty lame-o club roped off at the door with a long line—a place that had worked the con of convincing a certain group of people that it was the place to be.

While this scene describes more than a few postgrad Hamptons houses, it by no means represents the broader sharehouse phenomenon. When I was twenty-seven, I had begun dating a woman who had taken a share in East Hampton, one of a handful of women in a house full of gay men in their thirties. After dinner on Friday night, someone began assembling brownies à la mode with sliced strawberries and fresh whipped cream. Someone else cued up *Titanic*, which had just come out on video, and we all crowded around the TV. The boys scoffed at the movie, offering up Mystery Science Theatre 3000-esque commentary that would drop off precipitously during long takes of Leonardo DiCaprio. The movie became incidental, a conversation piece that allowed them to cattily cut one another down, to bitch, to laugh at themselves, to unwind.

That Saturday, my girlfriend and I capped off a day at the beach with a long bike ride, pedaling out of town on the wide-open country roads. Our group dinner back at the house, served in courses with different wines, reminded me of the exquisite meals I had enjoyed on the French Riviera. On Sunday night, one of the guys pulled all the uneaten produce out of the refrigerator and then phoned in a couple of lobsters. We sat down to the most superb lobster pasta salad I've ever tasted. Near the end of our meal, the chef picked up the bowl, which contained another serving.

"Who wants the rest?" he called out.

"Give it to Straight Boy," the guy next to me said, topping off my glass with chardonnay. "He's still growing."

He was absolutely right. I was still growing. They were ten years older than me and I wanted to grow up to be more like them (minus the cocksucking). I wanted to roll the way they rolled, to combat the overload of Manhattan with regular access to the beach, to belong to a community that ate and drank like kings.

Anyway, that house couldn't have been any more different than that flophouse in Quogue, which unfortunately is the kind of sharehouse that dominates the popular imagination: overcrowded with postgrads; fur flying as warring cliques fight over too few beds; bathroom sinks clogged with puke. I like to watch people's faces whenever I tell them that I own and manage a sharehouse on Fire Island; I can almost see their false impressions brewing. The All-Of-Fire Island-Is-Gay stereotype joins forces with the frat-boy sharehouse stereotype until they imagine me as the love child of George Bush and Nathan Lane.

After explaining that the house is neither gay nor a fraternity party, I then have to combat another negative connotation. Unfortunately, many sharehouse managers will take money from whomever wants in, resulting in wholly disparate personalities placed beneath the same roof. I explained that Chance was structured, that people knew where they were sleeping, and that I met everyone before letting them join. While it took a lot of time to meet everyone and weed out people who might not know how to play nice, it paid off. Upon first coming to the house, most people were blown away by how well this large group got along, and most of them just wanted to reinforce this dynamic, creating a larger, more compelling sandbox. This, for me, was the most rewarding aspect of running the house.

When it came time for the returnees from my inaugural season to re-up for 2005, many of them colluded to sign up for the same weekend series. There were forty-seven reasons why I didn't want returnees to close out one series. Since a majority of newbies have never been to Fire Island, having returnees spread out evenly would save me a lot of trouble, as they could serve as information resources about the house, Kismet, the ferries, and Fire Island in general, saving me from having to field the innumerable questions that crop up during the first weekends. With all the returnees loaded into the C series, I would have to teach the better part of the A's and B's how to do and find everything. I tried to explain to returnees that by closing out a single series they would be sequestering themselves from a lot of the new people; I joked that on the romantic front, they might lose out to the better scheduled. Still, most of them crowded into the C series and closed it out. I couldn't blame them—they wanted to continue hanging with people who had become good friends.

The first returnee to arrive for that kickoff C weekend was Joo-chan, a former pitcher who once dished heat from the mound of a Major League farm team until an unsuccessful surgery on his arm put an end to his stadium-sized dreams. He was of Korean descent, and his fastball was clocking high in the nineties at a time when recruiters were going ape-shit over Asian pitchers (even though he was American-born). It hardly surprised me that Joo-chan was the first to show up, because he didn't have a job. He loped upstairs and tossed his book on the couch, pouring himself a glass of Coke and grabbing a cylinder of Oreos before settling down in front of the TV. It was great fun to watch baseball with Joo-chan, as he could field every random question about the game. He was also well informed about Iraq, our trade deficit with China, and was by any measure a pretty smart guy; when you consider that he was one step away from becoming a Major Leaguer, really, he was like Einstein. In 2004, I overheard another house member ask Joo-chan if he wanted to play cards. Joo-chan replied that he didn't know how to play cards except for War and Crazy Eights.

"What do you mean?" I cut in, under the impression that baseball players knew every card game imaginable. "What do you mean you don't know how to play cards?"

"I don't know." He blushed. "I never learned."

"How the hell did you pass the time during all those bus trips?"

"Guys do one of three things on the bus: They play cards, they watch porn on their DVDs, and they drink. Most guys don't make it to the Majors and when I first started playing, I decided that I didn't want to be thirty-five years old and not have anything to fall back on. So on long trips, I would crack open a book."

I liked that about Joo-chan. Growing up, there were plenty of times that I found myself in guy-guy situations when to do something intelligent instead of pissing away your time moving sideways with the boys was seen as subversive or downright faggy. So I'm sure Joo-chan found himself razzed for being "a reader." Now, at thirty, hooked on the twin teats of TV and junk food, he was getting flabby and didn't seem in any particular hurry to find a job, subsisting on his baseball pension. He traveled and spent a lot of nights in bars, still transitioning to a life that wouldn't involve the roar of the crowd. Still, he didn't seem the least bit inclined to "fall back" on his mental superiority in any way that would result in a paycheck.

Next to arrive was Dani, a five-nine, model-esque blonde who had skipped out early from her office where she worked as an executive assistant. Despite being quite a dish, Dani was hardly a SHMILF. When we first met before the 2004 season, my little voice was screaming in my ear, only to settle back down after Dani's first weekend. From then on, she possessed all of the allure of a loud younger sister. At twenty-six, Dani (like Rufus) fell below my age range. She was the consummate party girl who put in long stretches sipping fruity cocktails in the hot tub while enlisting the closest male to massage her neck. Still, she was fun and made regular appearances at meetups—something that certainly didn't hurt the drive to recruit men. Besides, in the circus that is a good sharehouse, you need a couple of people like Dani—meat-and-potatoes party people—to counterbalance those high doses of cerebrality that I also love.

In Dani's tow was one of her coworkers who ended up joining the house. Let's call this woman "Joy." I first met Joy before the '04 season when Dani had brought her to one of my recruiting parties. I asked everyone to fill out an information sheet. After their contact information, the first question on the sheet is "What is your favorite kind of cheese?" It's a great and telling question. Whenever people trip over it, or think of it as a test question that must be answered correctly, I wonder whether they are right for the house. These people know that I lived in France and think they need to list a sophisticated-sounding cheese. They almost always put "Brie." I like when people treat the question like the goof that it is and answer "Toe Cheese" or "Fromunda Cheese" or "Velveeta." What I immediately liked about Joy was how she goofed the whole form. On the age bracket at the top, she filled in "37—But I feel like 36!" It went on from there. In the end, she started dating some guy and passed on the house that first season, but I felt lucky to have her join in 2005. A dozen years older than Dani's post-grad friends, Joy had actually experienced life as an adult. She had put in long hours at a Manhattan law firm, had been married, decided that she wasn't happy in her marriage, got divorced, and then decided that she no longer wanted to be an attorney. Still trying to figure out her next move, she was working alongside Dani as a ridiculously overqualified executive assistant.

A critical mass arrived on the eight o'clock ferry. While this returnee-heavy group oohed and ahhed over the transformation of the house from leaky shack to lush crib, they quickly set about getting their grooves on. Although I hardly expected the C returnees to produce the same fizzy overflow that occurred with the mostly new B people during Memorial Day weekend. Most of these people already knew each other and knew what to expect.

Maggie boiled kielbasa and bratwurst in a pot of beer and then laid them out on the grill, finally assembling a platter of beer-soaked blackened sausages in buns on the table. I sat down to eat next to Martin. If Take Your Sharehouse Manager to Work Day existed, I would hands down choose to spend the day with Martin. As a successful private investigator, he was chock full of vivid stories about liars and scumbags and paranoid celebrities. Martin, PI (as I liked to call him), had a knack for looking sharp without appearing overdressed for Fire Island. He also possessed the absolute best MP3 in the house, his iPod loaded with an array of world music ranging from Afro-Cuban jazz to South Asian dance music—a much-welcomed change of pace from Kelly Clarkson.

"*Mazel* on the house, Johnny!" Martin exclaimed. A rather charming disconnect existed between Martin's language and appearance. Despite his youthful hipness, he grew up in Brooklyn, and his Yiddish-sprinkled English was that of a seventy-five-year old man complaining about his back.

On the romantic front, Martin had had a rough off-season. The previous summer, he had become entangled with Charlotte, a house member now sitting across the table from us. Unfortunately for Martin, a situation that he had hoped might develop into a relationship, was, for Charlotte, less serious. I liked Charlotte a lot—she was one of those perpetually happy people, a walking, blooming sunflower, and the kind of person whose good mood rubs off on you. So I was glad to see no trace of residual weirdness between them— something that might have had to do with Martin's recent romantic fortune. Right before the summer, Martin had met Sonia, and Sonia Changed His World. I had asked him if he wanted Sonia to join the house. After a bit of juggling, I found three weekends during which they would share Baltic, the loft. Sonia was set to arrive the following morning.

There were only three couples in the house. Friday night's last boat brought in one of them: my friend Joe and his girlfriend, Tina. I had known Joe for years. We used to live across the street from one another in Hoboken, where our Sunday-night barbecues of calamari and shark (after playing bocce in the park) became prototypical sharehouse experiences. He and Tina had been dating for three years, and they shared the mark of a Good Sharehouse Couple, that is to say that they weren't attached at the hip. A stranger would assume that they were both single. They never came close to committing the cardinal sin of a Bad Share-house Couple, which is to treat a singles' sharehouse like a hotel, a place to carve out their own romantic nook at a discount.

As the plates began to clear, Dani connected her iPod to the stereo. Unfortunately, Dani had the shittiest taste in music of anyone in the house. She had the iPod of a sixteen-year-old. Among her fluff was that strain of gangsta rap that combines child-like cacophony with lyrics that reinforce the worst stereotypes about African-Americans for so many suburban white kids. Having grown up in a predominately black neighborhood in Paterson, New Jersey, I'm regularly amused by "wiggers." (White kids who fetishize urban blight.) Paterson, at times, was a rough place, but my brothers and I somehow didn't end up spouting off Ebonics to make a fashion statement. Nevertheless, I recognized that I was on the intellectual fringe in this area, that this "music" would continue to exist in its PC loophole that allowed it to print money for mostly white record execs. Aside from finding much of this music racist, I simply couldn't stand it on an auditory level—just as I'd go nuts if I were forced to watch repeated episodes of Barney. I never thought I'd lament the disappearance of the generation gap, but this music was for kids. (I'd suggest that the music I listened to at sixteen could kick this music for sixteen-year-olds' ass, only the people making this music are armed and actually do kill each other.) Still, I tried to bear in mind that at twenty-six, Dani was just as close in age to the kids whom all of that shit got foisted upon as she was to my age. While I was prepared to endure an overabundance of teenybopper music, I did undertake a restrictive measure to protect my sanity. This involved completely banning certain songs from play in the house. That list of songs, as it existed at the end of the 2005 season, is as follows:

AC/DC – "You Shook Me All Night Long"
Bee Gees – "Stayin' Alive"
Bob Marley – All tracks from the *Legend* CD, except for "Redemption Song" and "Exodus"
Jimmy Buffet – "Cheeseburger in Paradise"; "Margaritaville"
Neil Diamond – "Sweet Caroline"
The Eagles – "Hotel California"

Gloria Gaynor, Cake – "I Will Survive"
Gorillaz – "Clint Eastwood"
James Taylor – "Fire and Rain"
Lynyrd Skynyrd – "Sweet Home Alabama"
Puff Daddy – "Every Breath You Take"
Sugar Hill Gang – "Rapper's Delight"
Usher – "Yeah!"
Van Morrison – "Brown-Eyed Girl"

While many of these songs are bona fide members of the classic pop canon, repetition dulls the senses. "You Shook Me All Night Long" and "Rapper's Delight" still evoke fond recollections of my youth, but I've been subjected to them a few hundred thousand times too many. Some of these songs, however, just plain suck. If a great pop song is like cognac, then the Gorillaz song "Clint Eastwood" is like cough syrup. (That Gorillaz named their cloying drip of a song after such a great American like Clint Eastwood is as much an affront as if Chef Boyardee were to rename their product line after Julia Child.) Meanwhile, "Cheeseburger in Paradise" is just about the stupidest, most annoying song ever written and fuck it all if it's ever going to be played in my house.

Most people appreciated that these songs were banned and understood the list as an expression of my aversion to everything that is predictable and reflexive. More than the music, I wanted people in the house to be different. In a culture dominated by over-marketed, recycled bullshit, those who refused to drink the Kool-Aid were our first line of defense. This C group, however, weighed down with returnees, began reflexively acting out the same old script, behaving, unfortunately, like one huge clique.

*   *   *

Sonia, Martin, PI's girlfriend, arrived on Saturday morning. A cute little pixie fresh out of college, she was even younger than Rufus. I'm an ignoramus when it comes to describing women's clothes, so let's just say that she looked far more East Hampton than Kismet. Sonia wore an uncomfortable expression during the brunch hour and Martin entertained her exclusively.

The term "high maintenance" comes from cars, and a guy's car can be a decent gauge of the level of maintenance he is willing to tolerate in a girlfriend.

Suffice it to say that Martin drove a vintage Jag. At the beach, Martin set up an umbrella for Sonia and himself apart from everyone else.

The ocean was still at a temperature that turned nipples into coat hooks and intrepid bathers didn't last more than a minute. Joy stood and removed her iPod headphones. A swatch of opaque fabric hung beneath the cups of her bikini top, covering her belly. She had the feminine figure of a Playboy bunny circa 1966, back before Twiggy pissed in the pool. Still, her covered belly and her rather conservative bikini bottom made me wonder if she was self-conscious about her curves. Joy pulled a scrunchie from her hair, and her long, dark curls fell over her shoulders. When she invited the group to join her for a swim, I sat forward.

"Stay down," my little voice said.

"It's just a swim," I grumbled.

"Forget it."

I relented. Joy didn't last long in the water, marching up from the surf while wringing out her hair. Covered in goosebumps, her body displayed other telltale indicators of the water's temperature. Behind my sunglasses, my gaze fell upon the line of the curve from her waist to her hip.

"Time for your swim."

"What?!"

"Just do it."

I sighed and pushed up from my chair and stared at the surf. There was only one way to enter the ocean at this time of year, and that was to commit to doing it and then get a running start.

*   *   *

For dinner that night, Martin was grilling ribeye steaks, which Costco amazingly sold for eight bucks a pound. Ribeyes used to be a Friday night standby for Martin, who would generously spring for a couple of steaks and then treat whoever was smart enough to hang out near the barbecue when he carved up those hot, greasy strips that we'd eat with our fingers while standing around the deck. Given Costco's amazing price, we decided to upgrade ribeyes to a sit-down Saturday night dinner accompanied by spinach mashed potatoes. At the barbecue, Martin mentioned that Sonia was uncomfortable being in the house with Charlotte.

"It's always weird to meet someone's ex," I said. "Once she sees for herself that both of you have moved on, she'll relax." I wasn't sure if I was so much trying to convince Martin of this as I was myself.

"Yeah, but you know what, Johnny?" Martin shook his head and tapped his temple with four fingers. "She's young."

Natasha and Joe set up a long folding table at the end of our wooden table, creating an eighteen-foot landing strip of a dining area that extended into the kitchen beneath a tarnished crystal chandelier that once hung in the dining room of my paternal grandmother's house. (It's funny for Matt and me to see this chandelier in Chance; while Nana was a vivacious woman who loved to eat, and we enjoyed classic southern Italian meals with our extended family in that house, Nana never danced on the coffee table and no one ever did body shots with Aunt Theresa.) While it may seem strange to have a chandelier in an airy beach house, it just worked, casting its soft, elegant glow over our immense dinner table.

Unfortunately, when we sat down to dinner, Dani's iPod was still plugged into the stereo. I didn't want to make a fuss and hoped that Martin might step up and plug in his music. The intro to some other overplayed, noxious track cued up and Dani started to groove in her chair before cutting herself off.

"Wait." She shot me a look of faux concern. "Is this song banned?"

This Dani asked as though the list of banned songs were a far-reaching library that included every single track that she might consider good. Of the billions of songs that exist in the world, I simply requested that two dozen of them not be played in the house. People who couldn't manage to rock out without that handful of songs only proved my point. While most house members got a good laugh out of the list, some of them didn't understand that it wasn't a joke; I really did have to ban those songs. Since I was at the beach every weekend, I endured a fair amount of shitty and/or repetitive music, both at The Out and in the house. Every culture that has ever walked the earth has had music, songs and dance, so obviously there is something intrinsic that we derive from it. It is tragic and unhealthy that an abundance of worthwhile music—whole genres of which I remain ignorant—gets crowded out by so much corporate shit.

As much as I would like to, house members would never stand for my banning all corporate music, so I have to put up with such luminaries as Eminem, Justin Timberlake, Britney Spears, and Sean [Insert Current Infantile Nickname Here] Combs. Instead, I try to stake out certain limitations. One of my other musical pet peeves involves loud music of any kind being played during dinner. When eating, music should be ambient background noise. I deplore having to shout a dinner conversation. (If you were to find Jay-Z more compelling than the person seated next to you, Chance might not be the right beach house for you.) When Martin carried over the tray of ribeyes, I went and lowered the volume on the stereo. Then, while our plates were being cleared for dessert, Dani, unconscious that I had ever turned the volume down, strode over to the stereo and gleefully cranked it back up.

Before the table was cleared, Dani led the transition to the dance party in the living room. But I wasn't worried about the cleanup because Natasha had sprung to action. Since she never cooked, Natasha made a super effort at cleaning, a walking and breathing example of a tenet from "Belief & Technique for Epicurean Sharehouse Management":

"In sharehouse caste system those who clean are Brahmins."

Natasha was our sergeant-at-arms, a most important role in a sharehouse like ours. GE has spent tens of millions of dollars weaseling out of its commitment to clean up the PCBs it dumped in the Hudson River. If that "winner" Jack Welch would have just zipped up Natasha in a hazmat suit and promised her seven days at a luxury spa, I'll bet she could have had that fouled riverbed scrubbed down in a week. She attacked the dirty dishes, and the other cleaners deferred to her command. With the table now cleared and the dishwasher humming, Natasha joined a half-dozen people crowded onto the coffee table, including Matt, Maggie, and Tina's guest, Susan. From behind, Matt threw an arm around Susan, who began grinding back against him. When it comes to horizontal refreshment, guests are golden opportunities, as house members can then avoid post-horizontal weirdness. Of course there was no one for whom a guest hookup was more desirable than me, so while watching my brother do the butt with Susan, part of me felt an odd, recurring longing. It's not that I wanted to hook up with Susan; rather I was sad to be missing out on the idea of it.

Unlike the 2004 summer, when I regularly returned to the City during the midweek, this summer I was living out at the beach. My whole social life would unfold under the Kismet microscope and I suddenly felt as though I were wrapped in an emotional condom. Across from me, Martin sat on the couch, a wistful look on his face as he stared up at the women dancing on the coffee table. Last summer, he would have been right up there with them, only now he had different matters to attend to. I understood how he was feeling.

I crashed down on the couch next to Joy. "How come you're not dancing?" I asked her.

"Sometimes it's fun just to watch," she said. "Check out Charlotte."

I caught Charlotte exchanging a look with Joo-chan; it was nothing ostentatious, but it was a look I had seen before and Joo-chan's face flushed red, although Joo-chan was one of those Asians whose face and neck turn red when drinking. Still, an extra glow gave him away; maybe it was good that he didn't play poker...I could almost see something brewing between them, but I doubted the likelihood of horizontal refreshment, as both of them knew the perils of an in-house hookup so early in the summer.

Joy finished her drink. "Would you like a cocktail?" I asked her.

"Kind of a dumb question, dontcha think?"

"What would you like?"

She flashed an impish grin. "Whatever you'd like to give me."

I approached the wet bar and shook her a drink I'd invented called a "Christo." It's a variation on a Cosmopolitan, with some of the cranberry juice displaced by OJ to give it a saffron color similar to The Gates exhibit that the artists Christo and Jeanne-Claude had mounted in Central Park a few months earlier. I poured myself a snifter of brandy and returned to the couches.

Joy sipped her drink. "This is really good," she said. "Did you learn how to make this in France?"

"No." I laughed.

"Why are you laughing?"

"Despite their love of food and wine, the French don't know the first thing about cocktails."

"Really?"

"No one knows cocktails better than Americans."

"Well, alright then," Joy said. She polished off her Christo.

"How did you like that?" I asked her.

"It was terrible." Her eyes glistened as she handed me her empty cocktail glass. "Can you make me another?"

At the wet bar, Martin sidled up to me and grabbed a bottle of vodka.

"Johnny, what's up with this *fakakte* vodka?"

Our liquor store on the mainland offered a little-known brand of vodka at half the price of Stoli. The year before, I had asked the owner about it, wanting to make sure it wasn't nickel-plated Popov.

"That vodka is just as good as any a those other vodkas," the owner said in his rich Long Island accent. "They just don't spend the money on the advertising."

Seeing no reason for him to down-sell me, I bought a bottle and we gave it the Pepsi challenge. No one could taste any difference between that vodka and its pricier, sexier, over-marketed brethren. As the house dropped four figures on vodka, this brand saved us hundreds of dollars.

"You drank it all last summer," I said.

"Come on, Johnny. Can't we get a little Grey Goose or Ketel One?"

"Do you want to pay for it?"

He shrugged and mixed two Seabreezes, carrying them over to Sonia, who still hadn't socialized much beyond Martin. (I wondered if she had anything to do with Martin now finding the vodka unacceptable...) She seemed to perk up, however, once people mobilized to hit the bars.

The Inn was packed and I broke away from the group to talk to Doctor Stern, a dentist who lives on the bay block of Pine Walk. Doctor Stern's house is the wildest house I have ever had the pleasure to visit. There's an outdoor sculpture garden that includes half-buried mannequins adjacent to a Mongolian yurt tricked out into a sexy, sultry lair—and that's just the outside. The interior of Doctor Stern's house was jam-packed with display cases and natural wonders—it was as though a band of thieves looted the Museum of Natural History and then holed up with a crack team of decorators tripping on acid. I have met few people who give less of a fuck about what anyone else thinks of them than Doctor Stern. Tonight, she was wearing a feather boa and a fluorescent pink wig. We began to chat when I noticed Martin leaning against the bar facing Sonia, holding her hips. Elton John's "Your Song" was playing on the juke, and Martin and Sonia began singing the chorus to one another.

It was ghastly.

During the signature line, Sonia placed a finger over Martin's lips, as though to say, No, it's YOU who has made MY life wonderful, while Martin shook his head as he sang, insisting to Sonia that No, truly, it's YOU, who by being in the world has rendered life wonderful for ME.

Holy Christ Jesus.

In that instant I understood why our firearm death toll dwarfs that of all other developed nations combined; it's not that people in other countries aren't subjected to sickening PDAs during overplayed Elton John songs, they just aren't packing heat at the time. I am largely sane, but had I been armed and red-brained upon witnessing that display with that treacly soundtrack playing in the background, I'm just not sure that I wouldn't have taken the express route to the front page of the *Post*.

I bid adieu to Doctor Stern and dropped by The Out, where I found another group of house members clustered near the dance floor. Deee Lite's hit "Groove Is in the Heart" was playing and I stood along the wall, watching Natasha tear up the floor. Nearby, Johnny Thunder was cranking his fists in the air. Joy bopped over to me and grabbed my wrists, pulling me onto the dance floor. Thanks in part to the two Christos I had shaken for her, she was drunk. Not sloppy, falling-down wasted, but solidly, squarely drunk. We began to dance, and her arms fell out of time from the music until they swayed at her sides. She moved closer to me, staring hard into my eyes. She draped her wrists over my shoulders, and her smile fell away as though something inside of her was trying to fight its way out. My hands came to rest on the tops of her hips, rousing my little voice:

"What the fuck are you doing?!"

Glancing over at Natasha, I remembered how I had steeled myself not to hit on her all through the '04 season; now I would have to do the same with Joy. It would be incredibly stupid to do otherwise. Like, imagine you were the President of the United States and you thought it might be fun to score a couple BJs from an emotionally unstable twenty-one-year-old intern. It would be almost as stupid as that.

"Groove" wound down and then that eurotrash dance remix of "Cotton-Eyed Joe," that horrendous stadium anthem, cued up. This may well be the worst song that the world has ever known. I told Joy that I was going to take off.

"Why did you TELL her you were leaving?"

"I'll come with you," she said.

We walked out along the bay, passing The Inn and the Kismet Market and turning onto Pine Walk. After crossing the main road, Joy stopped in front of the house.

"Let's go to the beach," she said.

"No!" my little voice thundered.

"It's kind of chilly," I said.

"What's that thing you said in that list of stuff?" Joy said. "Never go straight from bar to house but always stop at the beach?"

"I'm kind of beat," I said.

"You know, I'm just trying to follow your rules." She shook her head. "You're pretty complicated, John Blesso." Her devil grin fell away, once again morphing into that look that I had seen in The Out. We trod past the house and over the dune crossing onto the sand.

"Are you listening to me? No! Absolutely fucking NO!"

It was cold and windy and the stars were out, the constellations overlaid like a Pollock painting. We sat down on the sand facing the surf, and she grabbed my arm, nuzzling against my shoulder.

"Don't do it, Johnny! Don't fucking do it..."

A gust blew in from over the waves, and Joy leaned her head against mine. Her dark curls blew across my face. I couldn't believe how good she smelled. Breathing in her scent, I again harped upon the realization that I was now living at the beach; this *was* my social life. What was I supposed to do? Become a monk?

"No! Just don't stick your dick in the house!"

Joy smiled at me again, her stare locking mine like a tractor beam, coming together in a look that was damn near devastating. After the whirlwind of the past year and a half, a red-tape morass of paperwork, permits and people-people-people, it just felt nice to be sitting next to Joy watching the surf roll in on a starry night.

"Don't do it!"

Older than most of the women in the house, Joy's life had already taken a few turns; she had perspective and maturity. That's the thought that settled in my mind as our fingers locked together. After fending off my SHMILF temptation for more than a year, I could feel my defenses crumbling. I felt like Muhammad Ali dropping his hands in front of Emmanuel Lewis.

Unless you didn't realize until that numbnuts Charlton Heston did that Soylent Green was made out of people, you'll not be surprised when I tell you that despite my little voice's barrage of epithets impugning my intelligence and judgment, Joy's stare was just too much for me to bear. My hand slid up her back and my fingers got lost in that jungle of curls as we began to kiss. From now on you will know Joy by her real name: Rule Number One.

Belmont Breeze

The following morning, my eyes peeled open to the sight of Rule Number One lying next to me, asleep.

"Nice work."

"Thanks," I muttered in response to my little voice. Indeed, I thought I had made a huge mistake—until Rule Number One's eyes opened and her starry look came into focus on mine. I slid my hand over the curve of her waist and pulled her closer. Breathing in her scent, it didn't feel like a mistake at all. She placed her hands on my chest, separating herself from me.

"Did we just royally screw up?"

"No," I said. "It's fine. At least I think it is."

"Don't worry," she said. "I just want to be your C-Weekend Girl." Her devil grin returned. "So what are the perks that come with being one of the sharehouse manager's hookups?"

Her punchy humor seemed to be masking something else—nervousness, apprehension—but pulling her back against me, I was no longer thinking about any of that. I was thinking about morning sex. I dashed off to the bathroom, but when I returned, Rule Number One was putting on her clothes. A few hours later, she boarded a mid-afternoon boat back to the mainland.

On Monday, I thought about calling her but my little voice warned me against it:

"She wrote it off as a hookup and so should you."

We didn't speak at all that week, and I soon became distracted with troubleshooting the new plumbing and responding to rounds of e-mails from excited house members. They wanted to sign up to cook meals; they wanted to trade weekends; they wanted to reserve guest spots. Tracy e-mailed me about organizing a Belmont Stakes happy hour. In addition to a house pool, she wanted to serve a cocktail called the Belmont Breeze, a drink created by the legendary mixologist Dale De Groff—the Belmont's answer to the Kentucky Derby's mint julep. As a recovered Catholic, I still love fanfare and ceremony—especially when traditions are celebrated through eating and drinking. So I included Tracy's Belmont Stakes happy hour in the rundown of culinary events scheduled for the weekend.

On Friday morning, I gathered up my cooler, two soft-cooler bags, two thirty-gallon plastic bins, and a large knapsack, pulling them on my garden cart down to the ferry dock. It was time for my run to Costco, where I dropped more than $600 a week on food. I arrived at the end of the ferry dock just as the hulking passenger ship nosed in at an angle. The bow was a few feet from the pilings when the captain threw the engine in reverse, swinging its stern right up alongside the dock. I boarded the boat and walked up to the deck, lying down on one of the benches. Sometimes it was hard for me to nap in the house, as I was too easily distracted by loose ends. On the ferry, however, I was blissfully helpless for the next twenty-five minutes. Once I lay back on the bench, the vibrations from the motor knocked me out like a baby until the boat slowed down to dock at Bay Shore.

After disembarking at the main terminal, I picked up my car. Driving out, I stopped at the freight terminal to snag the empty keg I had sent over on the freight ferry the day before. I dropped off the empty at the distributor and rolled over my deposit onto a new keg that would be delivered on Saturday morning. Then I hit the liquor store and paid for all of the wine and booze that would also get delivered on Saturday.

At Costco, I wheeled a towering cart of food and supplies out to my car, where I packed everything into bins and coolers. Back at the ferry terminal, a college-aged woman was loading freight alongside a guy who was a couple of years older. Most people who rode the ferries on any kind of regular basis knew this guy, at least by sight. Trim with close-cropped auburn hair, he called out the destinations in a loud, clear voice:

"All aboard! Fair Harbor, Saltaire, and Kismet!"

While I've heard people complain about the ferry crew's surliness, those people forget that in trying to keep the boats on time, the crew was perpetually playing against a clock at a job that involved heavy lifting. Still, I was hardly the only passenger who noticed the pride this one guy took in his job. His courtesy and professionalism were top-notch, and it was always a pleasure to be served by him. When I presented my bins and cooler, his voice took on an apologetic tone as he charged me a mere four dollars for my freight. I carried my backpack and two soft coolers upstairs and crashed down on the upper deck.

Jeannie, Kismet's columnist for the *Fire Island Tide*, shot me an exaggerated come-hither glance as she came up the stairs. I'm not sure how old Jeannie is; suffice it to say that she has a couple of decades on me. She sat down next to me and asked when I was going to have a party. I told her about the Belmont Stakes happy hour and invited her to drop by. She didn't hear me, though, distracted by a handsome college-aged lad walking toward the back of the boat. Jeannie, you see, is infamous.

According to rumor, during the seventies, Jeannie hung a beach towel from her deck railing that bore her phone number. If you were a man—especially a younger man—and you spotted that towel, you could just walk right on in. Running Chance had taught me something about myths and rumors though, so I always considered this bit of Kismet lore suspect. What is true, however, is that the towel did and does exist. (Keeping up with the times, Jeannie's current towel bore her e-mail address.) So Jeannie was hardly shy about still possessing the sex drive of a teenager. And why the hell should she be? I could only hope that I'll still be able to get my soldier to salute when I'm her age—whatever indeterminate age that might be. I once sat next to Jeannie at The Inn during the hurricane season of 2004; the TV was tuned to the news of storms, one of which was named Jeannie.

"I'm a hurricane!" Jeannie proclaimed, bringing her hand down on the bar.

"Actually, Jeannie," I pointed at the TV, "you're just a tropical storm."

"Really?" She looked disappointed.

"Although it's possible that you could turn into a hurricane." I took a sip of my beer. "But you'd have to blow harder."

I liked Jeannie because it took courage to be a pariah in a small town, although Kismet was a crazy place during the seventies. (Of course, it was crazier everywhere during that decade, but from the stories I've heard, Kismet was truly cranked up to eleven.) Jeannie once described being met at the Kismet ferry dock with a cocktail. From the dock, she moseyed over to the bars and then to a party, not actually arriving at her house until the following morning. I met a guy who had been a share in my house back then—when the house was called Apples—and he described the scene like this:

"Back then, every house you went to had marijuana sitting in piles on the table. There were single people everywhere and everybody was fucking everyone else." He shrugged and shook his head. "Then the eighties happened and they all got married, had kids, and voted for Reagan."

In Kismet, a near seamless tolerance exists between the sharehouses and the families. Many of these parents, like my next-door neighbors, Nick and his wife, Nicoletta (who were shares in my house years before I bought it), were not far removed from the scene. Across the walk from me, Dick and Heidi shared their communal deck with their friends and extended family. While they could certainly hear our acoustic jam sessions and after-dinner dance parties, their grand-kids sometimes made up for it in the morning. We all got along. Certainly it helps that Kismet is a hard-drinking town. I'm talking Mickey Mantle–John Barrymore–Ernest Hemingway hard-drinking. Drinking in Kismet reminds me of the way people drank during my first two years at UConn—only Kismet drinkers aren't distracted by having to learn anything. I am, by any measure, a good drinker. On any given Saturday, I might down a gin martini at sunset, drain the better part of a bottle of wine during dinner, follow that up with a healthy snifter of armagnac or calvados, and then switch over to beer at the bars. In Kismet, however, that regimen—and its pacing—makes me something of a lightweight. Kismet's serious drinkers don't pace themselves. In fact, they would laugh at the whole notion. They just start drinking at some point late in the morning, and, well, whatever happens, happens.

As the ferry began its approach to the Kismet dock, Jeannie informed me that she wanted to write about Chance in the *Fire Island Tide*. I reminded her of the Belmont Stakes happy hour and she promised to stop by. The ferry crew began to hitch the boat to the dock and people filed downstairs. Jeannie, ever the social butterfly, fluttered off to chat with someone else. After stepping off the boat, I fetched my cart and loaded up my bins and coolers. Pulling the cart off the dock, I felt a mild ache in my shoulders. In deciding to set up an epicurean house, I couldn't have chosen a location with worse logistics. Everything comes in on the boats. Either you lug your stuff on and off the passenger ferry, or you drop it off at the freight ferry for delivery the following morning (not an option for perishables). Either way, you schlep. I sometimes told myself that having to schlep everything the house consumed was good exercise (although it wasn't aerobic and involved heavy lifting). Still, I jokingly accepted that such were the travails of "The Hardest Working Man in Sharehouse Business."

I first gave myself this title as a gag, tipping my hat to James Brown. After inserting this line in my e-mail signature and website, people began to refer to me as such until I quickly grew sick of hearing it. But its sheer repetition had created a self-fulfilling prophecy.

If you were to ask a group of seven-year-olds what they'd like to be when they grow up, very few of them would cough up "sharehouse manager," and my own rise to that esteemed post was rather circuitous. While working at the Authors Guild, I published a book of alternative fiction and then began writing a novel called *Killing Mercutio* (not knowing then that I would spend the next seven years writing and rewriting that draft). In 2000, I left the Authors Guild for an ill-fated six-month stint in corporate publishing, hated it, and then, at twenty-nine, became a nanny, once again, in Manhattan.

While I may well have been "The Hardest Working Man in the Aspiring Novelist Business," I never afforded my day jobs the same intense dedication that I showered upon my writing. Still, I can look back at some real achievements during my years at the Authors Guild. I campaigned hard to write an investigative piece that exposed unscrupulous "book doctors" who sang songs of imminent publication to aspiring writers, only to then charge them extortionate fees through bogus third-party editing services. The article was reprinted in other publications, and led to an investigation by the New York State Attorney General. As a nanny, I like to think that I provided a decent example for the children I've looked after, although I was hardly The Hardest Working Man in the Nannying Business.

In November 2002, after two years of nannying in the City, the boy I was looking after outgrew me. I tried to find another post, but the dot-com bubble had burst and nannying wages dropped back down from the stratosphere. I began looking for another in-house job at a magazine or a publisher, but with the Dow having dipped back down to 7,000, I couldn't even manage to land an interview. While people joke about kicking back and collecting on the easy street of unemployment, being jobless can throw a good number of people into full-fledged identity crises. I don't care what anyone says—it is neither fun nor healthy to be unemployed, and a confluence of events made my own experience all the more trying.

That winter was when George W. Bush began building the NeoCons' bullshit case to invade Iraq. While no shortage of military and regional experts decried the pitfalls of "breaking" Iraq, all of them were fired, kneecapped, or silenced. Once Colin Powell drank the Kool-Aid, things started to get scary for me, and I began spending too much of my free time—which, unfortunately, was all of my time—watching and reading the bold and grim news. This only depressed and alienated me from my worker-bee friends, who, spending long days at the office, were too preoccupied to realize that Bush was gearing up to drive world stability into a ditch. Watching those NeoCon chicken-hawks—none of whom had ever seen a day of combat—cobble together that ill-fated adventure was like watching a train wreck in slow motion. I marched. I wrote letters. I signed petitions. But it was all too clear that preemptively invading Iraq was a foregone conclusion. In the fear and anxiety of the post-9/11 world, reason was now dead and George Bush was creaming in his pants. I felt like I was chained to a post, unable to collar a ten-year-old marching toward the barn while striking matches.

So aside from the funk of unemployment, I was further dispirited by our looming invasion of the *wrong...fucking...country*. Were we really going to do that? We were. Holy fucking shit...

Meanwhile, after seven years of gamely wrestling with *Killing Mercutio*—now a dense, 700-page draft—the novel's numerous themes, story lines, subplots, and characters overwhelmed me. I felt like a heart surgeon whose hand had gone numb. Not wanting to butcher the draft in my compromised state, I knew that I needed to wait until I felt better. Only I had organized my life around *Killing Mercutio* for so long that without it, I no longer knew what to do with myself. I felt as rudderless and adrift as our misguided foreign policy, which was ramping up for the biggest strategic blunder in American history.

So, there I was: A thirty-one-year-old unemployed male nanny who had frittered away his career-building years chasing after a pipe dream. I thought about my friends who had created sensible careers for themselves—like my brother Matt, who was preparing to hire his first employee. I didn't envy their jobs or salaries; during all of my years of lean living, I dreamed only of earning enough money to eat or drink whatever I wanted. That was my goal in life, and I always thought it modest. Now, I felt as though I were back at square one, staring down another decade of meager living, only I didn't even know which path to follow.

This anxiety made fast friends with short-term worries about money. Since disposable income was never something I had had in abundance, being cut off from that meager teat led to too many Friday nights alone in my apartment, the trumpet intro to the *Newshour* sending me into the kitchen, where I'd drop a package of chicken thighs into a baking pan and coat them with cumin, cayenne, and coriander in a desperate effort to taste something. I'd toss them in the oven on high heat and then crash down in front of the TV, cracking open a tall can of Old Milwaukee and spearing up whole thighs with a fork in front of *Washington Week in Review*. Once the credits rolled it wasn't long before (to paraphrase Tom Waits) I had thoroughly taken advantage of myself, capping off another cheap night alone, further alienating me from my friends, who seemed to think that everything was just fine.

Killing Mercutio lay scattered across my desk among notes, files, clippings, and other materials. The mere sight of it all tormented me, highlighting my inability to make sense of it. Meanwhile, the NeoCons had conned us with their shell game, swapping Saddam Hussein for Osama bin Laden. This was when I asked myself a hard question: How could I forge ahead with a novel—something that was made up for people's enjoyment—when we weren't paying attention to things that were true and that really, really mattered?

Not wanting to face that question, I gathered my notes and materials into a manila folder and began magic-markering "KILLING MERCUTIO" across the cover. After drawing the E, however, my hand froze. I stared down at the words I had just penned in block letters: KILLING ME.

I became short of breath. That's what this book is doing, I thought. It's killing me. Like George Bush, I didn't understand that steadfast determination was hardly admirable when you're headed down the wrong track. Glancing over at the mirror, I was astounded by the cowed look on my face. I felt impotent and disoriented, as though I was thrashing about in a dark cave. Rising up from my desk, I walked over to the mirror and asked God, or my subconscious, or whatever that entity is that knows all the shit that I don't figure out until much later on to please, please lift this burden from me. I then closed my eyes and let go of my book, shelving seven years of my life.

In that moment of surrender, a swirling lightness rose up in me as though I were being drained of a heavy liquid. I felt the way I imagine one might feel after a long-suffering relative finally passes away. While a monumental relief, it also brought great sadness. The characters in *Killing Mercutio* had been with me longer than many of my actual friends. I felt as though I had forsaken them, as though I were watching them pull away on a train, not knowing if I was ever going to see them again.

As the TV and the Internet led me to the looming invasion, I avoided them, spending most of the day reading, pathetically lying in bed curled up with my cats as the sun rose and fell during those short days. The speed with which I was burning through books only heightened my sense of not having anything else to do, so I decided to read an outlandishly long book.

I choose *Roots* and loved it. Wanting more of Alex Haley, I then read *The Autobiography of Malcolm X*. This led to James Baldwin's *The Fire Next Time*, which then sent me reading and rereading a good part of his canon. I then reread *Invisible Man* before cooling off with Walter Mosley, wondering why I kept turning to African-American literature. I now realize that I gravitated toward those books searching for strength, for answers, that immersing myself in the literature of a people who had been fucked over for 400 years gave me some perspective as a property-owning white male temporarily finding himself on the wrong side of history.

I knew that what I most needed was to get back to work, only I still couldn't land so much as an interview. I scanned a popular new site called Craig's List and drummed up freelance editing projects. I also became a focus group habitué—a job that I absolutely loved. I started bartending for a catering company, getting over the hurdle of working alongside postgrads ten years younger than me. I began tutoring my doctor's son in French, bartending at private parties, working as an assistant for a friend's wife, doing whatever odd jobs I could get while trying to establish myself as a freelance editor.

In the spring of '03, after landing a huge editing project that lasted a number of weeks, I decided to reward myself with a summer share, something I hadn't done in three years. Unfortunately, that cool Southampton farmhouse was no longer being shared out, so I checked out Craig's List and the Village Voice in search of another downscale house. But now a lot of Hamptons half-shares were going for three grand and up. Aside from being priced out, a lot of those managers seemed wholly preoccupied with scoring tickets to polo matches, or figuring out how to make the guest list at Puff Daddy's parties. I quickly realized that my Southampton farmhouse and its bohemian crew were an anomaly. After informing my brother that I was going to look at the Jersey Shore, he suggested Fire Island.

"Isn't Fire Island gay?" I asked.

"I think only parts of it are," he said.

I began researching Fire Island on the Net. After learning that it was overwhelmingly straight, I was further astounded by its geography—no matter where you are on that barrier island, you are always close to the beach. Also, the island banned cars. No more angling my motorcycle between Mercedes convertibles or standing around waiting for people to coordinate their rides. There were few celebrities, and polo was not being played. Then I saw that Fire Island half-shares were going for considerably less than in the

Hamptons, where you pony up a premium just to penetrate the red velvet ropes of Route 27 East. If social-climbing and star-fucking aren't your bag, to do a share in the Hamptons, in many cases, is to set the first thousand dollars of your share price on fire.

Matt and I ended up joining a house in Kismet run by a real character. Like Johnny Thunder and Jeannie, this guy is as familiar a part of the Kismet landscape as the dune crossings or the rusted wagons. For some reason, he was known as Bicycle Bill. (In Kismet, nicknames are so pervasive that after a while they no longer faze you. I've never wondered what Johnny Thunder's real name is, nor did I blink upon first hearing about the legendary impresario "Punk Rock Pete," or that the propane was delivered by a friendly, soft-spoken man who went by the most misleading moniker "Boomer.") While Bicycle Bill is old enough to remember where he was when he learned of the Kennedy assassination, I often think of him as the World's Oldest Twenty-Three-Year-Old. He's got a great, weathered face like a sea captain, and despite battered knees, Bicycle Bill still danced and partied like a ninth-semester college student bounding out of his last class on Thursday. I first met Bicycle Bill at a meetup that he hosted in his apartment. A vast array of cheese was laid out across his coffee table. I sat down next to a guy who was the math consultant for the movie *A Beautiful Mind*. He was explaining to a bohemian-looking woman just why Thai basil and regular basil were wholly different animals. When I learned that Bicycle Bill taught cinematography, I asked him his favorite director. He treated me to an impassioned argument as to why he thought Hitchcock was the best. Listening to these disparate, offbeat conversations while hitting the cheeses, I remembered my old farmhouse in Southampton and knew that I wanted in.

My first visit to Fire Island—as is the case with many people—blew me away: the wild, green growth of the dunes and the pristine beach just steps away from the house; Kismet's working-class and bohemian crowd spilling willy-nilly from weathered houses. While I fell hard for Kismet, Bicycle Bill's house turned out to be what I did and didn't expect. The group's heady eclecticism certainly held up, although they were a bit couple-heavy that year and the age range spanned a couple of decades. Still, I met a lot of interesting people and was most impressed by how well Bicycle Bill combated Fire Island's logistics, providing house members with as much of what they needed as possible. No one had to lug sheets, towels, or beach chairs onto the ferry. There was house shampoo and toothpaste, sunscreen and bugspray. (Costco's large sizes and low prices make the box store ideal for these purchases.) Most importantly, there was plenty of food.

After learning that houses in Kismet were relatively cheap—at least compared to the Hamptons and other Fire Island towns—it wasn't long before I started thinking that *I* could run a sharehouse in Kismet (one that had more singles in my age range) and that maybe I could take it to a new level. With gentrification sweeping through upper Manhattan, my West Harlem condo had appreciated considerably. I told Matt that I wanted to look into buying a house and sharing it out—once I was working more steadily. While this is the way rational people think, when your brother is an ambitious, up-and-coming developer, you hear a different tune. You hear things like, "When interest rates are so low, *debt is your friend!*" and "Now is the *perfect* time for you to buy a house because you have the time to renovate it."

I thought of the growing pile of equity in my condo and how I was just sitting on it...

Boys and girls, can you say re-FI-nance?

We began plugging numbers into a spreadsheet. Once it became clear that I could cover costs on a house by sharing it out, finding one became my central focus. That fall, I began bartending at a restaurant in the Village. Still hustling up editing work, I continued to participate in focus groups while scouring Craig's List for odd jobs, keeping busy and pulling in cash wherever I could. I eventually signed a contract on the house that would become Chance, but would not close on it until March 2004. I would only have ten weeks to suitably fix it up while also recruiting all the shares. Knowing I would have to hit the ground running, I spent a good part of that winter researching all my purchases on the Net until everything was just one click away. The house, previously known as "Echo Beach," was foul. It had been a sharehouse rental for years. I built up the walls of a ten-yard dumpster by lining it with old box springs and then filling it far above the rim with trash. Captain's beds (without drawers) had been built in to every room; I spent long days swinging a prybar and a hammer to tear them out. (I easily scraped up two dozen crusted condoms from beneath those beds amid enough stubbed-out roaches to have stayed high for a week.) I tore out the carpet and then painted everything white, doing whatever I could to make the house presentable in that short time frame. I've never worked harder than during those first six months of 2004, putting in sixteen-hour days, seven days a week, renovating and recruiting house members right up into the high season.

Once again, I had developed a somewhat perverse notion toward work. A job, for me, was just something to pay the bills, something that enabled me to write. While it probably seems obvious and Boy Scout-y to most people, I was older than Jesus before truly understanding that you should always do your best at whatever job you're lucky enough to have. Not to put too fine a point on it, but throwing myself full-force into renovating, recruiting, and running Chance was ultimately what pulled me out of a pretty rough place.

While I still hoped to one day take another crack at *Killing Mercutio*, I learned to consider that possibility gravy, realizing that it wasn't healthy to peg my happiness to something beyond my control. What made me happy now was fostering the fun, interesting community of people with whom I lived large in Kismet. While I sometimes felt like a pack mule or a glorified super, to be sitting on the ferry on a sunny, breezy day, my muscles pleasantly aching from my Costco run, and an e-mail inbox filled with house member requests waiting for me back at home was nothing to complain about. Running Chance felt like a natural extension of my years spent nannying. The "kids" now under my care were just larger and required a different kind of juice box. In fact, Machiavelli once said, "the distinction between children and adults...is at bottom a specious one. There are only individual egos, crazy for love."

I was met at the door by some house members who helped carry the bins upstairs to be unloaded. We have two refrigerators—the main one in the kitchen and a reserve fridge in a shed (as well as a counter-high fridge next to the kegerator for open beverages). After we finished unloading, all of the refrigerators were jam-packed, save for the bottom half of the outdoor fridge, which was ready for the new keg arriving on Saturday morning.

I checked my e-mail. CrackBerry Troy was bagging that weekend. That was fine by me. His co-worker, Wayne, a house member, wanted to know if he could bring a friend to take Troy's place. Of course, he was hoping that his friend wouldn't have to pay guest fees. I e-mailed him back, explaining that all guests must pay guest fees. Wayne e-mailed back his okay, informing me that he and his guest would be arriving on Saturday.

Wayne was a bright and witty guy who initially expressed an interest in cooking Asian food, and after meeting him and seeing that he knew how to play nice, I offered him a spot. He told me that he wanted in, adding that his friend (who turned out to be Troy) was also interested. As an officially licensed jackass, Troy remains a perfect example of why you should never let friends join in stages. If you offer a spot to one person, and then you meet the next person and you don't like them, it makes for a rather awkward situation. I hosted my meetups at the White Horse Tavern, a literary dive in the West Village. Sharehouse meetups—especially for postgrad Hamptons houses— are often held in loud, swanky clubs, the manager out to impress potential shares as a socially connected impresario upon whose coattails they can ride. Since my Q-rating fell somewhere south of Wilfred Brimley's, I couldn't get people in to such places; besides there's no place to "get in to" in Kismet. The White Horse—where Dylan Thomas fell off a stool and died after drinking two dozen whiskeys—is very much a bar. The back room is a great place to converse—unlike loud clubs—and it was usually empty at six o'clock, so I'd stake out a couple of tables in the corner. The bar itself was a good filter, as people underwhelmed by the White Horse's lack of swank were probably looking for something different than what I was offering at Chance.

I could sometimes be out-of-sorts by the end of these gatherings, as I usually ended up talking for about two hours straight, replaying verbal loops and answering the same questions over and over, marketing Fire Island, Kismet, and my house to whomever was in earshot while trying to gauge whether or not our interest was mutual. I am only able to spend so much time with one person. Troy dropped in during the end of the meetup, when the questions come fast and furious. Troy and I didn't get to talk much, but he seemed (as I put it earlier) "minimally acceptable." Had he come by himself, I probably would have negged him, but Wayne, whom I liked, was already in, and, as I've explained, it's not easy to find suitable guys in March or April.

A few days later, however, Wayne began to sing a tale of financial woe. He had just gotten beat by the IRS, had moved into a new apartment and had to pay first and last months' rent, blahbety-blah-blah... I'm continually amazed by the number of yuppies—earning salaries I've only dreamed about—who still live hand to mouth. (Although the so-called "conservatives" spending our tax dollars like drunken sailors were hardly setting an example...) I offered Wayne a very favorable arrangement: I requested $300 cash to hold his spot, while allowing him to pay his balance any time before July 4. He thanked me profusely, and we set up a time for me to pick up his deposit.

The following day, I was eating lunch at my parents' house in Paterson. Instead of taking the direct route back across the lighter traffic of the GWB, I drove down to the Lincoln Tunnel to meet Wayne in midtown at 4:30. Why would I go through such trouble? Because men are far more likely to flake, or to continue shopping around for another house, and once I've offered them a spot, I want to lock them in. Unfortunately, after sitting double-parked on 42nd Street for fifteen minutes during rush hour, I got a call from Wayne, who explained that he was being called in to a meeting and couldn't come down to meet me. He once again apologized. I gritted my teeth and told him it was no problem; I was soon hosting a pizza party where returnees would be paying for their shares, so I suggested that he pay me at the party. He agreed. You won't be surprised to learn that a few hours before this party, Wayne e-mailed that he wouldn't be able to make it, but that he definitely wanted in and would catch up with me later on to give me cash.

"*Cut your losses.*"

"Really?"

"*Do it,*" my little voice implored me.

"But—"

"*If he's being a pain now, he isn't going to get easier later on.*"

While I knew my little voice was right, Troy had already paid a deposit and was bringing his balance that night. So when Troy arrived, I pulled him aside and explained why I was going to neg Wayne and that if he wanted to back out, I would gladly give him back his deposit. I invited him to hang out with everyone, have a slice of pizza and let me know what he thought at the end of the night. Troy gravitated toward Vanessa and seemed to know how to play nice. Additionally, two other promising male prospects were no-shows, and with four guy spots left to fill, I was only too happy when Troy told me that he still wanted in.

The following morning, Troy e-mailed me asking if I would reconsider my decision to neg Wayne. He promised to keep on Wayne and make sure that he paid promptly. I opened up my spreadsheet and saw four guy spots that I still had to fill. I was still behind schedule with renovations that had to be completed before the start of the season. (This was even before the water-heater fiasco.)

"*Don't do it.*"

Treating my little voice to a sharp elbow, I re-invited Wayne to join.

Wayne then promptly paid his deposit. Now he was coming out to the house for the first time. The Belmont Stakes happy hour was already underway when he arrived late on Saturday afternoon with his guest, Leon. Wayne presented Leon's guest fees in cash. (That he made this transaction easy couldn't have gotten him off to a better fresh start.) Meanwhile, Tracy was already mixing up round two of her Belmont Breezes. At first I questioned whether this would be a good house cocktail, as its laundry list of ingredients included both whiskey and sherry, but cranberry juice gave it body and it was finished with a splash of soda (instead of 7-Up), a strawberry slice, and a mint sprig. It was quite refreshing, solidifying Tracy's culinary creds. Someone else had made a batch of virgin Bloody Marys (to allow for different potencies of vodka).

"I gotta get caught up here," Wayne joked. And that's just what he did. He was on his third cocktail when Jeannie came up the stairs. She began mingling straightaway, and I was putting together a Belmont Breeze for her when Wayne stepped in front of her. Now, bear in mind that Wayne didn't know anything about the towel rumor; still, he drained his glass and said the following to Jeannie:

"What's happening, hot stuff?"

I had never seen Jeannie light up quite like that, and in that moment, all was truly forgiven with Wayne. I thought him pure Chance material.

Tracy scurried about, arranging one more last-minute pool over yet another round of Belmont Breezes. The race began, and we all screamed at the TV as my randomly drawn horse, Afleet Alex, passed a half-dozen other horses, making his way to the front of the pack. During the last turn, Andromeda's Hero, Rufus's horse, was still in the lead, and Rufus began smacking his own ass as Afleet Alex passed Andromeda's Hero on the final leg for the win. As the winner of Tracy's pool, I promised everyone that I would buy drinks later that night at The Inn.

Jeannie wanted to take a picture of us for the newspaper, so I herded a bunch of house members outside. We crowded into the corner of the deck. At the last minute, Wayne scurried over and dove across the plastic table in front of us, lying on his side like a model for a Dutch master. Possibly Wayne had been inspired by Afleet Alex, because by the time we sat down to dinner, Wayne had definitely caught up. In fact, he had lapped everyone. I could hear my little voice whistling smugly to himself.

In the movie of Steven King's *Misery*, Kathy Bates plays "the number one fan" of novelist James Caan, whom she rescues from a car accident. Kathy Bates takes him home and begins nursing him back to health, but there is an ominous moment when the viewer realizes—along with James Caan—that he is not in the care of a good Samaritan; he is being held prisoner by a lunatic. During the '04 season, we had a woman named Roberta who was a smart, gregarious, and rather attractive brunette who knew an awful lot about wine. Once she arrived at the house, however, she began to complain. During her first Sunday morning, a number of us were eating brunch out on the deck over the Sunday *Times*. Roberta, hungover, joined us. Setting down her cup on one of the plastic tables, she lit a cigarette and then pulled the table closer. One of the legs dragged, knocking over her coffee.

"MOTHER*FUCK*ER!" she screamed, trashing a peaceful morning, cursing up a storm over having to go inside to get another coffee. That was Roberta's Kathy Bates moment, and she only became an increasing buzzkill as the summer wore on.

Wayne's Kathy Bates moment occurred after we sat down to a dinner of glazed ginger pork chops and wasabi mashed potatoes. We were just digging in when Wayne stood, raised his wineglass, and slurred the following:

"John Blesso is...the hardest...motherfuckin'...workin' man...in the sharehouse business!"

He then fired off a pitch-perfect impersonation of the James Brown scream. People laughed and the conversation moved on. At least it tried to, only Wayne then cut off whoever spoke with another scream:

"*Yeah!*"

I laughed it off and someone else tried to pick up the thread, but Wayne gave another yell and began muttering in James Brownspeak, crushing any attempt at conversation.

"Jump back! Kiss myself!"

Wayne was wasted.

Hey, it happens. We've all gotten faced and said and done things big and small that we've later regretted. This is just a small thing, I told myself. It's his first weekend at the house, and he's excited. After all, half the house was so off their chairs during Memorial Day that the juggling of cooking utensils became incorporated into the dance party. Every Saturday morning I hauled six hundred bucks worth of booze from the dock, so it should come as no surprise when someone gets wasted. What did concern me, however, was the nervous look on the face of Leon, Wayne's guest.

Out of nowhere, Wayne launched into a haranguing monologue about Dr. J, Julius Erving. He was seated next to Rosemarie, the girlfriend of our resident stoner, Jeffrey. Now, Rosemarie was blessed with a set of cans so eye-catching that no single guy in the house ever once commented on them. There was just no need to. It would have been like acknowledging, upon a glass crashing to the floor, the force of gravity. Besides, she was off-limits. The funny thing, however, is that the women in the house wouldn't shut up about Rosemarie's breasts, providing all manner of commentary on the geometric perfection of her tatas. So a good deal of what Wayne had to say was delivered to this nonauditory portion of Rosemarie's body. Jeffrey looked on nervously as Wayne continued to blather:

"Because man you know what? *Fuck* Michael Jordan! Doc J was the greatest motherfucker that ever *lived!* When you gave Doc J the ball, it was like fucking *poetry* man! When that motherfucker charged the hoop it was like a motherfucking sonnet in motion!"

Rosemarie, who was from Germany, probably didn't even know who the 76ers were, let alone Dr. J, but that hardly fazed Wayne.

"One time I went to this Philly cheesesteak place and guess who the fuck was standing in front of me getting a Philly cheesesteak? Guess?"

Rosemarie ignored him.

"The *DOC!* That's who! Do you know what that motherfucker got on his Philly cheesesteak?"

"Actually," Rosemarie said, "I couldn't care less."

We tried, as a table, to move on, only Wayne kept foisting over-intellectualized diatribes upon us—such as likening iconic power forwards to Shakespeare. Still, we soldiered on. Someone was telling a nightmarish hotel story when Wayne once again cut in:

"How many people have ever found a human thumb under their hotel bed?" He then raised his hand earnestly. "No one? No one?"

"Oh yeah?" Someone called him on it. "Where was that?"

"Where was it?" Wayne paused. "At the hotel."

"What hotel?"

"Best Western. Cedar Rapids."

During a dessert of homemade plum-and-mango ice cream, Wayne bragged that he had gotten himself kicked out of three bars the night before. While he had already established that he was full of shit, I saw no reason not to believe this to be true.

Once people transitioned to the dance party in the living room, I almost couldn't believe my eyes when I saw Jeffrey pass Wayne a lit bowl. While I wouldn't know, personally, I've been *told* that getting high once you're already lit can put you in a strange place, so it hardly surprised me when Wayne began breakdancing on the living room floor. Now, that floor had already experienced its fair share of breakdancing, much of it courtesy of Matt and me, but Wayne didn't seem to notice stuff like furniture and other people that he kept knocking into. People spread out around him, and he dove toward the floor, planting his palms for a handspring. Only when his legs kicked over, he began to collapse on himself, his face on the floor and his shoulder blades folding toward his head. For a split second, I thought he was going to snap his neck. I remember feeling an odd sense of relief that at least he would no longer terrorize the house.

Wayne regrouped near the sliding door on the eastern end of the living room and began waving his arms for people to clear a path. He dove onto his stomach and began doing the worm, writhing across the living room and then actually turning a corner in the kitchen, making his way toward the deck when he crashed into the kegerator. It was pretty impressive—I have to give it up to him for that. Still, for me, the symbolism was a bit much. Having already established himself as reptilian, he had now literally slithered across the breadth of the house. I squatted down and slid my hands beneath his armpits, clutching his ribcage and helping him up. He was scrawny as all hell. I wondered if he got hooked on the junk habit of negative attention as a boy, growing into the kind of loudmouth who found himself the regular recipient of ass-kickings, one of those guys for whom getting laid out by a burly motherfucker in a bar becomes the ultimate affirmation that they exist.

I spun him over and he snarled at me, his green eyes meeting mine with a vacant, simmering look that I've only seen a few times—the look of a cornered animal in the throes of rage. He looked as though he were having an out-of-body experience.

"Wayne." I squeezed his ribs and brought him to his feet, pulling him close to me. "You've got to calm down."

His guest Leon approached wearing a genuine look of apology.

"No problem, dude." Wayne laughed and a sudden lucidity came over him. "It's cool."

It was far from cool. Wayne's row in my spreadsheet was beyond red. It was fucking fuchsia. He would certainly be leaving Chance to spend more time with his family. I contemplated calling a water taxi, getting him on the boat, and then trying to convince the skipper that Wayne wouldn't blow the vessel out of the water. (As a nanny, I had long ago learned how much harder it was to negotiate a kicking and screaming child; it was always best and easiest to psych them out and defuse any potential tantrums.) Leon escorted Wayne out to the deck and I eyed them from the sliding door, not at all surprised when I overheard Leon pleadingly exclaim, *"Why do you always have to do this?"*

With Leon effectively assuming the role of babysitter, I figured it would be best to let Wayne stay the night and then boot him out in the morning. While Leon's time-out succeeded in calming Wayne down, house members were approaching me with tight smiles, exclaiming that Wayne seemed really fucked up.

"Don't worry," I said. "It will all be taken care of."

Ready to hit the bars, a critical mass began filing out onto the walkway.

"I'll catch up with you guys later," I said, when a tiny comet trailing smoke arced from the deck over our heads, landing in the dead grass in front of the house. I jumped under the railing and stomped out the butt. Above me, Wayne leaned over the deck railing, lighting another cigarette.

There are two events that bring out in me the rosy glow of reactionary extremism, and those events are Rape and Fire. Just a few days earlier, a house in Saltaire, Kismet's neighboring village to the east, was destroyed by fire. It's the kind of thing that rattles homeowners. If my condo in West Harlem were to burn down, it would suck in the way that it would suck for anyone else, but if Chance were to burn down—after all the work and heartache and stress that went into transforming the house from leaky shack into lush, fortified playground, well, it would take me a long time and an awful lot of gin to get over that. I flew up the stairs and onto the deck faster than Carl Lewis on crank, getting in Wayne's face.

"Just what the fuck is wrong with you?"

"What?" His playing-dumb indignance infuriated me, and I began to experience an odd sensation. Time seemed to slow, bringing on what felt like my own out-of-body experience; it was as though I were watching myself from a short distance, clutching Wayne by the neck and the scrotum and tossing his scrawny ass over the side of the deck. I must have looked like I was about to blast off, because Leon grabbed Wayne's arm, pulling him back.

"Come on," Leon said. "Let's go to the bars."

*   *   *

One of the 932 fascinating things I've learned about people since running Chance is that if you're a certain kind of person or you behave in a certain kind of way, and then someone else is more of that kind of a person than you are or they take your kind of behavior to the next level, it freaks you out. We are all like this. During the '04 season, Jeffrey was a party animal. Perpetually stoned, he was always beating the drum to do tequila shots alongside gaggles of Ocean Beach party girls that he'd invite to the house on Saturday nights, their rambunctious jacuzzi sessions sometimes lasting until dawn. On Sunday mornings, I would regularly find half-empty magnums of tequila out on the deck, the cap rolling on the ground among spent lime wedges and a half-dozen dirty rocks glasses. While dating Rosemarie had settled him down, he could still be a handful. So it surprised me—and then it didn't—that he was the house member most troubled by Wayne.

"Dude." Jeffrey approached me at The Inn. "Where did you get this guy?"

I glanced over at Wayne being minded by Leon near the pool tables.

"Don't worry," I said. "Everything's going to be taken care of."

While this would be enough information for most people, stoners sometimes require bolder strokes and brighter colors.

"Dude. Is he going to be like that all the time? What's his deal?"

"Dude," I said to Jeffrey, raising my brow for a pregnant pause, "everything is going to be taken care of."

I could see the lightbulb pop over his head. "That's cool, Johnny." He grinned. "Right on."

"Come on." I threw an arm around his shoulders and motioned toward a cluster of house members near the bar. "Let's do shots." I pulled out my Belmont Stakes winnings, waving the bills in the air like a gangsta rapper. "Who wants a tequila?"

I don't normally do shots, but right then I needed a drink and sometimes there is something to be said for expediency. I approached the bar and caught the eye of Mugsy, the younger of the Cole brothers, and delivered a favorite line from a Kinky Friedman novel:

"Bartender!" I called out to Mugsy. "Nine tequilas!"

"You got it," Mugsy said, never breaking his deadpan as he set up nine shot glasses. We drank, and I was relieved to hear people joking about Wayne. While they were having fun in spite of him, they were wondering how I was going to handle him. My sole objective was to cleanly separate Wayne from the house. Not wanting any kind of chatter getting back to him and disrupting that process, I thought it best to be oblique, to reassure them while not explicitly telling anyone that I was going to kick him out. So I stuck with my earlier statement to Jeffrey:

"Everything is going to be taken care of."

Still, they were questioning how a guy like Wayne passed the screening process. Even before the money difficulties, my little voice did indeed shout out in protest—although I had chalked this up to his name. I hate to admit it, but yet another one of my prejudices has to do with certain names; suffice it to say that my lifelong experience with Waynes has not been positive. I've found 67 percent of Waynes to be irredeemable assholes, while an additional 16 percent of them are just flat-out dicks. If you go through the list of Waynes with whom you've crossed paths, you'll likely come up with similar numbers. Possibly it's a by-product of growing up with a name that rhymes with "pain," "insane," and "a drain." For this Wayne was all of these things. I try to overcome my prejudices. I really do. And in having asked Wayne to join the house, I think I was trying to do just that. Unfortunately, this Wayne only reinforced my bigotry toward all Waynes. Certainly there are a number of upright, decent Waynes in the world bearing their collective bad rap, and I hope that one of these SuperWaynes might one day change the way I feel about their ilk. Until that day, it is very, very unlikely that I will ever allow another Wayne to join Chance.

While it was a relief to have Wayne absorbed into the crowd at The Inn (instead of burning down my house), I certainly didn't want him doing anything there that would result in one of the Cole brothers putting a boot in his ass while he proclaimed to know me. I approached the pool tables, where Wayne was fumbling the balls into the triangle.

"How's he doing?" I asked Leon.

"Oh, he's fine," Leon said dismissively. "You know, he gets like that when he smokes. Sometimes the best thing is to just give him a little coke. It kind of puts him in his groove."

As a guest, Leon didn't know that I banned coke from the house. There are thirty-seven reasons why I do this (some of which I'll explain later on). Given Wayne's behavior, however, it had crossed my mind that he could be cruising on something other than pot and booze, although it hardly mattered. I'd have been just as perturbed if all of this were the result of him having ingested a five-pound bag of sugar.

Turning around, I spotted Rule Number One standing in front of the juke and my heart began to race. What the hell was she doing in Kismet? Why didn't she tell me she was coming? Was she upset that I hadn't called her? Did she find another house? I strode over, startling her—only she wasn't Rule Number One. This woman grimaced and I backed away. It was uncanny. They had the same build and the same mass of dark curls scrunched up genie-like at the crown of their heads. From behind, she still looked like Rule Number One, but when this woman turned again, any resemblance disappeared like a mirage.

While relieved that Rule Number One hadn't come to Kismet without telling me, I wished that she were there—her combative sense of humor might have defused Hurricane Wayne. Feeling spent, I slipped away from The Inn. Stopping near the walkway to my house, I could hear Rule Number One repeating that tenet about not going straight from the bar to the house, but stopping at the beach. Only the anticlimax of the Rule Number One mirage had trashed me. As soon as I lay down in bed, a wave of sleep washed over me. So it was something less than a treat when I was woken up at three a.m. by gangsta rap pumping from the stereo.

"*Yo! Yo! Yo! Yo!...*"

"You've gotta be kidding me," I said. One way in which I tried to maintain the balance between raging house party and civilized respite were quiet hours. After 12:30, people who still wanted to rock out were supposed to hit the beach or the bars so that anyone interested in sleep could sleep. Bleary-eyed, I rushed upstairs. While there were twenty-one people in the house, I knew that it was Wayne. I would have been just as surprised to find Jesus Christ himself cranking the bass were it anyone other than Wayne.

"TURN THAT SHIT *OFF!*"

Wayne reached over and lowered the volume.

"NOT DOWN! *OFF!*" I charged over and hit the power button. "FUCKING *OFF!*"

"Sorry, dude." He once again shot me that indignant look as though I were a madman.

Back in bed, I realized that I had just given Wayne the nightcap he had been craving. The guy had been grooving on negative attention all night long and if I had just gone upstairs and politely asked him to turn the music off, he wouldn't have gotten his rocks off and I wouldn't have further fueled his fucked-up neurosis.

Livid, I lay awake considering the logistics of booting Wayne. What about CrackBerry Troy? He and Wayne were friends and coworkers. Something told me that Troy wouldn't want to stay in the house after Wayne got the boot, but you never know—especially if he thought he might make time with Tracy. A number of women had mentioned that they found Troy skeevy, but he hadn't tried to rape anyone or burn the place down, so I'd have to refund a prorated amount of his share. Still, it's not worth any amount of money to keep someone in your house who makes people uncomfortable. This was a lesson learned when I was a share at Bicycle Bill's.

It was the pre-season, and I was out at the house for the 2003 Kentucky Derby when a guy named Todd showed up just before the race. His first time coming out to the house, Todd was, quite literally, falling-all-over-the-place drunk. When he did manage to hook together a subject and a verb, what came out of his mouth was pure shit. Wanting to escape his sphere of belligerence, I grabbed a guitar that was lying around and carried it up to the roof deck. Ten minutes later, Todd sat down next to me and asked if I had ever heard of Jimmy Buffet. Todd didn't know that I was hardly a fan of Jimmy Buffet and all of that parrot-head crap that adds up to second-rate stoner music for Volvo Republicans.

"Didn't he write some song about a popular tequila cocktail?" I said.

"Yeah...well...I played guitar in his band...for three years."

"Really? That's awesome." I passed him the guitar. "Play something."

"Nah. Maybe later."

"Come on," I said. "I'm just a hack. You're a professional. Maybe you can teach me something."

He drained the rest of his Corona and—like that psychopath Begbie from *Trainspotting*—blithely tossed his bottle over the side of the deck toward the main road, where it could have landed on someone's head. I brought this to the attention of Bicycle Bill, who explained that Todd was under a lot of stress because he had been spending a lot of time at the bedside of his elderly father who was dying. Fair enough. Only Todd ended up being perpetually faced and abusive to anyone in close range. Whenever he went too far, he would play the trump card of his dying father as though it were a license to be a royal asshole.

Just before the beginning of the high season, however, a woman named Maureen joined the house. She was a quiet, attractive woman whose biological clock must have been ticking like a time bomb. It's the only explanation as to why after knowing Todd for fewer days than could be counted on the fingers and toes of Def Leppard's drummer, she agreed to marry him.

Nevertheless, being engaged did settle Todd down. No longer getting fucked out of his mind, he at least became bearable. Then, during a weekend late in July, something disastrous happened. Maureen wasn't out at the house, and Todd got faced. There was a woman in the house named Donna who, after a long night of partying, woke up at four o'clock in the morning to find Todd on top of her, raping her.

Donna called the police, and Todd was arrested. Last I heard, he was in jail. (While I normally share Don Corleone's view on the pointlessness of vengeance, if Todd were to have found himself bitched out behind bars to the point that you could park a Pinto in his rectum, let's just say that I wouldn't lose any sleep over that ironic twist of fate.) Anyway, the Todd fiasco taught me that if someone is bad news, don't even think about your bottom line—just boot 'em out. Even if he's just a jackass, he's still going to cost you returnees.

So Troy's toast, I thought. Don't worry about the cash—just get rid of him. Unfortunately, this resoluteness did not send me back to sleep, so I got out of bed and did something that rarely fails to make me drowsy: paperwork. I opened my spreadsheet and hit my piles, capping off my session by painting the rows for Troy and Wayne red. Still not feeling tired, I wandered out to the beach and watched the eastern sky turn purple as the sun came up over the silvering crests of the waves. Back inside, my stomach began to rumble. I grabbed one of the large commercial pans that hung from hooks above the kitchen and dropped it over a medium-high flame, filling the bottom with olive oil and coating that pool with crushed red pepper. I grabbed two eggs from the fridge and then sliced up a red pepper, tossing the rings into the sizzling oil.

Most peoples' idea of comfort food is warm, hearty meals. While a proper *cassoulet* is one of my pet dishes, during such moments I'm usually craving simplicity. One of my absolute favorite things to eat is a big plate of linguine (boiled in chicken broth if there's some lying around) covered with fried garlic, olive oil, and fresh grated parmesan. If Italian-Americans lived in trailer parks, this is what we'd eat. (It's probably no coincidence that I think Italian during these moments, because the Italians understand simplicity in cooking better than the French, and maybe better than anyone.)

While waiting for the peppers, I rimmed a beer glass with Old Bay seasoning. Then, instead of tapping a Killian's from the kegerator, I poured a can of Budweiser into my glass, added a shot of tequila, and gave it a splash of the leftover Bloody Mary mix. (If I'm feeling like a lightweight, I'll instead have a lager with a splash of cranberry.) At the stove, I plated my peppers, then dropped two eggs in the pan. After flipping the eggs over easy, I laid them on top of my pile of peppers and broke the yolk. I then mopped up whatever oil and dregs remained in the pan with a slice of ciabatta before sliding it in the toaster. My "breakfast" was magically delicious. I added salt and hot sauce to what remained on my plate before licking it clean. After downing the rest of my "Buddy Mary," a blessed sleepiness came over me. It probably comes as no surprise that I suffer from acid reflux, eating and drinking the way that I do, and so I popped a Zantac-75 knockoff before lying down in bed, finally falling back asleep.

*   *   *

Unfortunately, I didn't have a cancellation policy. I had avoided stating that there are no refunds, or that if you were kicked out your share price wouldn't be refunded because I thought that calling up such scenarios was not the best way to attract good people. This was a mistake. Stating a policy of no refunds is like having a pre-nup—an ugly but sometimes necessary thing. Besides, if you refund share monies for bad behavior, it could encourage assholemanship on the part of someone who developed a string of scheduling conflicts and wanted to weasel out.

The first thing I did was to update the content on my website, explaining that there were no refunds of share monies. Next, I informed all house members via e-mail that Wayne had decided to leave Chance to spend more time with his family. Then I had to figure out how to ditch Troy. After a long round of e-mailing among Wayne, Troy, and me, we agreed that Troy would also leave the house and that I would refund a prorated remainder of their shares, minus a modest cancellation fee.

Before hitting Craig's List to recruit someone to fill Wayne and Troy's vacated spots, I e-mailed the house and offered those spots up at a discount, figuring that whatever cash I lost would be worth the security of known entities. There were still enough ecstatic new house members who had wanted to add on to their shares, and the open spots were snapped up.

I have an odd relationship with money. I once walked eight blocks for a Chinese lunch special that cost $4.95 instead of ponying up the gouging price of $5.95 for sesame chicken, pork fried rice, and an eggroll. So why did I resist totaling what I lost in ridding the house of Wayne and Troy? How could I walk eight blocks for a buck but not want to know the particulars of a four-figure transaction?

Part of me feared that if I kept an eye trained too closely on my bottom line, the house wouldn't be as good. I was going to miss Wayne and Troy about as much as I missed a staph infection. They would never come back to the house and sit down at our table. That I might have been able to spend six days eating and drinking on a brown sand beach in Costa Rica in late January with the cash I lost by getting rid of the two of them never entered my mind. At least not until now.

Later that morning, I ran into Jeannie on her bike in front of the dock.

"Hey, hot stuff," I called out, stealing Wayne's line. We chatted for a bit and she told me how much she liked my group. "So," she blinked. "Is *Wayne* still out at the house?"

I told her that I had to kick him out.

"Why?" A truly disappointed look came over her face. "He was such a nice guy..."

"Don't worry, Jeannie. There are many fish in the sea."

She sighed. "That's what they all say." She turned and pedaled away.

Grilled Shrimp Tacos

I still had not talked to Rule Number One since her last weekend at the house. She wouldn't be coming back out for another two weeks. I wanted to call her, only I kept hearing her say, "I just want to be your C-Weekend Girl..."

"Keep it casual," my little voice insisted. *"That's what she wants and that's what's best."*

I began composing my weekly e-mail to all house members, noticing that two other romantically crossed house members would now find themselves in the same cage: Risa and Colin. Colin worked in sales. He traveled a lot and was one of those overworked, over-gadgeted, over-communicated City dwellers so steeped in their corporate environments that when they finally make it out to Kismet, they're not searching for an epicurean respite; they're primed for oblivion. Not surprisingly, Colin and Jeffrey became fast smoking friends. Thankfully, however, Colin was more considerate than Jeffrey about getting his groove on. I'll always remember an exchange we had during his first night in 2004:

"Hey, Johnny? Can I ask you a question?"

"Sure."

"It's totally okay if you say no."

"Okay. What is it?"

"Umm...well...I was wondering if...umm...if it would be okay if maybe I smoked some pot out on the deck?"

I laughed. "You can smoke it right here."

Colin wasn't the kind of guy with whom you were going to debate third-world debt relief, but he was easygoing, fun, and always considered his weed and bowl—which were never more than a few feet away—to be your weed and bowl as well.

At a party the previous winter, I spotted Risa conversing with Colin and their conversation, at least from a distance, appeared to be Heading In That Direction. A few weeks later, Mandy was having her birthday party. At the time, Mandy didn't really know Colin and so she didn't invite him, but she invited Risa, who then asked Mandy if she could bring Colin as her date. Mandy agreed. After dinner, we transitioned to a nearby club where Mandy, being a good birthday girl, got faced. Mandy didn't seem to mind at all that Colin was there. And Colin didn't seem to mind that he had come to Mandy's party as Risa's date. In fact, the two of them felt so comfortable around one another that they began making out on the dance floor in plain sight of Risa, who, before leaving, informed Colin that he was acting like a board-certified jackass.

Both Mandy and Colin later apologized to Risa. Still, I wondered how things might play out between the two of them that weekend. Yet part of me also welcomed a bit of house-member weirdness that didn't involve me or Rule Number One.

*   *   *

Late that Friday afternoon, I was clipping together my receipts for that weekend's bacchanalian excesses when Chris knocked.

"Hey John?" He wore a sheepish look. "Do you mind if I talk to you for a minute?"

"Not at all."

He stepped inside my room and closed the door.

"What's up?"

"Well, I read your e-mail about Wayne—and I'm really sorry you had to deal with that. But I guess I'm just... I don't want to accidentally do something stupid that would get me kicked out of the house."

I did everything I could to suppress a fit of laughter. Of all the house members who should be worried about getting kicked out, Chris was absolutely the last. It was more likely that I'd have to kick myself out first.

"Chris. I am never going to kick you out of the house."

"Well, that's good." He let out a nervous laugh.

"People fuck up all the time. I fuck up all the time. Wayne didn't get kicked out because he fucked up. He flat-out didn't belong here."

"That's cool." His shoulders dropped. "But you might want to tell other people that. Because we weren't here and we didn't see what happened. I was thinking, like, suppose I accidentally pissed in the hot tub—is John going to kick me out?"

"Chris, I'm not ever going to kick you out." I wondered if such a categorical statement was in my best interest. "But please don't piss in the hot tub."

"Okay." He laughed and closed the door. I opened my inbox, watching it scroll down with guest requests, weekend trade confirmations, and other house-related e-mails interspersed amid a tidal wave of spam. I began to plow through them, once just pasting the URL from the house website that answered that person's question. These people who are too lazy to find answers on their own can reduce the Information Age to so many newfangled mediums in which they don't have their shit together, and so many devices with which they can pester you. (This is reason #67 why I am thankful to no longer work in an office.) I wish there was a correlation between these people and how much I liked them, but there wasn't. Unfortunately, a lot of them were my friends and I simply had to accept their helplessness. I'd be a lot more enthusiastic about the tech revolution if someone invented a device that cured flakiness. Unfortunately, the only way to combat flakiness is, and always will be, through fear.

I wish that I could curb the Machiavelli in me, but I can't. It is simply more effective to be feared than loved. Still, I tried to limit my Machiavellian side to collecting money, an area where I had no problem being a prince in the extreme. Since I have taken on the responsibility of not just managing a sharehouse, but also feeding everyone (and trying to feed them well), my role required a much higher level of organization than traditional sharehouse managers, and thus required a higher level of compliance by house members. To paraphrase John Lennon, the structure you take is equal to the structure you make. No one will ever accidentally sit down to a twenty-person dinner of ceviche followed by grilled pork tenderloin and homemade mango ice cream for dessert. That happened because people in the house were willing to get on the same page. So while I asked for a lot from house members, most of them understood that we all got a lot more in return.

I closed my inbox and wandered upstairs just as a few more people strolled in from the latest ferry. Vanessa and Risa had cobbled together a dinner of mixed grill and a crunchy Thai coleslaw made with red cabbage, raisins, and raw ramen noodles. I sat down next to Dani, who began to fidget. Other people were quiet and I could detect a mild tension at the table. Chris was right: None of them had been there, and they didn't understand that axing Wayne wasn't a choice but a necessity. I sat down and poured a glass of shiraz, skeptically forking up a bite of that cole slaw, disbelieving that broken ramen noodles might work, but they did.

It was cool and crunchy and spicy and sweet. John Coltrane spun from the speakers at a perfect dinner volume. In fact everything was perfect. Dani shifted, and I spotted her iPod tucked in her pocket. Considering the teeming gigabytes of crap crammed into that little device, and how it wasn't currently plugged into the stereo, I considered saying nothing about Wayne, letting them all chew over the prospect of getting kicked out. *The Prince* has survived for 500 years because Niccolo Machiavelli had more than a clue. Still, it was a passing fantasy. Having a majority of perfectly good house members exist in fear of getting kicked out was no way for them or for me to enjoy our summer together.

I've worked really hard at not being a dick. It's hard. (Not being a dick, that is.) Unfortunately, the more you structure your house, the more you have to be somewhat of a dick. Someone will always test your limits, either through bad behavior or by being a pain in the ass, forgetting that they are one of many and making too many requests.

Accepting this inevitability was precisely why I re-upped Jeffrey. He had a foot in both camps of bad behavior—he could be an inconsiderate partier, while his last-minute demands masked as requests rendered him a mild, yet persistent pain in the ass. Yet you almost have to have someone in that role, and Jeffrey was the devil I knew. Stoners are a funny breed. I know many high-functioning people who smoke bales of marijuana but who don't behave like stereotypical stoners. They are thoughtful and considerate and don't speak as though they are retarded, their range of emotion not limited to inflecting the word "dude." I suppose the difference between a pot smoker and a stoner is that stoners are flakes, and it was this—not the Pigpen-like cloud of pot smoke that followed him around—that rendered Jeffrey an unruly house member. Still, he was a twitching, giggling goofball and could be fun in the way that seven-year-olds can be fun. Unfortunately, it was also like dealing with a seven-year-old. If I still wanted to deal with seven-year-olds, I'd go back to being a nanny.

So it was people like Jeffrey who made being loved an awful lot of work. It would be easier to follow Machiavelli's advice and just make them all fear me. Still, my business plan was based on bucking conventional sharehouse wisdom. And Machiavelli also had this to say:

There is nothing more difficult to take in hand, more perilous to conduct, or more uncertain in its success, than to take the lead in the introduction of a new order of things.

So part of my new order consisted of my desire to be an effective manager of a well-organized house while still being friends with house members. Also, most people don't realize that Nicky Mack actually said, "it is better to be feared than loved, *if you cannot be both.*"

So I tried to be both. Tasting another bite of that sweet, crunchy cole slaw, I broke the silence:

"So last weekend was pretty dramatic."

They stopped eating, and I regaled them with my account of the previous Saturday: the haranguing bullshit conversations; the near-broken neck; the lit cigarette flicked off the deck. Now that Wayne was gone, it was funny to me—and them. A lot of nervous laughter dissipated the tension, and they loosened up, giving free flow to the pinball-like energy that characterizes most Friday nights. Late arrivals spiked the mood as they crashed down at the big table for their first beer or glass of wine and a plate of grill. There was an antsy-ness that reminded me of grammar school when you finished your math test early; checking your work was such a drag, yet you didn't want to be the first kid to hand in your test. So you sat there, trying not to fidget, until some brave pioneer cut a path to the teacher's desk and dropped off her page. The second person was never far behind, then the third, and by then it felt comfortable to join in the parade bottlenecking at the teacher's desk. Hooking up in the beach house was no different, and I was hyper aware of how Rule Number One and I were the first ones to have handed in our tests.

Before July 4, most house members were still sizing each other up. Despite the redlining of flirtometers, bikini bottoms and drawstrings had remained fastened, mostly. Still, I've seen some things. Nothing concrete, but little things—like Charlotte and Joo-chan making eyes at one another. I'm almost always at the house and usually the first one awake, so I see the continuum of small gestures, or a person exiting someone else's room. Still, I maintained a rule of never being the one to break news of anything brewing between house members.

While gossip is unavoidable, my low tolerance for it is one of my biggest shortcomings. It's as though I were a ship's captain who regularly suffered from seasickness. I most deplored gossip because in a sharehouse there is no greater enemy of sex. All of us would give a freer rein to our libidos if things could be kept confidential. Since many gossipers were burning off sexual frustration, this just becomes a vicious circle; if they would go out and get laid, they might be less interested in picking over other peoples' sex lives. Fundamentalist fanatics—whether they are of the flying-planes-into-buildings variety, or the bombing-women's-health-clinics types—all talk a good game about God, but what these people really care about is controlling our sex lives. While no such people would ever end up in Chance, the gossipers unwittingly do their bidding. Since no one spent more time in the house than me, no one resented gossip more, because these gossipers impinged upon my horizontal refreshment.

Amazingly, no one said anything about Rule Number One—although a lot of people had still yet to meet one another. People from different letter series were just starting to mix up through trading, so the lines of communication were still being constructed. By July 4, an advanced fiber-optic gossip network would be up and running—just in time for when everyone and everything becomes unbuttoned.

Rufus arrived and I remembered another weird situation: Uptalking Nancy would be returning to the house for the first time since Memorial Day. Surely she had seen Rufus's name on the schedule, which may have pushed her toward not arriving until Saturday morning. (Though being a financial analyst was maybe not the kind of job where you breeze out early on Friday afternoons for beach weekends.) Nevertheless, Nancy had reserved a guest spot, and I wondered if she felt the need to come back with a friend.

I knew that Nancy would be more bearable if she could manage to enjoy herself, and the first step was to make sure that Rufus laid off her. I approached him on the deck.

"Listen," I said. "Nancy's coming back out tomorrow."

"Nice!" His face lit up.

"No-no-no. You really put a bug up her ass with your saving-the-whales comment."

He started to laugh uncontrollably.

"Rufus, listen, she's coming back out with a guest, and I can all but guarantee you that she's warned her guest about you. So here's what I want you to do: I want you to formally introduce yourself to her guest and offer to make her a cocktail. Ask her if she's hungry. Just be the total opposite of the obnoxious dick that Nancy has undoubtedly told her guest that you are. Can you do that?"

"Absolutely!" He was beside himself. "It will totally fuck with her!"

"*JOHN*-NAY!"

I turned. It was Colin, walking in from the last boat.

"How you doing, buddy?" He shook my hand. Already stoned, he made a beeline for a glass and tapped himself a beer. He greeted some other people in the house, including Risa, who didn't seem the least bit fazed. I pulled her aside and asked if she was okay being there with him. She laughed, explaining that she considered Colin a dodged bullet. While this was great to hear, it only heightened the fact that in the weirdness department Rule Number One and I were all alone.

*　　*　　*

On Saturday, I dragged my garden cart down to the dock to pick up our booze delivery. After unloading, I sat down to lunch when Uptalking Nancy arrived with Rory, her guest. Rufus sprang off the couch. I shot him a look, and he patted down the air in front of him as though to say, Don't worry. I stood and greeted Nancy, who introduced Rory to me. Rufus approached, standing back deferentially.

"Hi, Nancy," Rufus said. "How are you doing?"

"Umm, pretty *good?*"

He then offered his hand to Rory. "My name is Rufus and you are—"

"Rory." I could see the flash of recognition—Nancy had warned her.

"Have you ever been to Fire Island?" Rufus asked her.

"No, this is my first time."

"Welcome to Kismet. Can I make you a margarita?"

Rory looked tentatively at Nancy, who was stone-faced.

"Sure," Rory said.

"How about you, Nancy? Would you like a margarita?"

"Uh, *yah?*"

"This is such a great house," Rory said to me, looking around. "Oh my God!" She had stepped into the upstairs bathroom, the walls of which were completely tiled with U.S. currency. I had wallpapered the upper half with dollar bills above a border of three rows of nickels. The bathroom's bottom half was covered with pennies, although I had only finished pennying one of the four walls before glossing everything over. It was a slow process that I had made even more tedious by placing each penny in the twelve o'clock position and then alternating heads and tails. I had posted them up a hundred at a time, dumping two rolls out onto a board, segregating heads and tails, and then giving each one a dollop of construction glue. A vast range of colors exists between the shiny new ones and the blackened old ones, and the random pattern of the different shades created a mosaic effect that reminded me of Italian glass tiles.

"That is so *cool*," she exclaimed. "What possessed you to do that?"

I gave her my stock answer: "Temporary insanity."

During my renovations, I had been dealing with such staggering sums that at times it felt as though I were throwing money out the window. Meanwhile, we had invaded Iraq while giving the ultrarich a lopsided tax cut. We couldn't find the cash to provide health care for millions of uninsured American children with working parents, while the people getting the biggest tax cuts were paying thousands of dollars to inject botulin toxin—a chemical once stockpiled by Saddam Hussein—into their faces. After watching a news segment about people dropping five figures on pet funerals, I realized that we were just setting our money on fire. While I was hardly rich, I wanted in on the game. I wanted to do something really frivolous with my money. So I used it as wallpaper.

"How much money is it?" Rory asked.

"It's about two hundred dollar bills, thirty-five bucks in nickels, and when I'm done, there'll be about a hundred and fifty bucks' worth of pennies."

It worked out to four bucks a square foot, which is really not bad for a bathroom. (And when you use currency in place of tiles, you can spend your overages.)

While pennying was slow going, I found it oddly meditative. That spring, when I was still dealing with my contractor and with the Town of Islip to get them to approve my deck permit, as well as recruiting new house members, I spent a lot of time on the phone trying to get other people to do stuff. Whenever I felt overwhelmed, I'd grab the construction glue and kid myself that I would just do two rolls, only to end up doing ten, tuning everything out for a little while.

I approached Rufus at the wet bar as he scooped ice from the below-counter icemaker. "Do you know what you're doing?"

"Absolutely."

And so it went, with Rufus playing the part of the fawning gentleman all afternoon. I was about to hit the beach when Colin informed me that the keg had run out. We went down to the fridge in the shed and carried up the new keg. I was running some cleaning solution through the lines when Grace called out to me from the cappuccino machine.

"What does this red light mean?"

"Well," I said, "it could mean a lot of things." I approached the machine and saw that its disposal was not properly in place. This is how many of my weekend days go, stringing together loose ends—only they were all of my own making. Managers without kegerators don't have to deal with people not being able to open their bottles of beer, while American drip coffee makers are far more reliable than Italian push-button cappuccino machines. I regularly maintained the jacuzzi throughout the weekend, tweaking the temperature and adding water after the latest group-of-eight summit sent the level over the side. On these days when the sleeve-tugging never ended, it's easiest just to ride it out. So after hooking up the new keg, I dropped eighteen hot dogs on the grill and filled up a thermos with beer. I stacked the dogs in an empty cardboard produce tray and carried them all down to the beach. If you're ever in a sharehouse—especially if you've done something that might have put you on the shit list—try bringing everyone on the beach beer and hot dogs. People love this. After crashing down on one of the sheets, I tapped a beer from the thermos and loaded up one of the dogs with mustard. Beer and dogs on the beach taste even better than in the ballpark. It just works. And during such days, enjoying a hot dog out in the sun while watching the waves roll in may well be the highlight—and not a bad one at all. I took a sip of beer and watched a pair of birds circling upward in a thermal.

*   *   *

Before dinner, Vanessa and I transferred our first batch of beer from a glass carboy to our five-gallon pony keg. She brought out some bottles of orange-coriander wheat beer that she had brewed at home and put them in the icemaker to speed-chill in time for Risa's dinner of grilled shrimp tacos with pineapple salsa and grilled corn served with chipotle butter. Among Risa's sous-chefs, Grace was hunched over a cutting board, dicing a pineapple. While her row had been painted red since attempting to read the *New Yorker* during the juggling dance party, I was glad to see her at least making an effort. After dinner, Colin offered up his bowl. I partook and then poured a snifter of armagnac, grabbing a handful of peanut M&Ms before heading out onto the deck, where I sat down on the porch swing I had constructed out of an old fence.

Rory came outside and sat down next to me.

"Dinner was amazing," she said. "This is such a fun house, and I was wondering if you have any open spots during upcoming weekends that I could buy."

"I'm sorry, but we're booked. It's too bad we didn't meet earlier, because Nancy just sold Labor Day weekend—" I took a sip of armagnac. "—when we do the Cajun shrimp boil out here on the deck."

"Really? Huh. Well, if anything opens up, please let me know about it."

"Sure," I said, beginning to feel the effects of Colin's bowl. With the dance party cranking up in the living room, I finished my armagnac. "Come on," I said to Rory. "Let's dance."

We stepped inside, and Vanessa pulled me toward the fray. For some reason I remembered her asking me why I wasn't married yet. Age is a funny thing. There were times during the past couple of years when I momentarily forgot my age, or had it in my head that I was still in my late twenties. It was an easy thing to do when you lacked a career track, and I wondered if, like Bicycle Bill, I didn't have a touch of the Peter Pan Complex. I then wondered why my skin suddenly felt as though it were six inches thick. When Colin walked past me toward the kegerator, I hooked his arm.

"What did we just smoke?"

"JOHN-*NAY!*"

"Colin. I'm serious. Tell me what we just smoked."

"Just delivery service sprinkled with a little Special Sauce."

"What the fuck is Special Sauce?"

"It's totally cool, Johnny."

"Hey," I called out to Matt, sitting on the couch. "What's Special Sauce?"

"It's just Thousand Island dressing, which is really just ketchup, mayo, and relish."

I should have found it funny that Matt was perfectly serious, but I remembered the pot cookies Colin had baked the previous summer, sending a number of people into full-fledged freakouts.

"No," I said, finally laughing. "Not the Special Sauce that goes on Big Macs. What does Colin sprinkle on his weed?"

"I think he adds kif to it."

"Is that THC-based?"

"Yes."

"Dude," my little voice said. *"Kick back and enjoy the ride..."*

I turned to Vanessa.

"I am really high. How are you doing?"

"Pretty fucking stoned," she said, grooving to the music.

I hopped up on the coffee table and began dancing with Maggie.

"Uh-oh!" Dani called out. "The bossman's up on the table!"

I spun around and grabbed Dani's waist, moving with her as Maggie moved up behind me, sandwiching me between the two of them. For a little while I forgot that Maggie was my friend and that Dani was Dani and it was fun to just dance between them, rocketed out of my mind. At the end of the song, Matt paused the iPod and called out, "Let's go to the bars!"

"I am not going to the bars," I said, hopping down from the table. "I'm going to the beach."

"I'll go with you," Vanessa said.

My little voice might have warned me against this were he not also totally baked. Downstairs, Vanessa grabbed one of the beach sheets, and we walked out of the house and over the dune crossing. She spread the sheet out on the sand, and we lay down on it, staring up at the stars.

"This is really nice," Vanessa said.

"Does the ocean seem really loud to you?"

"I don't know. Kinda. Not really."

I spotted a shooting star.

"Did you see that?" Vanessa said.

"Yeah," I said. "Do you want to go for a walk?"

"Sure."

We left the sheet and began walking west where the City lights forty miles away bathed the lighthouse in a faint orange glow. It was one of those hazy, fuzzy nights when the beach just looked otherworldly—even without being zonked. We turned around at the sign signaling the start of the nude beach. Back near the Pine Walk dune crossing, I was still high, but normal high, and I could feel it getting chilly.

"Come on," I said. "Let's go inside."

She folded up the sheet and we walked back to the house where it was dark and perfectly quiet. Everyone had either gone to the bars or gone to bed. In my room, I took off my clothes and put on my bathrobe, grabbing my toothbrush and making toward the bathroom just as Vanessa, wearing pajamas, did the same. We stood together before the bathroom sink, brushing our teeth in the mirror and cracking up at the sight of one another's foaming mouths.

"Goodnight," she said, embracing me in the hallway. When I broke away, her arms were still wrapped around my chest. She shot up on her toes, giving me three quick kisses—one on my temple, the corner of my jaw, and then on my neck beneath my ear. They were elegant little kisses, classy and sweet and well-targeted, but my little voice had been roused:

"Hey-hey-hey!"

"Relax," I said.

"Huh?" Vanessa said.

"Goodnight." I gave Vanessa's waist a squeeze and stepped back.

"Goodnight." She turned and walked into her bedroom.

*   *   *

On Sunday, a few of the midweek house members arrived, including Maurice, a talent agent who had gotten hooked on working from the beach. He spent a good amount of time on his cell phone, but unlike CrackBerry Troy, he wandered out to the far corner of the deck or down by the sheds. Sometimes he carried his phone along with his fishing gear down to the beach or to the ferry dock, returning with the occasional barely legal bluefish for the grill.

For dinner that night, I surveyed the fridge and pulled out what remained of some vegetables: zucchini, sugar snap peas, green beans. I then grabbed what was left from a package of bacon, dicing it up for carbonara. After setting a pot of water on the stove to boil, I pulled down a box of farfalle from our collection of pastas.

We would have thirteen people staying at the house that night—a record for a nonweekend night. Part of the midweek spike resulted from the house now being wireless. A number of house members were coming out with laptops and cell phones and cobbling together work-from-home days between swimming breaks and bike rides, not exactly letting on that "home" was sixty feet from the beach. (Maggie purposefully never told her coworkers that she had joined the house just for this reason.) In addition to the WiFi, however, people were just having a really good time.

Many of the midweekers had ditched offices or were willing to work during the weekends. When I was nannying in Manhattan, my workday didn't begin until after lunch, freeing me from the crush of the morning commute. Scheduling appointments and errands in the late morning when the subway wasn't crowded, I began avoiding the masses whenever possible. This was when Friday and Saturday nights started to feel like a drag. If I planned to drop some coin on a nice restaurant, I would never dream of eating there during the weekend. Likewise, I avoided many of my favorite bars on Friday and Saturday (and sometimes even Thursday) nights. During my stint tending bar at a restaurant in the Village, I began to frequent some of the late-night bars and restaurants that fill up with other people just getting off work at one or two a.m. I found many of these people quite interesting. They too had decided that being free every Friday or Saturday night was overrated, managing to find life elsewhere.

On Monday morning, I came upon Risa in the kitchen rolling out a large swath of brown dough.

"What are you baking?"

"I'm making graham crackers."

"Graham crackers?"

"I didn't see any in the house, and I need a graham-cracker crust for key lime pie."

"You're making homemade graham crackers just so you can crush them? I could have picked up a box at the store."

"Oh, that's okay."

"Are you going to start raising chickens out back for the eggs?"

"You know," she punched my arm. "I like to bake."

That afternoon I went back upstairs to mop and found her leftover graham crackers on the counter. They were twice as thick as the store-bought kind and bore those same tell-tale toothpick holes. I sampled one of the scraps, disbelieving that graham crackers could taste so scrumptious. I popped another one in my mouth and then poured a dash of pine cleaner in a five-gallon paint bucket, dialed up Van Halen's "Women and Children First" on my iPod before grabbing the mop. Van Halen is quality mopping music, because Eddie and David Lee still rocked harder than any of the watered-down wussies who have risen to the top in this millennium and by the end of "Everybody Wants Some," I had finished the kitchen floor and moved on to the bathrooms. After having hired a housecleaner during my first season, I decided to just do it myself. I was still making all kinds of messes with my renovations, and with the abundance of midweek people, the laundering of sheets and towels was a never-ending project. I really didn't mind cleaning. Unlike procurement, cleaning didn't involve any heavy lifting, and when you're listening to Van Halen, it can even be aerobic. Cleaning also provided a constant survey of the state of the house, and if you suffer from OCD even a little bit, maintaining a seven-bedroom beach house allows you to really let it all hang out.

I was finishing up the downstairs bathroom when Cynthia, a cookbook editor, walked in. Cynthia stayed in a house farther up on Pine Walk and frequently came by to steal our WiFi.

"I've got these Morton's steaks from work," she said. "Do you want to cook them tonight?

"Does the Pope shit in the woods?"

"Cool," she said. "I'll come by around seven?"

"That would be great."

Later that afternoon, Rufus, who was still riding out the weekend, began his cocktail hour on the wee early side, mixing up a blender of strawberry margaritas. Cynthia came by with the steaks—soaking in a spicy Thai marinade—and threw them on the grill. She then placed a pot of mashed sweet potatoes over a low flame. Cynthia was one of those chefs who can tell if a steak is done just by touching it, and after poking them a second time with her index finger, she pulled them off. Curious, I pulled a carving knife through one of the steaks and was pleased to see that they were perfectly pink in the middle. Maurice set the table and we all sat down.

I preferred the midweek dinner conversations, as you can have a whole-table conversation with eight people—something that's nearly impossible when dining with twenty. One of the many running house debates concerned whether women could have sex whenever they wanted. While most of the men in the house believed this, only a few women accepted it as gospel. Risa was one of the more strident female doubters.

"I couldn't do that," Risa said.

"You mean you couldn't," I said, "or you wouldn't want to?"

"Oh, please, Risa," Rufus said. "You could walk down to The Inn, introduce yourself to the best-looking guy there and take him home."

"Suppose he's married?"

"If he were married, gay, or dead, the guy next to him would gladly oblige you."

"I don't think that's true," Risa said.

Maurice sat back, quietly observing.

"It's true," I said. "If you decided on a whim that you wanted a bit of horizontal refreshment, you could have it in fifteen minutes."

"Fifteen?" Rufus said. "Try five."

Risa shook her head, still not buying it.

"Risa," Rufus said. "Say these words to me: Rufus come downstairs and have sex with me."

Risa blushed and everyone laughed.

"Come on," Rufus insisted. "You don't believe it? Just say it: Rufus, come downstairs and have sex with me. And we'll put this question to rest."

Risa stood. "So," she said. "Who wants key lime pie?"

Everyone got a kick out of how I found Risa baking graham crackers to then crush for the crust. I repeated the joke about raising chickens, and Rufus asked if she had planted lime trees. Once we tasted Risa's pie, however, no one was cracking jokes. It was the best key lime pie I had ever tasted. Period. I then realized that making your own graham crackers is probably what you have to do to make the best pie. Risa had fulfilled the mission of the house, which was to prepare and serve food in the best way possible. I felt like a douche for poking fun at the high standard she had set to make such an amazing dessert for all of us to enjoy.

After dessert, Cynthia pulled out a bag of weed and rolled up a J the size of my middle finger. Remembering the fuzzy feeling the morning after smoking Colin's bowl, I only took a single hit. And then just one more little one...

"Hey," Maurice said. "Is the house shaking?"

"You're stoned," I said.

"No, I really think the house was shaking. Didn't anyone else feel it?"

A stiff gust had indeed shaken the house, and I came clean to Maurice. Most of the houses in Kismet sit four feet above the ground on posts. During the '04 season, before my renovations, the house shook like crazy. That spring, I crawled beneath the house with my nail gun and fastened a bunch of long boards diagonally beneath the joists to further solidify it. When it's really windy though, the house still shakes. There's one other event that causes the house to shake, and that's when people are getting busy in Baltic. It's the highest point, so depending upon the position(s) and vigor of the participants, two people can literally rock the house. You can really only feel it if you are lying in bed, but whenever someone mentions that they could feel the house shaking, and it wasn't a particularly windy night, I just tell them that the house does this sometimes. In a sharehouse, confidentiality is the ultimate aphrodisiac, and I live vicariously through whoever manages to pull off a bit of horizontal refreshment free from the gossip mill.

"There it goes again," Cynthia said. "Everything shakes." She got up from the table and bid us goodnight.

"That was the coolest thing," Maurice gushed after she was gone. "This woman just rolls in here, cooks us all steaks and then gets us high, too?" Maurice shook his head. "This place is going to ruin me."

"What are you talking about?"

"It's too laid back here. I'm doing yoga every morning, I'm fishing, strangers are cooking me dinner and getting me high. I'm gonna lose my edge out here. It's too—" His cell phone began to ring and he grabbed it, kicking the call into voice mail.

Fourth of July

Grand Theft Costco

Rule Number One and I still had not spoken. Now, three-and-a-half weeks later, on the Thursday night before the Fourth of July weekend—the biggest weekend in Kismet—I was going to call her.

An error in my spreadsheet, once corrected, revealed that we were going to have a whopping twenty-six people at the house, two more than I had initially planned. Aside from not knowing where to put all those bodies, I was having a dispute with Martin, PI. The larger corner rooms (Just Visiting, Free Parking, and Jail) were each going to house five people. Martin and Sonia were originally scheduled for Baltic, which contains the house's only queen-sized mattress (next to a huge mirror) and a twin at the other end. Once Martin told me that Sonia wasn't coming, I scheduled Joe and Tina in the queen and Martin in the single. Martin didn't think this was such a hot idea. He e-mailed back the following:

Not sure what you call the closet loft that I paid for, but pretty sure that it will not accommodate myself, Joe and Tina. Besides, there is still a glimmer of hope that I can persuade my girl to come out with me, so please make whatever changes are necessary...

The "closet loft" was my breaking point. He had paid for Sonia's share himself, and I had given her three spots, scheduling the two of them in Baltic for a song. He compared it to paying guest fees, but forgot that there was a guest limit (to prevent friends and significant others from acquiring de facto shares at a discount). And if Sonia had guested, they wouldn't have been in a room by themselves. I didn't hold back in pointedly explaining this to him, as well as the fact that it was the Fourth of July, when we packed the house to accommodate as many house members as possible during this most popular weekend, and that everyone had to make concessions. Martin held his ground, feeling that what we negotiated should stand. From his angle, he had purchased the loft during his weekends and it was his to use however he wanted (as was the case in a pricier house he had also joined in the Hamptons). Ultimately, it was a question of perspective. While I could see his point, it was another mark of a Bad Sharehouse Couple—considering their shares like a room in a hotel, forgetting the operative half of the compound word "sharehouse."

The blood was boiling on both sides. I hated feeling that way because I liked Martin and he truly believed that what he wanted was fair. At this point, I just wanted to turn off the heat. I called him, and we hugged it out over the phone. Now it looked like Sonia was going to come out after all, so I told him that Baltic was theirs. Alone.

"You're a *mensch,* Johnny. A fucking *mensch!*"

While my *mensch*-hood was debatable, being an upright person was not going to fix my scheduling problem. One of the primary reasons Nicky Mack believed that it was better to be feared than loved is that you'll always fuck over the people you love because you don't fear their retribution. Scanning the names on my spreadsheet, it didn't take long to figure out who I loved the most: Joe. I called him up and explained the situation. He couldn't have been cooler about it, agreeing that he and Tina would have one of the full-sized beds in Free Parking, sharing the room with three other women. Joe joked that at least he'd have other options if things with Tina went south.

*   *   *

After moving Joe and Tina, however, I still had to figure out what to do with the women I had originally doubled up in Free Parking. My older brother, Francis, and his wife, Jen, were coming and I had given them my room. Essentially, I needed to find a sleeping arrangement for me and one other woman. There was only one option: Mediterranean.

The cheapest property on the Monopoly board, Mediterranean was how we referred to the "room" when someone pitched the tent out on the deck. The advantages of Mediterranean, however, are that you can hear the ocean roaring and it allows for a bit of privacy when the house is jam-packed.

I picked up the receiver to dial Rule Number One. With the mounting stress of the July 4 weekend, I was more than ever looking forward to seeing her, hoping that that interest was mutual. Only calling her three-and-a-half weeks later to request that she join me in a tent made me feel like a dope. A fucking dope. I had known all along that I wanted to see her again. Why didn't I call her earlier? I wished I had remembered what Nicky Mack said about procrastination:

The wise man does at once what the fool does finally.

Not feeling particularly wise, I called Rule Number One and explained the situation.

"So you want me to sleep in a tent, huh?"

After razzing me about whether or not she'd be allowed to use the indoor bathrooms, she agreed to share the tent with me. This was a huge relief and only heightened my anticipation to see her. (I repressed the urge to tell her I was looking forward to seeing her, thinking it would sound like bullshit considering the time lapse and what I had just asked of her.) Now, with the bed arrangements taken care of, all I had to do was go to Costco.

*   *   *

Considering the pervasive lack of disclosure in our superconglomerate age, it is worth stating that I have never been compensated by Costco, nor do I own stock in that company. I mention this because I truly, with my whole heart, love Costco. The Kirkland line of products is simply top-notch at laughably low prices. Costco accomplishes this feat without jizzing all over their employees and the communities they serve—unlike Wal-Mart, whose stores destroy local retail property values, while they treat their "associates" almost as well as a pimp treats its hos. Costco's employees earn almost twice that of Wal-Mart's "associates," while receiving benefits with matching 401(k) contributions. This prompted a number of Wall Street analysts to give the company a mediocre rating. Some of those same analysts remain convinced that a company that treats its employees so well can't possibly continue to earn a profit for its shareholders. (Message to douche-bag analysts: During the last couple of years, Costco's stock has consistently outperformed Wal-Mart's and showed profits that almost doubled Wal-Mart's Sam's Club.)

Some people have called Wal-Mart anti-American, antiunion, and antifamily. Those people, frankly, are too nice. Wal-Mart, you see, is satanic. The company is disemboweling the American Main Street while pissing all over free-market forces and lowering the standard for all American workers. I wouldn't roll a cart down Wal-Mart's aisles laden with shoddy goods manufactured in Chinese sweatshops any sooner than I'd set an American flag on fire. I'd sooner set my nuts on fire. And if I ever did find my balls ablaze, I wouldn't buy a bottle of water from Wal-Mart to douse the flames. I'd just stand there in the parking lot and let 'em burn.

Conversely, shopping at Costco makes me feel like A Good American. Every year I proudly funnel five figures into a company that doesn't need to create a euphemism for the word "employees." Unfortunately, my adulation does not extend to my fellow Costco members, many of whom are retirees or parents with children—people that tend to be slow, sluggish, and unpredictable. These people don't have ferries to catch; they don't have to deal with container and refrigeration logistics. These people are Costco amateurs.

Today, I have brought my A-game, which was good because it was the Friday before July 4, and the parking lot of the Commack store was packed. Parking at Costco can be fierce, considering the store's slower-moving demographic. Seniors will drag for spots close to the entrance, their turn signals blinking as they wait for exiting shoppers to load their cars—instead of just parking further back and taking the cardio. Today, however, even the back rows were jammed, forcing me to park in the far corner. I snagged an abandoned cart and hunched over the handle, riding it down the hill to the entrance. After flashing my Executive Member card, I gasped at the thickness of the holiday crowd. I was going to have to squeeze past all of them to catch the 1:15 boat back to Kismet. Already famished, I would not have time for my regular snack of a quarter-pound Hebrew National dog and drink ($1.63, tax included) and would instead have to cobble together a meal out of the free samples. I considered running other errands to kill time until the 2:55 boat, but I didn't have anything else to do on the mainland and still had plenty to do back at the house. Besides, I had brought my A-game.

"You can do it, Johnny," I muttered, pulling out my iPod and dialing up Guns N' Roses.

I rolled past the towers of plasma-screen TVs, weaving around a cluster of old ladies eyeing the chandeliers. Stealing a glance at my inventory sheet, I swerved around the slow-moving shoppers, crossing the breadth of that massive box toward the food. I burned through the dry aisles, pulling items from shelves. Once the cart's undercarriage and top are brimming, that is just about what we need to get through a normal week; for a three-day holiday weekend with twenty-six people, proper cart arrangement was crucial. I was moving fast, anticipating the next aisle, never stopping except to negotiate the amateurs, some of whom can be straight-up comatose, abandoning their extra-wide carts and bottlenecking the aisles. On the other side of an abandoned cart, I spotted a comely MILF with one kid in the cart and another dawdling behind. She looked about my age and wore a harried expression as she called out to her child. At Costco I spontaneously fall in love with some of the finest MILFs in Suffolk County. They look sharp yet frazzled and could easily pass as extras on *Desperate Housewives*. We exchanged a glance of commiseration, and it was as though she somehow knew that I had my own brood waiting for me back at the beach.

I rolled into the refrigerated section: milk; half & half; whipping cream; four pounds of butter; 108 eggs; eight pounds of bacon. The cold and frozen section is where you can snag the best free samples, and I was ready to strap on the feedbag. I scored a double-grab of bourbon chicken fingers. Protein. Good. I then dropped seventy-two Nathan's hot dogs into my cart followed by six pounds of shrimp, pulled a U-turn and tapped the bourbon chicken fingers once again, not stopping as I swiped a Dixie cup of knockoff Gatorade, wishing I had grabbed a second cup to toss over my head. I followed up a wedge of salmon burger with a vegan portobello meatball and was now moving like a shark, picking up speed as I descended upon the produce, when, just ahead of me, a man abandoned his cart in the middle of the aisle to join his wife ogling the melons. Next to them, a grandparents-and-child team were blocking my flight. Feeling the full force of my load, my eyes zeroed in on the corner of that abandoned cart. In that moment, I wished that Costco would build an alternate set of box stores in secret, undisclosed locations where jet-propelled carts are equipped with bayonets, the wheels outfitted with spiraling spikes. If such a store existed, I would boldly compete against other professionals, people who don't take Costco's low prices and high quality for granted, patrons who shop with honor, never knowing if it might be the last time that they crouch down for a thirty-six-pack of toilet paper. It's fucking Grand Theft Costco, where you don't just over-sample the coconut shrimp, you grab super-luscious MILFs—and not those uptight Suffolk County MILFs, I'm talking down-and-dirty Nassau County MILFs—taking them down screaming over pallets of dog food and giving it to 'em Kirkland-style over a fifty-pound sack of Kibbles 'n Bits...

Just before ramming full-force into that abandoned cart, I gave a swerve-liftwrench, just nicking the corner—a shot fired over the bow that startled the melon-ogling couple back into conscious consideration. Powering through produce, I grabbed lemons, limes, a massive three-dollar pineapple, melon, strawberries, spinach, broccoli, snap peas, mixed greens, not breaking my coast toward the meat department, where the samples were off the hook.

It was like a fucking wedding. I refueled on kielbasa drizzled with honey mustard and chips with peach-mango salsa. I grabbed a whole ribeye roast, boneless, skinless thighs, tilapia filets and farmed catfish, before arriving at my terminus: the bakery. English muffins, hot dog and hamburger buns, seven-grain bread, croissants, asiago-cheese bagels, ciabatta, and baguettes that were still warm in the sack. My cart was now arced precariously high, my forearms walling in the sacks of bread. A time check revealed that I was behind schedule. With Axl Rose raging in my ear, I was accelerating toward checkout when yet another old lady wandered into my path. She was a tiny, Yoda-looking thing—someone's grandmother, probably—but fuck it all if she wasn't one little old lady too many. Still grooving on my Grand Theft Costo fantasy, I swerved and began picking up speed, drawing my right behind my ear when she turned and faced me just before I fucking decked her.

She was so frail that I sent her flying through the air, crashing into a shrinkwrapped pallet of kashi. Out cold, she slumped to the ground, an airy little smile set on her face. At first, I was like, oh shit. I just fucking snapped. I envisioned the other shoppers massing together and taking me down, bludgeoning my skull with an eight-pound tri-pack of Swift baby backs. Amazingly, no one did anything. They all just looked away or pretended not to notice or wore dispassionate looks as though they too had decked a couple of old broads before breakfast. Then it dawned on me that in Costco—with its overload of seniors and children—I was a bruising motherfucker. My eyes tightened, shooting them all a Who's Next look just in case anyone got any ideas, but none of them did and then, in that instant, I had an epiphany about our sorry state of affairs. I finally understood how those chicken-hawk NeoCon bullies ever managed to get us bogged down in fucking Iraq.

Halfway to the register, a child of three wandered into my path, and I swerved hard, creating an avalanche of bread crashing against my chest. I contained it, save a sack of ciabatta rolls that fell to the ground. Still moving, I decided that the ciabatta was expendable—collateral damage during a time crunch. Only a lump began to form in the back of my throat and I knew that I couldn't abandon the ciabatta, that to do so would dishonor myself, the store, and, most importantly, the ciabatta. Suddenly it was no longer about the ferries, or the Fourth of July weekend. My mind flooded with a singular notion:

No Ciabatta Left Behind!

Feeling the Costco Force, I let go of my rolling cart and spun around, dodging and rolling around the carts and shoppers like Tony Dorsett, fishing up the ciabatta and jetting back to my cart, still in motion, just before it crashed headlong into a display of Brita.

At the register, most amateurs choose the shortest line, dissing a queue four carts deep in which the shoppers only have a couple of items. Or they'll be scared to get behind two flatbeds piled high with cases of Poland Spring, all of which can be rung up in seconds. They also failed to consider the checkout person themselves. Costco's low turnover has resulted in me knowing most of the people in the Commack store by sight; I even know a good many of their names. There is a petite register clerk named Lana with long, raven-black hair who is amazingly efficient. I'm talking 1980s Japanese efficient. While scanning with one hand, her other hand reaches behind her to blindly group items on the register dock. I was looking for Lana, but the holiday-weekend lines were ridiculously long, curving along the candy aisle six and seven carts deep. From this distance I couldn't gauge the clerks, although I spotted a young, fast moving white male whom I didn't recognize. I got on his line and then checked the time: 12:35. I needed to cruise through checkout, load up my bins and coolers, drop them off at the ferry, park my car, and then hoof it back to the boat before 1:15. The only thing of which I could be certain is that the following forty minutes would not be pleasant. I checked my voice mail. Two people wouldn't be showing up until Saturday; there were special food requests; there were last-minute attempts to guest, which would be turned down. With twenty-six people, I was relieved that a few of them wouldn't be arriving until Saturday. Looking up, I saw that I had made little progress toward the register. I stepped to the side and saw why it was taking so long: The clerk was new. Despite his young, quick hands, he hadn't yet acquired the Costco muscle memory and was still being trained by the person loading the carts. By the time I got to the register, it was 12:47. The woman training this newbie sized up my load and called out for a second cart. *A second cart?*

"I'm all by myself here," I told her.

"Don't worry," she said. "Someone will escort you to your car."

While this was reassuring, I still had to get past the newbie. If only Lana were there. I was two steps away from calling out for her like that little kid calling for Shane. *Lana! Come back, Lana!* Lana wouldn't need a second cart; Lana could pack the fucking space shuttle. By the time I made it past the newbie, it was 12:54. My acid reflux was kicking in, and I could taste the kielbasa at the back of my throat as I popped one of Kirkland's Zantac-75 knockoffs (240 tablets cost only five bucks in Costco's pharmacy) as I rolled toward the door where Veronica was working the receipt check. I had been nursing a mean crush on Veronica for two years, her auburn curls and thick glasses coming together in this geeky/girly thing that works for her in a big way. While I normally loved how she questioned potential overrings—making sure that I actually purchased *four* sacks of avocadoes—I just didn't have the time for her excellent service; what I needed was some Wal-Mart grade mediocrity.

"Hi, Veronica," I said, throwing her off guard. "Oh, hi." She blushed, giving my cart a once-over before drawing a red line down my receipt. I threw my weight into the cart and raced up the parking lot, leaving the kid wheeling my second cart in the dust. At my car, I threw my bins on the ground and lined the bottoms with cranberry juice, coffee, pignoli nuts. My escort dropped off my second cart, and I began to fill my coolers, knowing that I wouldn't have enough room. Broccoli spears and spinach were relegated to my duffel bag. I jumped into my car and burned out of the parking lot, trying to catch the lights as I raced southward back to Bay Shore. It was 1:10 when I pulled in to the Kismet/Saltaire ferry terminal and gasped at the thickness of the crowd jockeying around the ferry loading dock. Seven or eight rungs of them were advancing ridiculous amounts of freight for the long weekend. It was like some kind of refugee camp, like Darfur in Birkenstocks.

I parked near the loading dock, dropped off my bins and coolers, and then bounded back into my car to drive back to the main terminal, where I kept a seasonal parking spot. After a quick head check, I put the car in reverse and gave a sharp cut to the wheel, hearing the distinct pop and crunch of broken glass. I slammed on the brakes, threw the car into park and jumped out, spotting a bag of broken jars of baby food beneath my tire. An older woman wearing a Saltaire shirt was yelling at me.

"Watch where you're going!"

I had already met my old lady quota for the day.

"You can't abandon stuff in the path of the cars! People are pulling in and out here! I can't see that!"

She started to rant and I checked the crowd. Eyebrows flipped and people looked away.

"Well…what if it were a dog?"

"Then your dog would be DEAD!"

A ghastly look came over her face, and I pulled the bag from beneath my tire and dropped it near the trash.

"Come on, mom, it's no biggie," a younger woman said, shooting me an apologetic smile. "We can get more at the store." I'd have loved to trade sorries and make nice with them, but I just didn't have the time. I raced around to the main terminal, parked my car, and then broke into a run back to the Saltaire terminal. While I'm a strong swimmer, I don't jog, and so I occasionally get shin splints. Feeling my calves begin to burn, I wondered, in our post-9/11 world, just what would happen if I ever had to run for my life. Suddenly, I could see that old Saltairean whose baby food I had crushed pointing a bony finger at me and delivering the answer:

Then the sharehouse manager would be DEAD!

"Fuck that," I said, ignoring the lancing pain beneath my knees. By the time I made it back to the ferry, I couldn't stand still, hopping from foot to foot like a child in need of a bathroom. My freight was squeezed into the hold and I boarded the boat and found an empty bench on the upper deck. In the run-up to the biggest weekend of the summer, I was now through negotiating factors dependent upon other people. Now I only had to count on myself. I pulled off my T-shirt and bunched it up for a pillow, lying back on the bench and pulling one of the sleeves across my eyes to blind them. Listening to the seagulls circling above, I wanted only to forget for the next twenty-five minutes that I happened to be the Hardest Working Man in Sharehouse Business.

The Whole Pig

Sipping five ounces of gin while sitting out on the porch swing would have been a most lovely way to wind down after my whirlwind on the mainland, but I still had to clean the house and cycle laundry. I was still zipping around when people began to arrive and was about to pull the sheets down from my clotheslines when Rule Number One came around the walkway. She was a sight for sore eyes, but when I embraced her, she didn't give in my arms.

"So I'm sleeping in a tent, huh?" She broke away from me. "Where are you going to sleep?"

"Let me go get those sheets," I said.

Upstairs, she maintained her air of detachment, but I could see that it was work and hoped that she wouldn't be able to keep it up for long. I was soon distracted, however, by the arrival of Francis and Jen, who came down from Boston. Francis is a competitive bicyclist, a former captain of the Tufts sailing team, and an all-around spatial desperado who, when we were kids during the early eighties, figured out how to solve a Rubik's cube. (He can still do it in a matter of minutes.) While he works for himself as a consultant, no one in our family possesses more than a vague understanding of what he does. I don't think Jen even knows. As best as I can recall, Francis installs large computer networks in places like banks and specializes in writing some kind of computer code. (If you were a drug dealer or a government spy or otherwise in need of a cover, just ask my brother what he does and then write it down word for word. You will snow everyone in one sentence. Not only will they not ask follow-up questions, they'll never even remember what you do in the first place.) Two years older than me, Francis was a model student and athlete who never got into trouble, moving through life with a peaceful contentedness that I have long admired and envied. His life has not been characterized by the tumult of my own and I took comfort in the fact that we shared much of the same genetic coding, that maybe there was still hope for me.

Since plenty of people have to contend with nightmarish brothers-and sisters-in-law, I feel doubly lucky that Francis is married to Jen, who is sweet and pleasant and with whom Matt and I regularly joke about Francis's absent-mindedness that sometimes drops him so deeply into whatever task he's performing that you have to call his name repeatedly until he snaps out of his trance. Francis and Jen make a charming couple and provide a decent buffer for Matt and me, and our parents can at least take comfort in knowing that they didn't raise a marriage-resistant strain of children.

While getting Francis and Jen set up in my room, however, Rule Number One regrouped and redoubled her efforts at jokey detachment. She reminded me of my cats when I've been away for a long time. I eventually coaxed her out for a nighttime walk on the beach, but still she kept a cool distance. With a number of people not arriving until the following day, Rule Number One informed me that she was going to sleep in Dani's room that night. I didn't try to change her mind.

*   *   *

On Saturday morning, Francis accompanied me down to the dock, the two of us pulling my handtruck and garden cart to collect our booze.

Of the many jobs I could never fathom doing—being a New York City police officer; a cardiac surgeon; Martha Stewart's personal assistant—near the top of my list would be managing the Fire Island Freight Ferry. That job is performed by a guy named Don Guinta, who cuts endless paths from the freight terminal to the boat to the business office, powering through the morass of loose ends that forever land in his lap. Just about everything I've purchased for the house—from the jacuzzi and barbecues and appliances, to all the materials for my renovations, down to our kegs and wine and booze— have all passed through Don's purview.

Getting things delivered to Fire Island can be frustrating. Whenever you speak to someone over the phone, you need to rouse them from the hypnotic glow of their computer screens and get them to understand that you're on an island, that large items have to be delivered to the freight terminal before nine-thirty a.m., and that you have to be able to track them, so that you can give Don a heads-up and make sure that you can be there when the freight boat delivers your item to the dock. So when that chipper voice on the other end of the line opens up with "How can I provide you with excellent service today?" you want to tell them that they can start by setting aside the cards listing their stock preambles and responses and to please just listen. You want them just to listen because you've been fucked over too many times and you need them to understand that you're on an island, a fucking island, and your situation is going to require some special instructions and independent thinking. They never fail to reassure you in condescending tones that your parcel will arrive at the freight terminal when it's supposed to, and this does happen almost half of the time. More often than not, however, a buggy e-mail based computer tracking system will force you to follow up your order with a phone call, whereupon you fight your way through one of those automated phone menus that leave you screaming YES! and NO! into your receiver, stringing you through a series of loops before dumping you on hold while maddeningly reminding you every thirty seconds that your call is important. You'll eventually speak to a human being and learn that your order is now in the hands of some delivery company you've never heard of, or has been pawned off to a local office who subbed out the delivery to some other driver, and you try to get a reassurance that that driver, who may or may not speak English, understands that the delivery has to arrive before nine-thirty. Communication breakdowns abound. I've had large items delivered to the freight ferry in the afternoon before the company has even sent tracking info. I'll learn of this via a phone call from Don, who wants to know if he can send it over on the next morning's boat (and then has to deal with my parcel that night). While my renovations were largely finished, there were still the weekly shipments of booze, as well as the endless string of empty kegs and propane tanks that I sent back. I relied pretty heavily on Don, and so I did my best to stay on top of my deliveries. Still, considering our overworked, disorganized populace that wanted everything at the last minute, I couldn't begin to imagine a day in the life of Don Guinta.

The ferry dock was mobbed, and as the freight boat pulled in, clusters of people advanced up the dock, bottlenecking it with their carts and wagons. These people were nervous because they didn't want someone making off with their crates of booze. Kismet runs on booze, and everyone feels better once they've been reunited with their stash. Francis and I hung to the side as the freight crew rolled out pallets of food and supplies for the Kismet Market, as well as for The Inn and The Out. Once these pallets were off the boat and their golf carts and pallet jacks were out of the way, the freight crew began unloading all of our stuff, much of it shrink-wrapped on pallets, our last names magic-markered on the boxes. One of the crew lowered a pallet down

from the jack, and Don whipped out a box cutter, splitting the shrink-wrap.
I could see my booze and other people recognized their booze, charging the
pallet as though recovering lost children. Looking exasperated, Don called
out, "Alright, back up folks!" After clearing a path, he spotted me and made
an example:

"There you are, Mr. Blesso, standing back like a gentleman." He then
personally unloaded each one of my six boxes onto my cart. I was not in a
hurry and would have given him a hand, but Don was an object in motion;
respecting Newton's first law of physics, I thought better of getting in his
way.

"Thanks, Don."

"Alright, have a good weekend," he huffed. "Your keg's over there," he
nodded toward the end of the dock and then charged back toward the boat.

I left Francis with the booze and wheeled the hand truck over to the keg.
As we walked back across the bay, passing The Inn and the Kismet Market,
people made the same stock friendly comments, telling us where they lived so
that we could deliver the keg, or asking what time the party starts. They didn't
know that we had a kegerator, that this is just what we did for beer, and so
they saw the keg and assumed that we were throwing a party, and in the end,
of course, we were. All summer long.

*   *   *

The house was now jam-packed with people milling about during the brunch
hour. Rule Number One was still cheekily brushing me off—something I
barely registered because I was starving. Risa had cooked a bastardized version
of *huevos rancheros*. I filled up a plate of eggs, refried beans, and bacon, and
toasted half of a ciabatta roll. It was a gorgeous day, and people filed down
to the beach after breakfast. I cooled off with a dip in the ocean and then lay
down next to Rule Number One, who had her iPod plugged in. I fell asleep.
When I woke up, Rule Number One was gone. On my way back to the house,
I ran into Alexis, Kismet's only topless female fisherman. While Alexis was
part of Bicycle Bill's house, she was also a de facto member of Motel-O, a
sharehouse that included a woman who organized sex parties in the City,
where couples pay a steep cover charge to participate, literally, in a Huge
Fucking Party. I've never attended one of these parties, but was fascinated
by the concept—especially the financial aspect—and I briefly considered

running sex-party weekends in my house late in September after my season ended. In the end, however, the idea of paying down my mortgage via dozens of people jizzing all over the place would have never allowed me to lie in comfort on my couch again.

"Hey," Alexis said, grinning. "Wanna come have a drink with me at Motel-O?"

"Why not?" I said.

At West Lighthouse Walk, the westernmost street in Kismet and all of Fire Island, we turned right and headed toward the bay. As we advanced up the walkway to the house, a man and a woman emerged from the outdoor shower wrapped in towels. Most of the visible parts of their bodies were covered with tattoos, while together they had about seven or eight pounds of metal punched into their faces and nipples and wherever else. Both of them gave me fresh-meat looks as Alexis hit them up for their share of a hotel room where a bunch of them had had group sex the night before. Alexis wanted $15 per couple. The guy retrieved his pants and pulled out a fiver. I stepped aside and began speaking to the woman, who was some kind of experimental artist, and so I didn't hear the conversation that ensued between Alexis and the guy. I wanted to, though. How fucking cheap do you have to be to decide that fifteen bucks was too much for group sex? Here's how I imagined him making his case:

"Well, I only fucked *three* women and sucked off *two* guys, so, like, I don't think it's fair that I should have to pay as much as Alistair, because he fucked *five* women and was a strap-on bottom for like four hours..."

My imagination regularly slips out from under me, and so when we walked upstairs, I expected to find a Caligula-like mass of contortions and felt almost let down when I came across a group of clothed people sitting out on the deck drinking mojitos. One of them fetched me a mojito and I sat down and chatted with them out on the deck, happy to be away from my house for a little while. I told them about the pig roast party I was hosting the following day and invited them all to come.

*   *   *

On the Saturday night of the July 4 weekend, people crowd the ocean block of East Lighthouse Walk for the block party organized by Elliott, an old-school Kismetian who had managed a sharehouse until acquiring a family. He's one of those links to that earlier, crazier era, and the block party is a free-for-all, with a blues rock band, Jell-O shots, gummy bears that have been injected with vodka, and lots of beer. It was already dark, and I hadn't been over to East Lighthouse yet. People were crashed out on the couch bank, listening to Dani's iPod. I announced that I was going to head over to the block party, and they said they would catch up. Francis, Jen, and I wandered over and found Elliott manning a large hibachi, cooking hot dogs. We grabbed dogs and beers and watched the band play through the rest of their set. No one else from the house showed up, and we wandered back. Upstairs, the house was just packed with people. The wet bar was a disaster, the whole surface crowded with capless bottles and half cut lemons and limes.

"Why don't you guys come to the block party?" I said. "There's a band."

They gave a collective shrug, and I looked at Maggie.

While Maggie had a decent epicurean sensibility, she also happened to be a throw-down party girl who usually went with the flow. She was probably the best bellwether of the collective mood of the house.

"I think we're just gonna hang here," she said.

"Hey, Johnny," Martin called out, approaching me. "What's going on with—" He shook his head, cutting himself off. "Jesus Christ Johnny, look at the *schvitz* on ya. You're sweating like a dog."

"It's hot in here, isn't it?" I went to crank up the ceiling fans, but they were already on full blast.

"It's fine," Martin said. "Look, Johnny, what's going on with the loft?"

"I told you, it's all yours."

"Somebody's stuff is up there."

"Joe and Tina stayed there last night." I looked around for Joe, but I didn't see him. "Look," I said to Martin. "When you see Joe, just ask him to take his stuff down."

Martin raised his eyebrows at being saddled with this task.

"JOHN-*NAY!*" It was Colin, yelling over Dani's music. "What's up with the red light on the espresso machine?" He was already drunk and high and now wanted to add caffeine to the mix. I approached the machine and dumped out the disposal and was looking for the bag of whole beans to refill the hopper when I heard the chorus to Puff Daddy's cover of "Every Breath You Take," a banned song.

I didn't need to hear this track a hundred thousand times to drive me batshit insane—once was all it took. That syrupy chorus is so disharmonic and shrill that it makes nails on a chalkboard sound like Sade. I spun toward the couch bank.

"That song's banned!" I pointed at the stereo.

Dani fumbled with her iPod until she managed to cue up the next track. Seeing the nervous look on her face, I felt like a piece of shit. It was not one of my finer moments and was probably so much frustration being vented in her direction. I pulled Dani aside and apologized to her, still feeling bad about it when she slunk away. I went downstairs and lay down in my bed, feeling the house shake from the dance party. When I emerged from my room, Rule Number One was coming down the stairs. I grabbed her wrist and pulled her into my room, closing the door behind us and pinning her against the wall. I was ready, if necessary, to initiate The Talk, the What Are We Doing Talk.

"How are you doing there, Mister?" She gave me a conciliatory smile.

"I'm fine." Upstairs, I could hear Matt rallying people to go to the bars. A train of footsteps began down the stairs.

"So." She shot me that devil grin. "Where's this tent?"

*   *   *

In the morning, I awoke from the heat in the tent and unzipped the vents. We had slept on two tri-fold cushions.

"How did you sleep?" I asked her.

"Not bad. So far I've slept really well with you."

"What do you mean?"

"Since we were little kids, both my brother and I have suffered from night terrors."

"What are night terrors?"

"Sometimes I wake up, but not all the way, and I think someone's in my room or someone's coming after me, until I wake up and then go back to sleep. This can happen over and over again in a single night."

"Have you seen a doctor about it?"

"Not in a while."

"Why not?"

"Because they all just want to send you to a shrink, who is going to tell you that you were molested as a child, and when you tell them that you weren't, they'll insist that you've repressed the memory."

I am, unfortunately, a very light sleeper. My slumber is regularly disturbed or compromised by my acid reflux as well as nocturnal teeth grinding. I wear a dental night guard, use a white-noise machine (or the ocean loop on my iPod), and a lavender sleep mask to block out the light. I resented having to employ all of this equipment to catch a decent night's worth—as though sleep has become some kind of trendy yuppie sport. So it broke my heart to imagine Rule Number One lying in bed as a little girl being repeatedly terrified, and that this condition had only persisted. I told her that I had considered going to a sleep lab, that maybe we could look into it together, but she wasn't interested, insisting that all roads of treatment would lead to a molestation-obsessed shrink. Her face became void of expression, and she waved away any suggestions, insisting this had always been her state of affairs, and that it was futile to hope that things might ever change.

* * *

I coffeed up and got to working on my mojo—a Cuban-style marinade of sour orange juice, garlic, oregano, salt, and cumin that I would later be injecting into the pig that we would be roasting out on the deck. Then I went to fetch my pig. Paul Whitney, who ran the Kismet Market with his son, Andy, had procured a whole pig for me. Paul was a friendly, soft-spoken man who never batted an eye at my strange requests. Whatever odd meat, fish, or fowl I needed to have sent over on the freight boat, Paul always made it happen.

"Hiya, John." Paul called out when I arrived at the market. "Have you come for Babe?" He winked.

"You read my mind, Paul."

Paul led me into his walk-in where I found the pig, wrapped in clear plastic, sitting perfectly well behaved in the corner next to the rest of the market's meat. I carried it out onto my cart.

While wheeling a keg down Pine Walk drew a certain amount of attention, pulling a dead pig on a garden cart is another thing altogether and I really wish that a particular stone-faced six-year-old boy hadn't seen that. At the house, I threw the pig over my shoulder, scaring the crap out of Tina when I carried it upstairs to the deck. I was sweating when I set the pig down next to the roasting box.

"Every time I see you, Johnny," Martin said, "you're *schvitzing*."

"It's good for the pores," I said.

"What the fuck are you gonna do to that thing?"

"Flay it," I said. I laid the pig on its back and put a hand on either edge of the rib cage, throwing my full weight down on it until I could hear a crack near the spine and the ribs gave as the pig flattened out. I then loaded my syringe with the mojo and injected the ribs, shoulders, butt, and thighs. Then I gave a squirt into each of the cheeks, which are about the most tender and tasty bites on the animal.

I placed the pig into the Cuban roasting box and covered it with its recessed lid that holds charcoal. (The heat radiates down from above, roasting the pig over the course of five hours, during which I'd have to add more charcoal on the hour.) After lighting and spreading out the coals, I went down to the beach, where I found Joo-chan sitting with Martin and Sonia, listening to the Yankee game on Martin's radio. I was glad to see Martin and Sonia sharing the house cluster. Next to them, Colin was sharing his bowl with Alan, a house member.

Rule Number One had told me that Alan had made a move on her the night before we took our walk on the beach and that she politely rebuffed him. Alan wasn't the kind of guy to sweat rejection, though, understanding that it was just a numbers game. On the other side of them lay Jeffrey and Rosemarie, along with two women from Bicycle Bill's house. I had forgotten that Rosemarie, like me, had started out at Bicycle Bill's and that she and Jeffrey had met in Kismet. While Chance was only responsible for one-half of the relationship, I liked that the house had something to do with putting two people together. Still, they were a curious couple. Rosemarie was quiet, understated, and imbued with a no-nonsense air (she was, after all, *Ger-muhn*), which made me wonder how she clicked with Jeffrey.

I returned to the house with Risa and Matt, who helped me flip the pig over. Risa began making rice and black beans, as well as a Colombian aji hot sauce made with jalapenos, cilantro, and scallions. People began to return from the beach at the appointed hour, and then our attendance doubled when Bicycle Bill brought over his entire house. We were also visited by Doctor Stern, clad in full S&M regalia and toting a video camera. I dragged an amp outside and plugged in my Ovation guitar, as well as a microphone. As planned, Risa joined me out on the deck, and I accompanied her as she sang "The Star Spangled Banner" to the roaring and cheering crowd. Matt and I then carried out the golden-brown pig, prompting a wave of delight (and horror from a pair of visiting vegetarians) as we began carving it up. Risa brought out the black beans and saffron-infused rice, as well as the aji.

The crowd picked that pig clean, leaving only the head, the spine, and four hoofs, a massive protein injection—following a rather savage presentation, consumption, and aftermath—that kicked the crowd into gear.

On the deck of Bananas, a house situated just to the north of ours, people were doing beer funnels. Bananas was a classic, old-school Kismet sharehouse (they called them "group houses") where members simply divided the rent and expenses among the group and everyone got to come out whenever they wanted. Bobby and Patty, the couple who ran the house, assembled a tight crew that had been together for years. Their house was like an anarchist's paradise, and I frequently envied their communal understanding that didn't require my rigid structure. Their group included a number of cops and teachers, and as they drained funnel after funnel, I considered that these were the people who were both protecting us and teaching our children. One of them called out to our deck, challenging our house to a funnel race. At Bananas, they regularly saw us out on the deck eating meals of grilled tilapia while drinking sauvignon blanc. So I could forgive them for thinking that a bunch of stem-pinching effetes would be no match for them in a funnel-off. They were seeing me and the group I put together years after the French gave me my gastronomic makeover; they didn't know that before I went abroad I was a pretty fucking lowbrow, Old Milwaukee-chugging, chicken-wing eating, dart-throwing, sports-bar drinker. I was the kind of guy who would have joined a fraternity, if it weren't for the sheep fucking. When it came to shotguns, funnels, and chugging, Matt and I have always possessed the quickest gullets in whatever circles we traveled, and while I can still burp longer than Booger in *Revenge of the Nerds,* in the competitive-eating department, I deferred to Matt, who just the previous year had competed in a qualifying round for Nathan's annual hot dog-eating contest. They tossed one of their funnels over to our deck.

"Give us your best," one of them called out, "and we'll give you ours!"

Matt was chomping at the bit. Both houses filled up the funnels with beer. At the sign, Matt dropped to his knees and drained the funnel at the speed of gravity. People cheered, further juicing the action. I went inside just as Alexis and some of the group from Motel-O came up the stairs. I set them up with drinks, and Alexis and I watched as a half-dozen people began vanilla-dirty-dancing on the coffee table.

"These people," Alexis said, "seem nothing like you."

When I had first considered running a sharehouse, I had imagined it as a quasi artists' colony, peopled with writers, musicians, painters, photographers, and other sundry artists on the verge of breaking out—the kind of people bounding with creative energy off whom I could bounce like pinballs. The problem with artists is that a lot of them just don't have the scratch to pay for a share. So I recruited a number of people who worked in creative fields, people who were artistic yet still filed tax returns, while a third of the house hailed from the corporate world. It was diverse.

"They're a little different," I told her.

"Why don't you have a house full of artists?"

"Because a lot of artists can be dicks about money. I'd rather hang around a banker who's a nice guy than listen to cheap bastard excuses from an artist any day."

I then reminded her of the hole-punched bi couple who could have paid for a share at Chance for the next decade with the money they had spent on tattoos, yet still weaseled out of their fifteen-buck share for a night of group sex.

"Money may not be everything," I said, "but these people present it when it is due, and that's the most important thing."

No sooner did I say this than did I realize that Mandy—who was among that white-collar gaggle gyrating on the coffee table—had yet to pay me for Uptalking Nancy's Labor Day spot.

"I'm going to check out the hot tub," Alexis said.

"Okay." I spotted Rule Number One flirting with Alan, but paid them no mind, moving out to the deck. Risa was introducing me to some of her friends when the crowd began to cheer.

"Hey," Natasha called out to me. "Your brother is naked in the hot tub!"

I approached the railing to see what Matt was up to, but when I looked over the side, these were the words that came out of my mouth:

"*That* brother?!"

Francis was seated in the hot tub next to Jen, along with Alexis and a few of the women from Bicycle Bill's house, all of whom were topless. Francis beamed up at me with his boyish grin, and I shook my head in disbelief. Francis was supposed to be the quiet one. (I would later learn that he was still wearing a pair of undies when he extracted his shorts from beneath the foamy surface and tossed them over the side.) Meanwhile, Alexis and some other women from Bicycle Bill's house had gotten down to their birthday suits. This was when a crowd of people I didn't know pushed up the stairs, when an Asian woman began dissecting the pig's skull, and when Rule Number

One fixed her smoldering glance on me and we ditched all that craziness to go downstairs.

*　*　*

By the time we emerged from my bedroom the sun had set. We rejoined other house members on the deck, where Martin, PI clutched a folio from the *New York Times* and began reading, out loud, the entire Declaration of Independence. I realized that I never really knew what was in that document beyond Life, Liberty, and the Pursuit of Happiness. He began to recite King George III's abuses of power, and this caught my ear:

"He has erected a multitude of new offices, and sent hither swarms of officers to harass our people and eat out their substance."

It was this passage, however, that floored me:

"For depriving us in many cases, of the benefit of trial by jury. For transporting us beyond seas to be tried for pretended offenses."

George W. Bush, King George III. Same shit, different century. Only back then we had the will and the courage to tell that particular George to go fuck himself.

*　*　*

We decamped to Bicycle Bill's roof deck to watch fireworks. Across the bay, a display lit up the sky over Bay Shore and, further to the west, Babylon. To the east, there was a show in Ocean Beach, and another spectacular one farther off, possibly coming from The Pines, one of Fire Island's two gay villages. (If it's possible to have a gaydar with fireworks, I do. The fireworks coming from The Pines just had more style...) I stood next to Francis and Jen, the three of us leaning against the deck railing and looking south toward the beach at an amateur show that was none too shabby, the fireworks lighting up Francis's face in pink and green. It felt good to have him there. He's lived in the Boston area since college, so I don't spend as much time with him as I do with Matt. Having leaned rather heavily on my family during the previous two years made me appreciate their support more than ever. When I was twenty-two and told my family that I was going to move to Paris, indefinitely, they didn't flinch. My parents even gave me the plane ticket for my college graduation. Other parents—so I was repeatedly told—would have considered this an insult, a rejection, not understanding that a wayward son will always return to a good home, that being away from your family only intensifies your love for them. (The same holds true for love of country.)

During those dark days after I had penned KILLING ME on that manila folder, when I no longer knew what to do with my life or how to earn my keep, I halted that emotional free fall by telling myself (as silly as this might sound) that because of my family, I was never going to starve; I was never going to end up sprawled out on the sidewalk begging for change. This meatball-down-the-middle realization was my first step in accepting as fact that Everything Would Be Fine. This was when I started to work again, not worrying about career choices or paths not followed, doing whatever work I could find, until I turned up in Kismet.

Once I began looking at houses, Matt consulted me through the purchase and my renovations, down through my first recruiting season. Since I saw him or spoke to him nearly every day, he was inadvertently keeping tabs on me, providing a constant reminder that I was not alone. Two years had passed since we first sat down in front of a spreadsheet, and from that moment on, the house had fully occupied my thoughts. Aside from having shelved *Killing Mercutio*, this whirlwind distracted me from the futility that I felt over the mounting number of flagdraped coffins being unloaded out of sight, as though they didn't exist, all of us being denied our duty to honor that sacrifice. I thought about the thousands of people alive now but doomed to die in the days ahead over a pack of lies. I thought of the trillion dollars of debt piled onto the heads of our children by those borrow-and-spend Republicans enabled by wussy Democrats. Looking across the federal preserve at my large red house, I knew that creating Chance took my mind off of all that shittiness. Somewhere along the way, I had accepted the morally hollow callousness that had pervaded our country just as I had accepted that *Killing Mercutio* was shelved. I decided that if we were hellbent on setting the whole barn up in flames, the best thing I could do was to get a bag of marshmallows. This was when I started to enjoy life again, once again taking pleasure from eating and drinking and conversing with the community of people I had assembled. At some point, I had resumed calling and e-mailing the White House and my representatives in Congress, my renewed level of civic participation making me feel, once again, like a Big Person. Now that I had regained some peace of mind and accepted what had happened, what was unfolding, and what was yet to come, I even held out a distant hope that our divided country might pull itself back together and send this God-awful cancer back into remission. Still, there was one final brick that I needed to lay: It was time to free myself from the whirlwind, to no longer run myself ragged with distraction.

The display in Bay Shore broke into its finale, and Rule Number One sidled up to me. I spun her around and wrapped my arms around her waist, dropping my chin onto her shoulder. With the sky lit up over the mainland, the display coming from The Pines segued into its finale until fireworks were exploding in clusters all around us. Other house members spotted us together, but I just pulled her closer, not caring who saw us. I kissed her beneath her ear, and she lifted her chin, holding her face against mine. My battered emotional state during the previous two years had been no kind of foundation for a serious relationship. Now, standing once again on terra firma, I began to wonder if it wasn't high time to Stop Fucking Around.

What had worked for me was to advance small certainties into larger ones, and all I knew for certain in that moment was that it felt great to have my arms around Rule Number One as we watched the fireworks blooming across the sky.

After the last finale, someone produced a digital camera. Rule Number One broke away from me to join in some group photos. She sat down on Alan's lap and grabbed his face as though about to move in for a seductive kiss. I thought about how she had rebuffed Alan and was now playing hopscotch along that line between flirting and being a tease. I decided not to get hung up on this, remembering some advice that Joe had given me years earlier about dating: Don't sweat one-time occurrences—it's all about patterns. Besides, how was Rule Number One supposed to know that I was having all these expansive thoughts? Still, from the subtle way she had responded in my arms, I wondered if Rule Number One wasn't also feeling something that verged on tenderness and if she just didn't care to make it last. More people crowded into the picture, and she leaned back over Alan's lap, basking in the glow of the flash.

Take the Cannoli

There is probably no factor more responsible for Fire Island's laid-back vibe than the ferries. The ferries help keep Fire Island—for lack of a better term— "real." If you're coming from the City, you have to carry your bag to Penn Station, get on a train, switch trains at either Jamaica or Babylon, get from the train station to the ferry terminal, get your stuff on and off the ferry, and then finally schlep it from the dock to your house. Having to confront your baggage so many times inevitably changes the way you pack. People start to wonder whether they really need that pressed collared shirt, whether they really need those shoes and all of that makeup. People scale down until downscale becomes standard.

A limited number of year-rounders have permits for cars, and during the high season, even these people must get rid of them. Since many people broadcast their status or station in life through their cars, taking cars out of the picture democratizes the mindset while providing an effective jackass filter. The kind of guy who can't be separated from his car is going to end up in the Hamptons.

And the towns in the Hamptons do an amazing job of drawing away these people who wear their status on their sleeves. Paris Hilton will never come to Fire Island; Prada will never open a store here; Donald Trump will never erect one of his tacky monstrosities on our pristine island, because our egalitarian social landscape deters this type of riff-raff.

The closest that Fire Island comes to red velvet ropes is Ocean Beach, Fire Island's largest town. On weekend nights, the bayside devolves into a fraternity party overrun with postgrads and kids from the mainland. Ocean Beach is the kind of place that I would have loved at twenty-two. Now, it just doesn't interest me. Ocean Beach is commonly referred to as "The Land of No" for its innumerable restrictions and its over-officious cops who reminded me of a band of Barney Fifes on steroids. Kismet doesn't have a police force or even a security team (as does Kismet's neighbor, Saltaire), relying solely on the Suffolk County Police who patrol from the mainland. Despite not providing private security, there are virtually no rules in Kismet—unlike Saltaire, which, until recently, banned barbecuing.

This blew my mind.

Why would any beach community anywhere ban barbecuing? Forbidding a man to barbecue on his own property is just un-American and an act of cruelty to men. People should be free to do whatever they want so long as it doesn't hurt anyone else, and that more enlightened sentiment is pretty much what governs Kismet. While drinking alcohol on Kismet Beach is technically not permitted, open responsible consumption is perfectly tolerated. Bass fishermen coexist with bathers, and most people manage to get along without existing under a laundry list of oppressive restrictions.

While I'm obviously biased, Kismet best embodies the spirit of Fire Island. No one in Kismet dresses up, and few women put on much makeup before hitting the bars. If women were to deck themselves out the way they do in the Hamptons, they would fit in about as well as an Amish preacher in Lil' Kim's posse. (My own Kismet wardrobe largely consists of clothes that other people have left behind.) A good percentage of people who join my house have never been to Fire Island. For a few of them, there is a funny moment during their first weekend when they do dress up to go to the bars. I refrain from cracking jokes because they'll figure it out soon enough and then scale back, content to have flip-flops double as dress shoes.

As a community, Kismet cannot be pigeonholed. It is a provincial, blue-collar enclave; it is also a progressive, bohemian paradise. There are retired people and families. There are sharehouses and old-school group houses. While Fire Island is overwhelmingly white, Kismet is probably the most diverse community and a place where many foreigners feel welcomed. There are surfers and artists and fishermen and construction workers and even a smaller gay population that doesn't care to deal with the scene in The Pines. While we're all quite different, what we share is a desire and an ability to make our own fun. We don't need red velvet ropes. All we need are the raw materials to enjoy beach living and Kismet has them all: grocery store, liquor store, ice cream and pizza parlors, tennis and basketball courts, and, of course, The Inn and The Out.

Kismet's carnivalesque air encourages original forms of expression—like that of Jeannie or Doctor Stern—and the town is a blank canvass across which anyone can boldly paint their own strokes, whether garish or muted, brash or elegant. All of Kismet's different kinds of people manage to coexist while respectfully doing whatever they want to do. In this way Kismet is the Fire Island community that I believe is also the most purely American.

*   *   *

Sitting at my desk, I became hypnotized by the flashing curser in my e-mail message. It was my weekly update to house members that included everyone's bed assignments. As it was a C weekend, I had gotten hung up on where to put Rule Number One.

Scheduling her in her regular room seemed silly. Still, it would be pretty awkward if she had met some guy in the City or had decided to pull the plug on our whatever-you-call-it. She had reserved a guest spot for her friend Elaine, and so I moved another woman around, scheduling Rule Number One and Elaine in Short Line, one of the smaller rooms. If everything was okay between Rule Number One and me, Elaine would end up in Short by herself—a pretty nice arrangement for a guest.

I hit "send" and then began fielding the requests in my inbox, including an e-mail from Clay, a new house member who had purchased two of the spots vacated by Wayne and Troy. Clay worked at a brokerage firm on Wall Street and was one of those guys who put off looking for a sharehouse until May. Having finished hosting meetups at the White Horse, Clay and I met up for a beer. He seemed balanced, smart, and considerate, and I offered him a spot. During his first night at the house, I walked past him on the couch bank where he was holding forth with four women. Speaking in a raging gay voice, he had them in stitches. The following day at the beach, I found Clay once again surrounded by women while doing his flaming voice, his wrists flapping and his eyes rolling as he became rather touchy-feely with them. When I spied him doing this a third time, I realized that it wasn't a voice he was putting on—it was how he talked. (To top it off, Clay had a Danny Bonaduce-like shock of orange hair, completing the overall flaming picture.) By the time we sat down to dinner that night, half the women in the house had asked me if Clay was gay.

I have a decent gaydar for a straight guy—something I credit to years of being wrongly perceived as gay myself. While I'm not effeminate, I was, at one time, a nanny who lived in my brother's building in Chelsea with my two cats. On paper, I was as gay as the day is long. Toss in the fact that I speak French, am into cooking, am involved in the arts, and that I own a house in

Fire Island, and people do the math. Even though no numbers are involved, they still do the math because when you add up all of those stats, you get ONE BIG HOMO.

Anyway, my years of being sexually profiled helped fine-tune my own gaydar, yet when I first met Clay, he did not register so much as a blip. As a stockbroker, however, I wondered if he was one of those gays capable of closing the spigot of their effeminacy in homophobic settings, and if now, in the free-flow environment of Kismet and Chance, he no longer felt the need to cover. If I were meeting him now for the first time, I would assume that he was gay. Still, even though again no numbers were involved, something about Clay hiding in the corporate closet just didn't add up.

"I don't think Clay is gay," I said to Mandy, the fifth woman to have asked me.

"Really?"

"Really," I said. "I think he's just fem."

Gay men have frequently gravitated toward me, as my stats rendered me the straight-male equivalent of the woman with whom guys can watch football. Clay, however, began edgily avoiding me, exuding a discomfiting vibe, as though he were stealing something. Possibly the different ways in which he had presented himself began to settle in my mind as dishonesty, creating a bad-vibe downward spiral. Now, however, in his e-mail, he wanted to know if it was okay to bring cash for his additional spots. At least Clay understood what many house members don't get—that being good about money is the foundation for anyone's standing. I decided to give him the benefit of the doubt; if he didn't feel comfortable being himself on Wall Street, I should feel flattered that he settled into his own skin at Chance. I e-mailed him back: *Cash would be great. Thanks.*

On Friday, I began to get antsy, wondering which boat Rule Number One was coming in on. As people started to trickle in late Friday afternoon, I busted out on an OCD tear, tidying up the house, refilling all the shampoo and sunscreen dispensers, doing anything that popped into mind. I was carrying out a bag of trash when Rule Number One wound around the walkway, flashing that devil grin. I dropped the trash. Two women called out to her from the deck above, but before she could answer, I had my arms around her.

"Well, hello," she said, breaking away from me. "Are we out?"

"I don't care," I said.

"Where am I staying?" She started in to the house.

"You're staying with me." I grabbed her bag.

"Oh, am I now?"

"Uh-huh." I carried her bag into my room, closing the door behind us, recalling the folly of the bed arrangement in the house e-mail. She was going to stay with me, in my room.

"It's nice to see you," I said.

Embracing her, my fingers got lost in those thick curls and I pulled down, raising her chin for a kiss before losing my balance.

*   *   *

Gwen, a creative director at an ad agency, was capping off her maternity leave. She had purchased a single midweek, marking the first time that she had been away from her six-month-old, whom she left at home with her husband. This was about the best way to experience Kismet, as it cost a fraction of renting even a tiny efficiency. Frequently, visitors like Gwen ended up liking the other people in the house, so sharing a renovated, well-equipped house with people like Chris and Risa, and dining with us, only accentuated their experience. (Gwen hoped to return in August with her husband.) On Friday after lunch, she packed up her breast pump—as well as the collection of white bricks she had massed in our freezer—to return to the City.

"It's such a beautiful day," she said. "I wish I didn't have to go back."

"You're welcome to stay as long as you like," I said.

"Well... Maybe I'll lie out for a bit."

She ended up staying through the afternoon. When Rule Number One and I emerged from my bedroom, Gwen was still upstairs, picking from a cheese plate with a few other house members. Unfortunately, Dani sat near the stereo, fiddling with her iPod.

"You're still here," I said to Gwen.

"I'm taking the next boat."

"Stay," I said. "Have some dinner."

Clay and Joo-chan were overseeing a round of cheeseburgers on the grill; Colin stood next to them, firing up his bowl. He held it up, offering it to me.

I signaled that I was good, remembering my last hit from his stash.

Stepping into the kitchen, Colin tripped over the threshold, knocking into the table. Already well on his way, I almost wished I hadn't encouraged Gwen to stay. It was kind of a boorish group, and I didn't want Gwen to end her week on a rowdy note. She was so easy, and it was no skin off my nose to have someone like her in the house during the midweek. I wanted her to come back in August with

her husband.

"Who's that?" Rule Number One asked me.

I told her about Gwen.

"She's pretty hot. Did you fuck her?"

I stared at her, curiously, not finding that devil grin so appealing.

"She's married," I said. "And she has a baby."

"So did you fuck her?"

Brazen was Rule Number One's speed, and it wasn't the first time she had asked me point-blank if I had had sex with someone. (During the Fourth of July, she had asked if my appreciation of Risa went beyond her superlative key lime pie.) It was getting to be a drag.

"I did," I said. "Twice last night and once this morning." I approached the wet bar and chilled a cocktail glass, preparing to lower the level in the bottle of gin.

*   *   *

Later that night, Gwen reappeared at the top of the stairs, clutching her bag. She hugged me good-bye and said, "Well, back to the real world."

People frequently uttered those exact words upon leaving the house. I think what they meant was that it was time to head back to that fast-paced environment where they earned their money. I took it as a compliment; stressed-out days at the office followed by nights forking up takeout in front of *Law & Order* were not as fun as the slower, epicurean days at the beach. The closest I came to hacking that so-called "real world" was when I left the pleasant work environment of the Authors Guild for an associate editorship at a large magazine conglomerate.

Insert here the sound of a needle screeching across the record, because here's what I traded in to: two weeks of vacation; an environment that valued the amount of time present over the quality of work; the worst watercooler conversations on the planet. All while being bunched up in that business-casual bullcrap. (I deplore wearing clothes that don't reflect my mood, and as you can imagine, it's pretty rare that I'm ever feeling pastel or beige.)

This office was one of those cutthroat corporate settings where possessing a moral compass and an ounce of self-respect amounted to little more than bad career moves. It was the mind-numbing conversations, however, that pushed me to the brink. I soon learned that there were rules to these conversations. For instance, if someone were to ask you what you did the night before, it was perfectly fine to reveal that you took full advantage of Tijuana Taxi's two-for-one margaritas, that you were dragging ass today, but still managed to get those pages over to the art department before lunch. People would nod their heads knowingly because not too long ago, they too had gone straight from work to that same crappy hour, downing two-for-one of those corrosively sweet, piss-yellow concoctions criminally represented as a "margarita." Like you, they made a meal out of free chips and salsa, paying the following morning for their excessive intake of well-grade tequila, corn syrup, and a dinner that consisted of yet more processed corn. They too managed to achieve a modest amount of work before rewarding themselves for overcoming their self-inflicted wounds by sneaking in an hour of online shopping. At this office, shopping was huge and the cubicle standard was to carry thousands of dollars in credit-card debt, paying late fees and sliding-scale interest rates that would make a leg-breaking loan shark weep.

Imagine, however, if you described your previous night this way:

"I went to a friend's house, we ordered some sushi, did a couple of bong hits, and then watched *The Deer Hunter*."

Now, while I've never done that—precisely—when you provide an answer like that in a corporate environment, people will look at you funny.

I found myself further ill equipped for workday chatter because a majority of the conversations had to do with prime-time television. With a few notable exceptions, I just didn't do prime-time television. Whoever decided, for instance, that "Everybody" loved Raymond, well, those people never asked me. So I never knew what anyone was talking about. Prime-time network television still pushes me within a hairsbreadth of full-fledged misanthropy. Believe me, I understand full well that I'm a nutjob for harboring the notion that in exchange for our getting to live in the world's sole superpower—instead of some corrupt outpost perpetually dry-raped by Texanoco—that we have the smallest responsibility to have some clue about the shit our government does in our name. I think a lot of people feel this way, only by the time they get home from work they're too tired to notice that what passes for "news" on their flickering TV screens is not news at all. When a corporate news program serves up a teaser on Michael Jackson, Botox, and kids snorting OxyContin, that's not news; that's infotainment fear-mongering bullshit feces designed to sell Range Rovers and Paxil. And you know what? If I were some CEO hellbent on finding newer and better ways of rimming my shareholders, this is exactly what I'd want my workers doing: tying one on until going back to work saves them from themselves, and hooking their minds during off-work hours on the lowest level of stimulation that instills fear—not a crippling fear, but a low-grade nervousness that scares them just enough to keep them afraid of losing their jobs and being unable to buy all the newfangled bullshit offered up by our turbo economy.

Amazingly, I lasted six months at that job. Thankfully, I got out of there before 9/11, because if I had had to deal with all of that middlebrow corporate know-nothingism during that hysteria, I would have cracked. Because this was when the river of bullshit breached the levees. After 9/11, George Bush addressed our nation and delivered a hard message: We would have to conserve energy and reduce our dependence on foreign oil...

Yeah. And I've got a fourteen-inch penis that speaks Dutch.

In the wake of 9/11, we weren't going to hear a message of conservation from an oil man any sooner then we'd hear an anti-drug message from a crack dealer. When my father was a boy during World War II, people grew "Victory Gardens" to save food for the soldiers. People lived with rations, proudly sacrificing to help the war effort. (During World War II, *no one* got a tax cut.) This is what Americans were *supposed* to do during a war. If George Bush had only asked, millions of Americans would have proudly sacrificed something to support our troops beyond a buck shelled out for a tailgate magnet saying that we supported them. The real sacrifice fell upon the shoulders of so many poor-and working-class kids. And what was George Bush's message to the rest of us?

Go shopping!

Considering the Bush Administration's extreme hostility toward homosexuals, I found it more than a wee bit ironic that he might implore us to go shopping.

I mean...*shopping?*

HOW FUCKING GAY IS THAT?

Still, when George Bush stood tall and made that call to action, we didn't let him down! We marched out of our houses and drove straight to our nation's malls, the American flags flying from the antennas of our SUVs flapping proudly in the breeze. We were going to show George Bush and the enemy just how much we supported our troops! We ran up credit-card debt equal to the GNP of Guam. And once our cards were maxed out, we refinanced until there wasn't enough equity left in our homes to buy a twenty-piece McNuggets.

I now understand that I turned up in Kismet at a time when I desperately needed a sanctuary from the so-called "real world." I pray that I'll never have to become a part of it again, because for me the "real world" was nothing more than a Company Store with consumer electronics. That's not the real world. It's just so many perverted notions strung together into an existence that has veered far off course. For thousands of years, humans have sat around a fire or across a table to eat together, taking stock of one another while unwinding and getting out of their own heads. A band of Senegalese peasant farmers crowding knee to knee in a hut around a communal plate of fish and rice that they eat with their fingers is far more civilized than what we've become. Too many Americans have been denied this part of being human because we've been made to spend too much time at work. That other existence in the City—as it has so degenerated—is not the real world. It's just a tawdry, second-rate theatre where we surrender the best part of ourselves, leaving fuck-all for our friends and family.

Please. Don't even get me started on that "real world" stuff...

Thankfully, many house members had great jobs at great companies whose bottom line did not depend on screwing people or fucking the planet. Some people, like Chris and Risa, worked for themselves. Nevertheless, many of them did indeed put in sixty-and seventy-hour weeks working for the proverbial Man. Frequently, the level of stifling corporatism endured was reflected in how people rode themselves over the weekend. As I've mentioned, some house members merely unwound while others inflicted upon themselves a punishing level of partying—the kind that sent them running back to the safety of their offices. This fairly summed up the day-to-day life of Colin.

Ever since that night on the dance floor at Mandy's birthday party, Colin had gone from gregarious drunkenness to getting regularly faced. He was now sitting on the couch next to Dani, firing up his bowl while telling a story about a recent medical visit. His doctor had told him that there was a serious problem with his liver. A few days later, he picked up a call from his doctor who told him that they had made a mistake. Colin, not wanting to hear anything further, said "Thank you" and hung up. Rufus insisted that he should have heard his doctor out, that there might still be something wrong with his liver, but Colin had no interest in compromising the clean bill of health that now existed in his mind with any inconvenient facts.

Despite the presence of people like Risa and Tracy, it wasn't the most epicurean crew assembled. The weekend was overloaded with people who just wanted to get their grooves on by any means necessary. I hated to admit that Rule Number One was also one of these people—someone for whom the future didn't span longer than the next five minutes. As Nicky Mack said:

Men are so simple and yield so readily to the desires of the moment.

Nevertheless, Tracy was scheduled to cook an Italian multicourse dinner of antipasti, a limoncello intermezzo, linguine with littleneck clams, and then can-noli and prosecco. Regardless of how the weekend played out, I thought, at least I'll have cannoli.

*   *   *

We played a fair amount of Scrabble. Some of the more hardcore players (the ones who have memorized all the two-letter words, as well as many of the obscure three-letter words) included Martin, Tracy, Chris, and Rufus. On Saturday afternoon, Tracy carried the board and the dictionary down to the beach and invited me to play. I liked playing with Tracy because we employed different styles. I hunted for bingos (when you lay down all seven tiles, scoring an extra fifty points), while the sexy librarian frequently beat out my occasional homeruns by consistently putting men on base. Midway through our game, I noticed Rule Number One flirting with Colin, but didn't pay her any mind because I was behind and had a rack of bingo-friendly letters.

We took a break when Rufus appeared carrying a tray of hot dogs, followed by Joo-chan clutching a thermos filled with beer from the kegerator. I spun around beneath our umbrella and watched the surf as we ate hot dogs and drank beer. It was sunny and breezy, and we were at that point in the season when the water was warm enough that you could bathe as long as you liked. I was already anticipating cooling off with a swim after our game.

Woody Allen once said you shouldn't expect too much from life. I used to think that was sad, but I don't anymore. Once I began expecting less from life, I became more conscious of when I had it good. Sitting in the shade with Tracy over the Scrabble board spread out between us, there was nothing else that I needed or wanted. I washed down the last of my hot dog with a swig of beer and turned back to the board and my letters, moving them around until I spotted my bingo.

*   *   *

Maybe my playing Scrabble with Tracy—followed by my sous-cheffing for her during a rather blender-heavy cocktail hour—had something to do with Rule Number One becoming increasingly flirty with a lot of the guys in the house. I remembered Joe's advice about patterns, advice that I had dismissed when Rule Number One sat across Alan's lap on Bicycle Bill's roof deck, only now I couldn't ignore a pattern that only grew more pronounced with each cocktail. I was scrubbing down clams while Tracy supervised Mandy and Charlotte rolling up the meats and cutting up peppers and artichoke hearts for the antipasti platters.

"What time should we eat?" Tracy asked me.

Normally we sat down at 8:30, but a lot of people were still in their bathing suits, feasting on guacamole. The jacuzzi is usually a good gauge, so I stepped out on the deck. The first thing I saw upon looking over the railing was Rule Number One standing up in the middle of the jacuzzi, doing an erotic dance as Clay sprayed her with the hose. Dani—whose neck was being massaged by Colin—egged her on, while Alan sat in front of her, red-faced. I considered cracking a joke about not leaving dollar bills in the tub and then informing them that we'd be eating soon, but there are few things you can say to a group of drunk people who have worked up a collective boner in the jacuzzi.

"What do you think?" Tracy asked as I returned to the kitchen.

"Let's bump it up to nine o'clock," I said, sending Mandy down to inform the hot tubbers that we'd soon be eating. When we finally sat down to antipasti, much of the table was faced. Normally we're well primed for dinner, but the punchy drunkenness was a bit much. Rule Number One sat at the far end of the table next to Dani and Elaine; I sat near the kitchen to help Tracy. Joo-chan was wasted, screaming over Dani's iPod while Dani grooved in her seat, pointing her fork as she mouthed the words, further emboldened by her guest, Karen, a thin, comely Asian woman who sat opposite her.

Dani's friends were so consistently attractive that I wondered if she might be prejudiced against normal-looking people. I especially remembered her friend Iylana, who guested during the '04 season. Iylana was a lithe Eastern

European model and just about every guy in the house was trying to take her temperature. On the dance floor at The Out, men circled her like sharks, and she grooved on the attention. I've long considered women the way I consider restaurants—many great ones are regularly overlooked by the masses who break their necks attempting to gain entry into a select, overrated few. (And to beat that metaphor to death, many of those restaurants never remain good for more than a couple of years...) So I ignored Iylana —until she stepped in front of me.

"I don't get you," she said.

"What do you mean?"

"I mean," she shook her head, "do you *like* me or *what?*"

"I like you a lot," I said. "You seem like you're really interesting." I walked away and rejoined some house members on The Out's outdoor deck, where I learned that Iylana actually had a boyfriend and probably wasn't so interested in me as she was rattled that someone who pees standing up hadn't gone gaga over her.

Karen picked at her plate while most of the rest of the table ate wolfishly, stabbing their forks into the antipasti. I busied myself helping Tracy plate the linguine and clams, as Mandy pulled the bottle of limoncello from the freezer. (While that sweet, lemony liquor is normally sipped, who was I to say that it shouldn't be thrown back as a shot?) Having filled up on guac before dinner, many people left half-eaten plates of linguine on the table, gravitating toward the living room, expressing little interest in cannoli and prosecco, which, to me, is like expressing little interest in oral sex. As we cleared the table and set up dessert plates, Dani cranked the volume on Eminem. (It was Eminem who made me first wonder if something was wrong with how I heard things. How else could millions of people enjoy this voice that to my ears sounded like a cat being strangled? It was just one of those things with me, and I didn't expect to ever understand the appeal of Eminem any more than I might ever understand why someone would voluntarily listen to the voice of Dr. Phil.)

Colin and Alan sat opposite Karen and Elaine, testing the waters with these two guests. Adjacent to them, Joo-chan slumped against Charlotte, while Mandy hopped up on the coffee table and began to dance.

"Hey, John?" Tracy called out. "How should we serve the cannoli?"

Watching Maggie hop up on the coffee table to join Mandy's ass shaking, I suggested that we just assemble the cannoli and then leave them on the table. We began filling the pastry shells with the cannoli cream, and Rule Number

One made a face at me as she wandered over to the table to snatch one up, before returning to the couches. Clay began dirty-dancing with Mandy up on the coffee table, and even Joo-chan got up to dance.

While Tracy either shook it off or didn't mind that people didn't pay proper attention to her lavish meal, I felt as though they had pissed upon the unspoken contract of the house—that in return for their willingness to be on the same page, they would get lavish, epicurean living. While people like Dani and Colin nudged the group toward fragmentation, Rule Number One's extreme flirtation had also pushed what was normally a fun, spirited level of sexual tension into something that felt almost treacherous. Having had enough, I remembered Clemenza's famous directive to Rocco after he whacked Paulie:

Take the cannoli.

I poured myself a flute of prosecco and grabbed a cannoli before retreating to the deck. Outside, I sat down and stared at the waves while rolling that sweet, creamy filling around in my mouth. I would have paid five hundred dollars to have had someone lower the volume on Eminem. When I finally went back inside, I found Rule Number One sitting on the couch bank next to Clay, her head bent over his crotch as she simulated oral sex.

Great, I thought. Fucking great.

I poured myself a snifter of grappa at the wet bar and went downstairs. A chorus of catcalls rang out as I closed my door and sat down at my desk. With the shitty corporate music still blaring, I plugged my earphones directly into my computer and cranked up my loop of ocean sounds. Gathering up my receipts, I figured that this was as good a time as any to total them. I began sifting through the piles on my desk and came across a DVD of *Casablanca*. Someone had left it at the house, and I kept meaning to watch it. I had only seen it once, when I was nineteen. Back then, I thought Humphrey Bogart had a pressure-treated two-by-four stuck up his ass. Why did his character Rick refuse to socialize with his patrons? Why was he so surly with people who, after all, were his bread and butter? Why didn't he lighten up? (When you're nineteen and you see a guy who can have sex with an unlimited supply of hot, drunk women, but chooses not to, you tend to think that something is wrong with him...)

I closed down the ocean loop and slid the *Casablanca* DVD into my computer, raising my snifter of grappa. I had forgotten what a great movie it was—Peter Lorre and Claude Raines and all of those classic lines. As

I now considered Rick—holed up in his back room while his patrons got their drinking, gambling, and black-market grooves on—his character made a lot more sense to me. There was a war going on, and beneath his amoral posturing, he managed to preserve a shred of humanity while surrounded by so many people whose shortsighted interests and appetites guided their every hapless move.

Men are so simple and yield so readily to the desires of the moment.

Guys who claim to identify with Rick, or who cite him as one of their heroes, are dopes. I would never want to be in their camp, but let's just say that, after that second screening of *Casablanca*, I developed a new appreciation for Bogart's interpretation of Rick.

*   *   *

On Sunday morning, when I confronted Rule Number One about her behavior, she was shocked, *shocked* to learn that anything was amiss. She claimed that her hardcore flirting was a cover so that no one would know that anything was going on between us.

"People know," I said. "They know. And I told you that I don't care."

She maintained that people didn't know and that her flirting was just a joke.

"Once you give a guy an erection," I said, "it's no longer a joke."

"It's just kidding around."

We went back and forth like this until our argument segued into spectacular morning sex. Then I fell asleep.

While I've tried my best to accurately portray our rather rocky romance, if Rule Number One were to publish a book entitled *John Blesso Is a Big, Fat Douche*, you would probably hear a very different story. For instance, during our first night together out on the beach, I had considered her the aggressor, whereas she felt it was the other way around. Again, since she can't give you her side of the story, I've tried to be as forthcoming as possible with my own mistakes. Chief among my many fuckups was to not have called Rule Number One for more than three weeks. (Then, when I finally did call, it was to ask her to give up the bed she had paid for to sleep with me in a tent—a move straight out of *Bill Clinton's Guide to Classy Moves on the Ladies*.) Again, I thought of Nicky Mack:

The wise man does at once what the fool does finally.

Why didn't I call her sooner?

I kept hearing her say, "I just want to be your C-Weekend Girl," while my little voice continued to berate me for having broken my cardinal rule. Still, I should have looked beyond her tough-girl posturing to the bare facts: I always knew that I didn't want that one night to be the last, while those three-plus weeks when I didn't call must have felt, for her, like a Mandela length of time. I could only guess that being left hanging had exacerbated her behavior, that her over-the-top flirting sprang from insecurity, that maybe she felt the need to accrue some kind of advantage.

Watching Rule Number One pack her bag later that afternoon, I considered pulling the plug. Only I'd be missing her next weekend at the house to attend a friend's wedding. Remembering our morning sex, I decided not to do anything rash. I kissed her good-bye and she boarded the same boat that brought Vanessa back to Kismet.

Vanessa had taken the week off and was spending it at the house, staying through the following weekend. When I hugged her, she jokingly wrapped a foot around one of my calves.

"It's so nice to see you," she said, her lip curling. My little voice didn't say anything. After everything that had happened with Rule Number One, it just wasn't necessary.

"You, too," I said.

She dropped off her bag, and we walked down to the beach.

Generally, the more epicurean house members stayed longer on Sunday, while the less sensuous didn't see much point in sticking around without another night of partying on deck. (Having ridden themselves harder, they also needed a quiet night at home to recover from their weekend before returning to work.) Some people stayed over Sunday night and took the "death boat" at 6:20 on Monday morning, or (as it was known in the house) the "near-death boat," at the more civilized hour of 7:45, capping off sunny Sundays on the beach with a smaller, quieter dinner. Even when weekends were fun, I still liked it when the house began to empty out on Sunday, when things would settle down—at least for a couple of days.

A sizeable group was still assembled beneath the late-day sun. Maggie was poring over the wedding announcements in the *Times*; Alan was firing up Colin's bowl; Dani, Clay, and Joo-chan were packing up to catch the next boat. Not since Fourth of July 2004 was I more looking forward to having a weekend behind me—but Rufus sat in the middle of everyone, holding

forth in a loud voice about a recent sex scandal involving the TV personality
Pat O'Brien. This was about the last conversation that I would ever care to
overhear. I'd rather listen to women talk about shoes. And truth be told, I
just didn't feel like being subjected to Rufus's marching-band energy at a time
when I was trying to wind down. An eastbound plane was flying a banner
advertising some new TV show and Rufus—without even a trace of irony—
complained about the noise from the plane and being subjected to advertising
while on the beach.

"I don't mind the planes," I said.

"Really?" Rufus said. "That surprises me. You're so staunchly
anticommercial."

"I don't know about that," I said. "The planes are just one of the sounds of
the beach. Like the seagulls and the waves. They've been pulling ads in front
of beachgoers for decades."

Rufus continued expounding on the pervasiveness of advertising, and
even though I agreed with him, I just didn't want to hear it. I just wanted it
to be quiet.

"I like the planes," I said. "I'd love to fly over Fire Island in one of those
Cessnas."

"Really?" Vanessa said.

"Yes." I thought about the amazing view of Fire Island from the top of the
lighthouse. "I'll bet it would be awesome."

Unfortunately, Rufus would not stop talking.

"Want to go look at a bunch of geriatric overweight naked men?" I asked
Vanessa.

"No, I think I'm good," she said.

"Okay. I'm going for a walk." I got up and headed toward the nude beach.
Just beyond Kismet, I walked past the brown sign that reads Entering Clothing
Optional Area. Unfortunately, eighty percent of the birthday-suit beachgoers
were men, a minority of whom were waxed and buffed gay specimens; the
majority, however, were just as I had described them to Vanessa. Why did
so many overweight men decide as senior citizens that now was the *perfect*
time to put their sagging, leathery bodies on display? For many of these guys,
however, the full monty was incidental, their stomach and crotch fat joining
forces to reduce their junk to drowning mushroom caps. (It's too bad we can't
somehow harness this excess of positive body image and beam it to thirteen-
year-old girls across the nation...) Aside from the scenery, I never stayed long

at the nude beach, as sand and scrotum were not exactly chocolate and peanut butter. I went there because I liked being in the ocean without a bathing suit. After finding a relatively secluded spot, I stepped out of my suit and waded into the surf, diving headfirst into an oncoming wave.

*   *   *

On Monday morning, I biked over to Fair Harbor, which lies to the east of Saltaire, and participated in a yoga class on the beach. You bring a towel and ten bucks, and Stephanie leads you through a series of fairly challenging poses. Biking back to Kismet after the class, I felt perfectly relaxed, and despite a number of time-sensitive items on the To Do list, I decided to instead build a wine rack. After lunch, I dragged the door and walls of my old outdoor shower out from under my house and began hammering my prybar, separating the two-byfours from the grooved, Texture 1-11 plywood.

Unfortunately, I never learned anything about construction until my late twenties. If my brothers and I had gone to public high school in Paterson, we would have ended up at Eastside High (which some people know from the movie *Lean On Me*), one of the most rough and neglected high schools in New Jersey. My parents instead scraped together to send us to a costly private high school where we were hit over the head with the arts and humanities. I had always considered this a fortuitous move by my parents—until my first attempts at home improvement. I then wished that I had attended a technical high school where I would have taken shop, learned something about electrical work and maybe even how to weld. Instead I was steeped in the humanities, something I blame for ending up as an English major. Back when I was an undergrad at the University of Connecticut, no one warned me that being an English major is fucking useless. If your children ever declare themselves as English majors, please call me and I will drop whatever I'm doing to talk them down. I'll explain the importance of studying something that has a practical application beyond teaching it to others. (In this regard, the only subject more futile to study than English is French, and funny how I happen to have a degree in that useless subject as well...)

Luckily, I cut my losses before going to grad school, where I would have been assigned crushing loads of texts to read. Being an English grad student is the literary equivalent of forcing down a ten-course meal in five minutes. (I could barely keep pace with my undergrad syllabi...) I didn't start doing any real reading until I got to France, free from the veal-calf cage that for me was college. So now, as an autodidact, I wish that I had studied something else. Because being able to diagram iambic pentameter didn't help set the angle on my chop-saw; my appreciation of Hawthorne's fascination with Original Sin lent no clues about the cleanest way to miter notches in my two-by-fours.

In the nature/nurture debate, I'm a genetics man. Gerard Chamberland, my maternal grandfather, was a prolific carpenter and contractor who built most of the houses and buildings in his town and the adjacent towns where my mother Jacqueline grew up in northern Maine. He was a quiet, gentle man— somehow I didn't end up swimming in that section of the gene pool—with fingers as thick as sausages and hands that looked as though they had been slammed repeatedly in a car door. (At the age of eighty-eight, he passed away in a convalescent home that he himself had built decades earlier.) Anyway, the men on my mother's side have worked in construction or building. Meanwhile, my father, a civil engineer, has worked for the city of Paterson for forty years, having dedicated his life to community development and urban renewal. Paterson was America's first planned industrial city, and my father loves its Greek revival architecture and historic textile mills and is fascinated by all things structural and architectural. Additionally, my brother Francis studied mechanical engineering, and Matt, of course, became a developer. Given my construction-and engineering-heavy gene pool, I learned to embrace my sudden desires to build stuff. I like how my left brain takes over and my right brain floats off on all manner of airy subjects. While jigsawing a curve in the T1-11 for the top of the wine rack, I remembered a sad incident. My paternal grandmother died when I was fourteen. That afternoon, my father drove to my grandmother's house in Hartford, Connecticut. My brothers and I rode up with my mom the next morning. I was the first one to hug my father, and I could feel his chest heave as he began to cry. We went inside. An old dining chair sat in the center of the living room. My father gestured at the chair and explained that it had been broken for years. Unable to sleep, he had spent part of the night repairing its framing. I guess it was something to do. I've since wondered if creating something out of chaos can help someone deal with their inner tumult, or if fixing something tangible can help repair something that is broken inside you.

Most of my materials consist of what the French refer to as *objets trouvés,* or found objects—as well as recycling materials that would otherwise be thrown away. On Fire Island there is no shortage of scrap lumber, yet I was still going through wood that was once part of my house, having used it to build my coffee table, end tables, a hammock stand, and much of my shelving. Interestingly, if you were to walk around my house and point out all the stuff I've built, I could tell you exactly what I was bummed out about that caused me to ignore my e-mail inbox to build it.

Late in the afternoon, I hooked a finish-nail gun up to my compressor and fastened the T1-11 back and top on my criss-crossing of two-by-fours, the falling sun casting a long shadow behind my finished wine rack. Admiring my work, I was hardly even thinking about Rule Number One.

*   *   *

The following day I hit my paperwork and then plowed through my inbox. That night, a bunch of house members were meeting up for a New York Philharmonic concert in Central Park. In the mood for a bit of live music myself, I headed over to The Inn to catch the Empire State Stompers, a Dixieland jazz band that performed there every Tuesday night. The Stompers brought out a good number of Kismet's retirees, the so-called "Greatest Generation." A number of older couples got up and danced. I liked watching them dance because I can barely dance at all. My staunch conviction that music was an intrinsic part of being human (and that overexposure to bad music was toxic) also applied to dance. Just about every culture that has ever existed practiced some form of organized dance. Except mine. While what we did in my house after dinner was, technically, dancing, I didn't know how to *dance*-dance, unlike these septuagenarians and octogenarians who all grew up dancing and whose brittle limbs still responded to that muscle memory. Watching them, I felt as though I'd been gypped and decided that once the season was over, I would sign up for a social dance class in the City.

Walking back to the house, I thought about all the house members from different weekend series commingling over uncorked bottles in Central Park, an event that I dreaded as a gossip feeding frenzy. My suspicion was realized when Rule Number One phoned me later that night. She had gotten sucked into the mill, repeating items she had heard about me, as well as gossip about other house members, all of which she geysered into my ear. I learned that Colin had been getting horizontal with Mandy, and that Joo-chan and Charlotte—something I had already suspected—were going at it as well. Rule Number One then told me that the women had ranked the guys in the house in the order of desirability and that my name was near the top of the list.

"They all want to fuck you," she said. "You know that, don't you?"

"That's not true," I said. "It's not true, and it's not something I'm encouraging."

"Oh, please," she said. "You totally flirt with them."

"Yes," I said, recalling Rule Number One's head bent over Clay's crotch. "I flirt with them. But I'm not simulating oral sex on any of them."

(No sooner did I say this than did I recall an incident from the previous summer. It was my first time tasting Maggie's peach cobbler, and it was so scrumptious that I actually grabbed Maggie and threw her down onto the dining table, mock-humping her in front of everyone who began laughing hysterically. Still, Maggie and I were established friends. And she really did make a hump-worthy peach cobbler...)

Rule Number One and I went back and forth until her accusations devolved into a disjointed stream of consciousness. So much fucking gossip and so much of it just wasn't true. Nicky Mack once said that *One who deceives will always find those who allow themselves to be deceived.* That was the truth, and with Rule Number One now flinging whatever she could grab, I suddenly felt exasperated.

"This was a huge mistake," I said. "And it's time we put an end to it."

She tried to backpedal, but I was having none of it.

"I can't believe we're talking about this over the phone," she said. "I just...I want to talk to you in person."

I was heading back to the City that Thursday to collect rent from the couple subletting my apartment, to meet with one of my editing clients, and for a dental appointment, so I offered to meet with her Thursday after work. I planned on taking care of all my errands and then driving back out after the rush hour, hitting Costco before they closed at eight and then taking a late ferry back to Kismet. I would get all of my shit taken care of in one scratch day.

*   *   *

When Grace arrived on Wednesday, she was about the last person I wanted to see. After unpacking her bag, she set to work in the kitchen preparing—as she had informed me via e-mail—watermelon chicken. She cut off the top of an almost spherical watermelon and scooped out most of the guts, dropping a whole chicken inside along with cinnamon, coriander, cloves, and Jamaican allspice, setting it to roast in the oven.

Later, when I came upstairs to take inventory for my Costco run, Vanessa was making a salad with chunks of watermelon, feta, and mint. A small bowl of the pulp remained; I chilled some cocktail glasses and grabbed the large shaker, pouring in some of the juice, adding vodka, triple sec, and lime juice, creating a pale pink watermelon Cosmopolitan, garnishing the glasses with a thick chunk of the pulp.

At the stove, Grace was doing the octopus, stirring her vegetables and then lowering the heat on her rice before opening the oven to check the chicken. A wonderful aroma wafted over to the wet bar, and my stomach began to juice.

"Come on," I called out to Grace. "Let's have a drink out on the deck." We carried our cocktails outside, and Chris suggested that we eat dinner out on the deck. He and Maurice pushed together two tables while Risa stepped inside to fetch plates. Grace carried out a platter bearing the slumped, roasted watermelon. A look of glee came over her face as she pulled off the lid and removed the pink, fragrant chicken. It was good to see Grace loosening up.

"Grace," Maurice said, "this is amazing."

She grinned like the Cheshire cat.

"And nice work on the watermelon salad," Maurice added.

"Vanessa made the salad," Grace said.

"To the chefs," Chris said, raising his glass.

We toasted them, and I pointed out the cirrus clouds cloaking the sky over the ocean, reflecting the sunset and broadcasting it down onto the waves, bathing them in a pink glow. Everything was pink. The chicken, the salad, our drinks, the sunset, the waves—even Grace's row in my spreadsheet.

*   *   *

Later that night, I was lying in bed checking my phone messages, when I heard a knock.

"Come in," I called out.

Vanessa stepped into my room and then closed the door behind her.

"What's up?" I said, half listening to a long-winded message.

"Nothing much." She approached my bed and lay down on top of me. "Hi," she said. Her eyes glistened and her pajama top hung down, affording me a clean line at her breasts.

"Now listen the fuck up!"

"Relax," I muttered to my little voice, flipping my phone shut. "Vanessa." I rolled her off me and flopped onto my side, facing her. "This is not a good idea."

"It seems like a pretty good idea to me," she said.

"I think that you're really sexy, and I really like you, but this would not be good."

"Why?"

"Oh, let me count the ways."

Amazingly, Vanessa had yet to meet Rule Number One. She wasn't keyed in to the house gossip circuit—something that further endeared her to me. Still, I explained to her that I had already broken my cardinal rule once, that it was a huge mistake, and that I wasn't going to do it again.

"I'm sorry," she said. "I'm sorry I came in here like that."

"Don't sweat it," I said. "Want to go down to the beach?"

We grabbed a beach sheet and sat down on the sand. It was a clear night, and the stars were out.

"Do you know anything about the stars?" I asked her.

"Not really. Just the basics."

"I don't think I even know the basics."

She spun around and pointed out the Big Dipper, and then showed me how to find the North Star using the bottom of the Big Dipper as pointer stars. We lay back with our heads to the ocean, and she explained how the North Star never moves, that all the other constellations revolved around it. I liked knowing that bit of information, knowing that I could now look up in the sky and find this one star that remained constant.

*   *   *

I didn't sleep well that night, and the following day I hit a number of snags in the City that left me running late for my appointments. Meanwhile, I had forgotten the inventory sheet for my Costco run. To top it off, the mercury in the City was punching the high nineties. By the time I found a parking spot and began up the muggy block toward Rule Number One's apartment, I was exhausted. She met me at the door of her studio, looking rather fetching in a pair of pumps and a floral skirt. A couple of dark ringlets escaped from her pinned-up curls, framing that devil grin.

"Thanks for coming by," she said as I stepped into her apartment. "I just wanted to—"

"Listen." I sat down on her bed and her AC felt heavenly. "Do you mind if I just lie down for a minute?"

"Go right ahead."

I cased her studio, but there was only a loveseat and her bed. I kicked off my Crocs, lay back on her bed, and fell asleep.

When my eyes peeled open to her drawn shades, I had forgotten where I was—until I noticed Rule Number One lying in the crook of my arm. She began to kiss my neck.

"Rule," I said, still feeling foggy. "Don't do that."

"You're so fucking serious," she scoffed. "Hello, I'm John Blesso and I'm *so...fucking...serious.*"

"No," I said, trying not to laugh. "This is a bad idea."

"Why? It doesn't have to mean anything."

I grabbed my cell phone to check the time—6:15. I bolted up and reached for my Crocs. I had to get back to Commack and finish my Costco run before they kicked everyone out at eight. If I hit any traffic, I'd be screwed.

"I gotta get going."

"But we never got to talk."

"We can talk another time. I gotta get to Costco before they close."

"Why? Why don't you just stay here tonight? We'll go out later and get a cheeseburger, and then you can go to Costco in the morning."

"No, I've got to get going."

"We can go to Big Nick's." She grinned.

Big Nick's is a legendarily nasty and delicious Greek diner on the west side of Broadway between 76th and 77th Streets. Despite their voluminous menu, I've only ever eaten two things there: their grilled, marinated chicken sandwich and their half-pound bacon bleu burger with crushed olives. Had I told Rule Number One about my love of Big Nick's? She had already proven expert at pushing my buttons, but injecting visions of a rare Big Nick's bacon bleu burger (in place of a rushed dinner of Costco samples) was just not fair.

So there were my options:

Coffee up and kick into gear, hoping for the best possible traffic situation on the eastbound L.I.E. only to then shop against the clock *sans* inventory sheet, wrenching a full cart around Costco's guerrilla army of kids and seniors.

Or...

Follow up my nap with a Big Nick's bacon bleu bounty before spending the night with Rule Number One in her air-conditioned studio.

Well, what would you have done?

Sushi

The following morning, I swung my cart around Costco with detached precision, recalling most of what the house needed from memory. Nevertheless, spending the night with Rule Number One hardly changed the way I felt about our incompatibility. She insisted that it didn't have to mean anything; having passed the halfway point in the season, I took her at her word.

Rule Number One did inform me, however, of something rather troubling: The previous Saturday night—when I was holed up in my room watching *Casablanca*—Elaine (Rule Number One's guest who had ended up in a room by herself) had gone to bed early, only to be woken up by Colin, who, fucked out of his mind, slipped into her room and attempted to crawl into bed with her. She promptly sent him packing, but still, it was bad. I would have to talk to Colin about it.

Back at the house, I began fielding e-mails. Rufus would be preparing sushi on Saturday night, and I was pretty excited for this Chance house first. Jeffrey, however, wasn't. It wasn't the first time that our resident stoner had complained about the food. While Jeffrey always got excited when ribs were being slow-cooked in the smoker, or when ribeyes were sizzling on the grill, he sniffed at a lot of our more ethnic fare. This time, he was concerned that all the fish would cost too much and that some people wouldn't like it. Some people. Jeffery didn't worry about "some people." Jeffrey worried about Jeffrey. I e-mailed him back, telling him that teriyaki steaks were already part of the menu.

Still, as I continued plowing through my inbox, a what-the-fuck feeling began bubbling up in me. Most people were quite happy with how well we ate and drank. Their constant suggestions helped fine-tune our dining, and their enjoyment of the meals is precisely what powered me through the bitch of procurement and organization. Jeffrey's repeated complaints were getting to be a drag.

Food is now bigger than it's ever been in the U.S. When I was nannying in the City, I couldn't believe that ten-year-olds might willingly eat sushi. (When we were kids, my mom strongly encouraged us to try all sorts of things, but if she had put sushi in front of me when I was ten, I would have raised high holy hell.) A downside of this new food sexiness, however, is an uptick in the number of people who profess an interest in food as shorthand for the level of sophistication they wish to project. Jeffrey would be content to eat cheeseburgers and hot dogs and drink tequila shots all night long. And that's fine. That's what happens at normal beach houses. But that's not how I marketed Chance. Both in Craig's List postings and on the website, I had outlined a different kind of dining experience. Now Jeffrey was essentially complaining about me delivering what I had promised.

Jeffrey, however, wasn't the first. During the '04 season, a woman had requested that I stock the house with Mike's Hard Lemonade. No way was I going to lug cases of that corn-syrup piss from the dock to the house or waste our limited cubic footage of refrigeration keeping it cold. (If underage drinking didn't thrive under our deadly joke of a legal limit, that loophole teenybopper beverage wouldn't even exist.) Another guy requested that I put Coors Light in the kegerator. (As an American, it pains me to accept that we invented "lite" beer. It's bad enough that we're responsible for N'Sync.) I told him flat-out "no," and it was pissing me off that these people—who were just not being honest with me or themselves about their own tastes—were now trying to wrench our consumption toward so much stuff that could be found in any other share-house. Every sharehouse except mine has shot glasses and lite beer. Every other sharehouse has a fridge filled with fruity malt beverages. Why did these people join *my* house?

I couldn't have been more specific about this niche focus of the house, although in describing our style of eating, I never once used the word "foodie," and have never described myself as such. Something about that word evokes, for me, a sense of highbrow passivity. I am an aggressive eater. I never cut fat from meat, getting downright pornographic with whatever carrion sits before me. Sometimes it's just me and the bone, and I have to remind myself that other people are around, that a certain level of decorum is called for, that the meat has already been defeated. Still, I sometimes fall into gnawing, masticating grooves until all that remains on my plate is a pile of bones devoid of flesh and cartilage to the point that they could be sharpened into prison-yard shivs. My fellow diners know to send the head of a whole fish in my direction. I order steak tartare whenever I see it on a menu. If any kind of meat or fish can be eaten raw, I will do it, preferably clad in as little as possible. I can count on one hand the number of days during the past fifteen years in which I did not ingest some kind of hot sauce or hot pepper. Whenever I eat barbecue, I order a beer, a glass of red wine, and a bourbon all at the same time. My tablemates no longer bat an eye when I sprinkle salt or hot sauce on whatever remains of my plate before literally licking it clean. (Yes, I have done this in restaurants.) I will travel far into the outer boroughs to sample culinary oddities. I like other people who take eating and drinking seriously in their own ways. For me, the word "foodie" just doesn't convey that eating is an exploration, an adventure, and that it might even be dangerous. The French word "gastronome" is better because it sounds like you might be wielding a sword in a steel cage as large hunks of meat are flung at you. It's an unwieldy word in English, though, so we're stuck with "foodie," which to me sounds complacent, pretentious, dissociated. Until a better word comes along, I'll continue to steer clear of what sounds to me like a misnomer.

I've also hit my fair share of snags with vegetarians and nondrinkers. I'm not sure why a vegetarian or a nondrinker would want to join Chance any more than an atheist would care to kneel down in a megachurch. I suppose they like the vibe and the people and they want to be a part of it, and I guess that's fine. In fact, some of my best friends are teetotalers or vegetarians. Amazingly, Natasha—one of the most fun and crazy people in the house—didn't drink, while Lauren, a midweeker vegetarian, didn't mind grilling vegetables on the same grill where meat had been cooked and regularly prepared great sides (for her they were main courses) that everyone else could eat. If all vegetarians and teetotalers were like them, I would have no problem finding spots for them in the house. Unfortunately, they are the exception, and all too often they want me to adjust their share of the weekend expenses, grumbling about paying $30 for an entire weekend of amazing food because they didn't drink or eat meat, forgetting that we spend about $100 per person, and that our guest fees take a huge chunk out of those costs. (Since it's such a small amount of money, I can only suspect that they're bitter, that despite their cheery optimism, their tofu burger just wasn't as satisfying as a rare, blackened ribeye.) Everyone pays the same thing, and I post all receipts both for full disclosure and so that people can see what stuff costs. Meat at Costco is really cheap, while cheese costs a lot more per pound, and vegetarians invariably hit the cheese. So I'm happy to accommodate vegetarians and nondrinkers, so long as they pony up and keep their holier-thanthou-ness to themselves. (I'll happily remind them, if need be, that the piece of fruit in their hand was probably picked by someone who, essentially, is a modern-day slave, or that the most notorious nondrinking vegetarian the world has ever known was none other than Adolf Hitler.)

Selecting what foods to stock is a balancing act. I buy plenty of items that I would never purchase on my own. Like ketchup. Kurt Cobain has ingested ketchup more recently than I have. Every tablespoon of ketchup contains a teaspoon of high-fructose corn syrup that crushes the subtlety of whatever you're eating. (Dubliners taught me years ago that when you put salt and vinegar on fries, you can actually taste the potatoes.) Nevertheless, I buy ketchup for the vast majority of people—whose eating habits I thoroughly respect—who would never eat burgers and fries without it. There are some items, however, that I just won't buy. Like American cheese. I challenge anyone to find a recipe that wouldn't taste better with cheddar. Cheese making in the United States has made a moon leap in the past decade, and I'm proud to say that Americans are now making some of the best cheese in the world. Independent fabricators in Upstate New York are making cheddar cheese that's better than it's ever been. If you're still peeling the plastic off those orange-number-five prefab squares, all I can say is get thee to a cheese shop.

Margarita mix is another item I refuse to purchase. Like Rufus, a lot of people who drink margaritas have only ever had fauxgaritas. Once you taste a margarita made with tequila, triple sec, and fresh-squeezed lime juice, a cocktail that walks that tart line between sweet and acidic, you'll never use those overly sweet mixes again. As I mentioned, there are no shot glasses in the house. Good tequila is now widely available in the U.S. and I don't even know Jose whatever-the-fuck-hisname is. Tequilas like Patron and Herradura are good enough to be sipped from a snifter as a digestif. And while I can't stop people from filling the bottoms of rocks glasses (as Jeffrey frequently did) not having shot glasses strips away the fanfare. If you want to do shots, go back to grad school and throw back those supersized thimbles until you can no longer feel the six figures of debt you just racked up.

Then there's cocaine.

I maintain, admittedly, a rather conservative and reactionary stance against coke. While I have friends who do coke, the drug just seems to bring out the flaky, aggressive asshole in them. With coke, conversation frequently falls casualty to a crossfire of monologues, all of them firing off barrages of pure shit. It's like being in a roomful of Bill O'Reillys, all of them sitting in a circle and screaming at one another. These are not the kinds of qualities you want to encourage in a communal environment. Cokeheads can also be a buzzkill the morning after. By noon, most people in the house have had brunch and are heading off to the beach for their first cool-down, while cokeheads would still be lying in bed, moaning about the sun and flailing about in their spent, sniveling misery.

I'd rather not be around that. Chance is a heady, epicurean, sexually charged atmosphere with unlimited booze, no shortage of marijuana, and a wide array of musical instruments. People who can't manage to have fun at the beach with all those considerable raw materials should find another house. Someone once challenged my hard-line stance, suggesting that since I've never done the drug, I just don't know what I'm talking about. Well, I've never stabbed a man to death with a barbecue fork, either (at least not yet), but I can still be a staunch opponent of the practice. During my twenties, I watched three close friends driven to the brink by that treacherous drug, and I just don't want it in my house.

The main reason I ban coke, however, is money. Aside from collecting share monies (the full amount not being due until the season begins), I regularly collect members' guest fees and their share of the food/booze shortfall. I spend far more time than I like collecting cash, and even under the best circumstances, it is a chore. Most people in my house know this and go out of their way to make it easy for me, paying what they owe when I am in front of my computer. Having to field cokehead lines of shit would not make that task any easier. During my first season, I recruited a guy named Nathan. He was an affable, all-around nice guy with a real interest in cooking. He was also quite good-looking, and many of the women—especially Maggie— were salivating over him. He did prove to be a great cook, and as the summer progressed, he also quietly made his way through multiple women in the house, only he managed to do it in a way that didn't cause drama or an excess of gossip, something that I greatly appreciated. Unfortunately, his expert management of on-the-sly hookups was not the only secret he was keeping. Near the end of the summer, Nathan came to me with a sob story about how he didn't have plans for Labor Day weekend. We already had twenty-seven people scheduled, and I contorted the bed assignments to create a guest spot for him. When he showed up that weekend, he fed me a line about rushing to catch the train and not having time to visit the ATM. In my holiday-weekend overload, I didn't think twice about it, not ever imagining that this cash would not be forthcoming. It never dawned on me then that he was an addict, probably because (as bad as this may sound) he was smart, personable, and handsome, and he masked his addiction with a thick veneer of impeccable p's & q's. I didn't put the pieces together until after the season when I learned of his problem. Then I saw the similarities between Nathan and my friends who had been ravaged by the drug, the mental cancer that wormed out their personalities and stripped away their true character. I then realized that despite the amount of time Nathan spent in the house, I never really got to know him.

*   *   *

On Saturday morning after brunch, I wandered downstairs just as Vanessa emerged from the bathroom in a baby-blue bikini.

"Hey," she called out to me. "Can you lube me up?"

"Sure," I said.

She turned and gave me her back.

"Do you want forty-five or thirty?"

"Thirty," she said.

I pumped the dispenser attached to the wall near the bathroom and began to cover her back. A funny thing about assisted sunscreen application is that, unless you shop at Big & Tall, there is really only a small area between your shoulder blades that you cannot reach yourself. Still, depending upon the lubee, their "back" can include their neck, shoulders, waist...

"You're good," I said, clutching her shoulders and rubbing in the last of the lotion down her triceps.

"Do you want me to do you?"

"That would be great." I spun around. She began working the lotion into my back, and I yanked down my bathing suit, presenting her with a few inches of butt cleavage.

"Don't forget the ass crack," I said.

I heard another pump from the dispenser and soon felt her hands rubbing the lotion into the top of my butt.

"I don't wantcha to burn," she said, laughing.

She was finishing up when I saw Rufus walk out of Just Visiting clutching his bag.

"Where are you going?" I said, rushing over. "You're cooking dinner tonight."

"I know. I forgot my bamboo rollers."

"You're going all the way back to the City?"

"Yeah, but I'll be back in time to get everything going."

Despite being a beautiful beach day, Rufus got on the 12:40 boat and went all the way back to the City, fetched his rollers, and then returned on a late-afternoon boat and set about heating up vinegar and sugar for the sushi rice.

* * *

Like Grace, Uptalking Nancy also came out of her shell, only she did it in a way that just caused her red row to bleed. While having never backpedaled on her initial assessment of the house, she had begun damage control, making fawning small talk with me in that grating intonation that only got on my nerves. Still, I had to laugh when she presented herself to Rufus—her Memorial Day Weekend tormentor—late on Saturday afternoon as a sous-chef.

"If you need help like *cook*ing the *su*shi? [Rapid-fire voice] *I-guess-you-don't-really-cook-it-because-it's-totally-like-cold.* But if you need help like, preparing it? I could totally help you?"

I cut a wide path around Nancy, who joined more than half a dozen souschefs that Rufus had assembled around the table making nori rolls. I had never seen a larger, more well-organized team in the kitchen. Rufus assigned different tasks and managed to teach a few eager learners how to pack tight Alaskan rolls of salmon and avocado. I've made sushi before, and while I can get the rice to have the right consistency and taste, I usually ended up making chirashi, a mound of rice with thick cuts of fish on top, as I've never been able to pack my rolls tight enough so that they don't fall apart after being cut. Not only did Rufus assemble trays of rice beds bearing lovely, angular pieces of tuna and salmon, he oversaw the production of tightly packed cut rolls that looked damn near restaurant grade.

Over on the couch bank, Joo-chan was watching the Yankee game next to Charlotte and Dani. If there is an opposite of PDA, Joo-chan and Charlotte were going at it hot and heavy. Even though they were out, you'd never have guessed it were it not for the gossip mill. Dani, mid-sentence to Charlotte, stretched out her legs across Joo-chan's lap. Engrossed in the game, Joo-chan began massaging Dani's calves. (A stranger walking past would have sooner thought Joo-chan was seeing Dani.) Meanwhile, a few people had begun to complain about Princess Dani, saying that she never lifted a finger. Having become obsessed over whether or not her iPod was plugged into the stereo, I hadn't noticed; whatever else Dani did or didn't do was fine by me.

Grace had figured out a recipe for green tea ice cream and made two batches of it for dessert. Out on the deck, I dropped two teriyaki steaks on the grill and then popped an acid reducer. (The sushi looked great, and I hoped to preempt my copious ingestion of wasabi and ginger.) After pulling off the steaks, we sat down to flutes of chilled sake garnished with pen-like spears of cucumber. I didn't eat more than a cursory taste of the steak, because I kept reaching for those tuna and salmon rolls. A scoop of the green tea ice cream capped off one of the best meals that had ever been served in the house. Even Jeffrey, to his credit, congratulated Rufus on a great meal.

As people began to clear the plates, I watched Dani. Indeed, she nonchalantly got up from the table and walked over to the couches, not so much as clearing a plate.

We arranged all the uneaten sushi on a single platter next to a mound of wasabi and a pile of ginger and carried it over to Bicycle Bill's. While walking on the main road, a full moon cast our shadows upon the ground. Up on Bicycle Bill's roof deck, members of his house were partying with a group from another share-house run by two women, Abby and Sabrina. Like me, Abby and Sabrina were lured to Kismet by Bicycle Bill's house and then broke away to run their own house. We became friends, and sometimes when I wanted to get away from the craziness of my house, I dropped by Abby and Sabrina's for a drink. Their group was a couple of years older than ours, almost all of them thirtysomethings, so they were a bit more sedate, which was a nice change of pace. (When Rule Number One first met Abby, she of course asked if I had had sex with her, and looked almost let down when I told her that I had not.)

Anyway, Abby and Sabrina were doing a bang-up job with their inaugural season, having assembled a crew that also walked the line between epicurean delight and unhinged spontaneity, as was proven the night before when a bunch of them shed their clothes on the beach for a midnight skinny-dip. Still cruising on the protein spike from all that raw fish and feeling the full-moon fever, I envisioned a larger, multihouse skinny dip and approached

Abby in the corner.

"Any chance you can get your house to go for another swim?"

"I don't see why not," she said.

Surveying the crew from Chance, I figured that I could count on Vanessa, Chris, Mandy, and Rufus. I doubted that Uptalking Nancy would do it, and didn't imagine that Grace would ever undress in front of all of us. Looking around at Bicycle Bill's crew—a number of whom were naked in my jacuzzi after the pig roast—I figured that selling them on group nudity would be about as hard as unloading a batch of OxyContin on Rush Limbaugh. Abby and I began to quietly spread the word, and at one o'clock, more than two dozen of us filed down to the beach.

The full moon illuminated the waves with a bright yellow swath, a glimmering, shimmering yellow-brick road that stayed with you, lining up perfectly between your vantage point and the moon. (This reflection sometimes reminded me of watching *Magic Garden* as a toddler, when I actually thought that those two women with the cooing voices could see me, had put on the show for a dozen of us, all of whom they were watching over.)

"This looks like a pretty good spot," Abby said.

"Yeah," I said, stepping out of my shorts. "Not too many families around."

Our house was well represented with Chris, Vanessa, Matt, Maurice, Mandy, and—amazingly—Grace, jumping around girlishly in a circle, all of us naked. I could see everything, the parts of the whiter bodies that didn't get tanned glowing like neon in the full moonlight. My eyes coasted over the bodies, but after a couple of minutes I got used to it—until Vanessa stepped in front of me.

"Are you ready?" she said. For once, that wild curl of her lip was no longer the part of her holding my attention.

We dashed into the gentle surf and were soon joined by another two dozen people thrashing and splashing about like children, dunking one another, doing the things that you do in the water when you're ten. I wanted to see what this looked like from the shore, so I climbed out to take in the sight of them all rising and falling in the long, slow rollers. Looking westward at the orange glow behind the lighthouse, I remembered a night on the beach from 2004—the worst night I had ever experienced as a sharehouse manager. It was the Fourth of July party, when Colin had baked those infamous pot cookies. As can be the case with novice marijuana bakers, they want their magic muffins to be a hit and so they spike their butter with a ridiculous payload of weed. That's what happened with Colin's chocolate-chip cookies. You couldn't taste the weed, and the cookies—from a pure baking standpoint—were delicious. It was as though they had been baked by someone's grandmother. Someone's really fucked-up grandmother. While I only ate one of them, an hour later I was seriously (pardon the pun) baked. Some people, however, had eaten two or three and had begun to freak out. One person was hearing voices; another thought someone was chasing them. This craziness led to a couple of reckless incidents with fire and fireworks—one of them involving Matt—that set me on edge. Stoned out of my mind, I resented that my own brother had forced me into a scolding role, although feeling pissed off provided some focus. I decided to herd the freak-outs away from the house and down to the beach, hoping that the rhythm of the ocean might have a calming effect. It helped, and I eventually left them there with a woman who had not partaken of Colin's cookies. I just wanted to go to sleep, only back then I didn't have my own room. So many stoned and drunk people were still rocking out upstairs that when I lay down I could feel the house shake. I tried to sleep, but was interrupted by someone coming into the room. I got out of bed, realizing that there was only one place where I might find some peace and quiet.

Back on the beach, I cursed what I had gotten myself into. Sometimes, weed heightened my enthusiasm and other times it exacerbated my self-criticism; that night, establishing the house felt like a colossal mistake, another bad move in a string of fits and starts. Recruiting an epicurean crew was so much harder than I had imagined. So many of those first-year members cared nothing for food. Walking westward along the surf, I did not want to be stoned anymore. Why, I thought, did I expend so much effort trying to do something differently? Why didn't I heed Nicky Mack's warning?

Suddenly, without thinking, I broke into a run, converting my frustration into full speed. After buzzing past the slip road, my lungs ached and my quads were on fire and I crashed down on the beach. This release was exactly what I needed. Watching the surf while feeling my heart slow, I understood that I was just having a rough night, that it would soon be over, and that the following season would surely have more epicures. (I also decided that night that I needed to have fewer people and my own room.)

Now, watching this collection of naked bodies all rise and fall in the surf, I couldn't feel any more different than I did during that night of extreme baking. Everything felt right and good—only I wanted that rush once again. Turning westward, I took off.

If you've never run full-speed while naked on the beach at night, try it. You don't need to purchase any fancy equipment, you don't need to train, and unless you were to suffer a heart attack and die, it's probably healthy. Passing West Lighthouse Walk, I was moving fast and wondered if I could go any faster, and then the thought itself gave me a turbo boost, further cranking my clip until I felt like an Olympian or like Carl Weathers, and with all of the houses behind me there were no signs of modernity, no chirping gadgets strapped to my waist, no e-mail inboxes, no gossip or restraint, no NeoCon fuckwads or adjustable-rate mortgages, nothing. I could have existed a thousand years ago, or a thousand years before Christ. There was no time, only my heart pounding like a jackhammer and my head engulfed with a buzzy lightness as I leapt in the breeze. I was high.

I looped around and jogged back toward the group, admiring the breadth of my footsteps in the sand and capping off my cool-down with another run in the ocean. Entering the water now felt like sliding on a silken glove. Spotting Vanessa, I drew a deep breath and dove under, swimming toward her until I saw her legs kicking in the moonlit water. Near the end of my breath, I threw my arms around her waist and pulled her down. She was coughing and laughing when we

came up.

"Where ya been?" she said.

"I just went for a little jog."

People began to wander out of the surf. Among the taut, glow-in-the-dark bodies, I spotted Grace hunched over and scurrying about. She looked like she was crying. I climbed out and approached her.

"What's wrong?" I called out.

She wasn't crying, but was in stitches and could barely talk. "I can't... find...my clothes!" she managed.

"Which walk did you come down? Pine or Seabay?"

"I don't remember!" She laughed.

Chris volunteered to help her, and I spotted Vanessa further east.

"I'll go check over by Seabay," I said, grabbing my shorts.

"How are you doing?" I said to Vanessa.

"Good," she said. "How are *you* doing?" Her eyes flipped downward.

"Well, it's kind of cold out," I joked. We stood there, staring at one another, giggling, until Grace called out that she had found her clothes. As we began toward the Pine Walk dune crossing, I stopped to put my shorts back on but then I thought, Shorts? We don't need no steenkeeng shorts! Grace and Chris rejoined us, and we all walked back to the house naked, parading up the walkway and past the front door, continuing down the ramp and around the back where we pulled the lid off the jacuzzi. I was always amazed by how long some house members could last in 103-degree water, and I was starting to get hot when Vanessa announced that she was going to take a shower. I watched her climb out of the tub and pad across the wooden platform to the outdoor shower. She slid open the handle and then faced me.

"Anyone want to join me?" she joked. Only I didn't take it as a joke. Preempting my little voice, I left Chris and Grace alone in the tub and slipped inside the outdoor shower with Vanessa.

"Whatever," my little voice said.

Under the lukewarm spray, however, I came to my senses and kept a literal arm's length from Vanessa as we scrubbed ourselves, respectively, in what was the co-showering equivalent of a sixth-grade dance. We joked about how it's a nice big shower, and when I finished up, I stepped over to the dry area and began toweling off, watching her finish as I wrapped the towel around my waist.

"Can I have a towel?" she said.

The hooks behind me bore no other towels.

"This one's kind of wet." I patted the one around my waist.

"I don't care."

I removed my towel and gave it to her.

"Nice showering with you," she said, padding herself.

"You too." I took the towel from her. "Let me get you a dry one."

"Okay." Her wrists fell over my collarbones just as my hands came to rest on her hips and when our bodies brushed together I considered how Vanessa steered clear of the gossip mill and wondered if she could keep it confidential...

"Don't be a douche!"

I stepped back and wrapped the wet towel back around my waist. The expression on Vanessa's face was such that I had to look away, the way you have to look away from the sun. I stepped out of the shower, averting my eyes from Chris and Grace as I fished a dry towel off the clothesline and passed it blindly into the shower to Vanessa.

Truffled Scallops Over Grits

Staring me down from the top of my To Do list was to call Colin. I finally resolved to do it when I picked up a call from Tracy, who informed me that Colin's uninvited entry that night wasn't limited to Elaine's room. Apparently—after turning in early following her underappreciated meal—Tracy woke up to find Colin lying on top of her with his tongue stuck in her mouth. (Thankfully, she woke up before any of Colin's other appendages could launch an unauthorized invasion.) When we spoke a second time, Tracy downplayed the incident, saying that she didn't want to create an uncomfortable vibe in the house. It didn't matter. All that I could think about was that most unfortunate incident at Bicycle Bill's house between Todd and Donna. I'd never forgive myself if I enabled Colin to drunkenly enter another woman's room—especially if she didn't wake up in time.

Sexual tension in a singles' sharehouse is like a guitar string; it needs to be taut enough so that it's not flat, but pulled too tightly it will become sharp and might even snap. If the women in the house began to feel as though they were being preyed upon, it would decrease the incidence of flirty dinner conversations and naked midnight swims, making the house less fun for everyone.

I dialed Colin, vainly clinging to the notion that there are two sides to every story, imagining how the frenzied gossip mill could have easily spun my near miss with Vanessa into something that barely resembled the truth.

"John-*nay*," Colin said.

"Hey, Colin. Listen...umm...can you tell me what happened during your last Saturday night at the house?"

"Uhh...what do you mean?"

His hesitation spoke volumes. I treated him to Joe Friday:

"Tracy says she woke up on Saturday night and found you lying on top of her with your tongue stuck in her mouth."

"Really? I...I..." He stammered. "I don't remember *that*. I mean, there was definitely some blackout time there, but..."

Blackout time?

"Well, Tracy says that that's what happened."

"I *really* don't remember that."

"Why don't you give Tracy a call and then get back to me."

"No problem."

We hung up, but I knew that whatever he had to report back didn't matter.

Colin was toast.

Later that night, Colin called me back and before I could do it, he beat me to the punch with class:

"Listen, Johnny, I think it would be best if I didn't come back to the house. I just want to tell you that I really appreciate everything you've done to put together such a great group of people. I was really glad to be a part of it, and I'm sorry about what happened. It's made me realize that I need to make some changes in my life."

I thanked him for his kind words and wished him the best of luck in making those changes.

*   *   *

On Friday morning, Lizzie, a somewhat difficult house member, e-mailed me that the two guests for whom she had reserved spots that weekend had cancelled. Aside from having hung on to two primo guest spots that other house members would have loved to reserve, I now had to find last-minute guests or everyone, including me, would divide a huge balance. After exhausting the waitlist (all of those potential guests had since made other plans), I then e-mailed the house to tell them that guest limits didn't apply, hoping to find someone to help underwrite our consumption. A few minutes later Vanessa e-mailed me, wanting one of the spots for a friend of hers. A male friend. This was especially good, as some of the women in the house had begun to voice their disappointment with the overall virility level in the house. Mandy went so far as to list the guys that she found lacking in the manliness department, capping off her list with "Gay Clay."

"By the way," Mandy said. "Is Gay Clay coming out this weekend?"

I picked up her unintentional joke before she did and tried not to laugh.

"Don't call him that, alright? You guys don't know that he's gay."

"Please, John. Clay is gay. Don't you think Clay is gay?"

I thought of that amoral genius poet Johnny Cochran who helped set O.J. free with his little rhyme.

"Just because his name rhymes with gay," I said, "doesn't mean that he is. By that rationale, you're a dandy. Or a piece of candy."

"Oh, I'm a piece of candy," she said, smacking her hip. "But this candy is for straight boys."

Natasha had also quipped, "There aren't many guys in the house who couldn't pass for gay," before exclaiming, "Next year, no more midget homos!"

I couldn't deny a sea change in the house's level of masculinity. The spots opened up by Wayne and Troy were purchased by pre-existing guys (including Clay), resulting in a net loss of two men. Then, Martin, PI and Jeffrey—two guys who had been on the make back in '04—now had girlfriends. Also, Matt had recently met an Argentinean woman (a bona fide Chance house connection, as he met her through Mandy) with whom he had become serious enough to no longer be on the market. Making this imbalance worse was the fact that women guests regularly outnumber male guests. Now, with the loss of Colin, the mercury in the house virilometer had sunk to a new low. To top it off, the mujahideen wing of the gossip mill had adopted this notion that I had filled the house with sissy men so as to have my run of the place like some coked-up member of the Saudi royal family.

After all of the trouble I had gone through to maintain the gender balance—from the guys that I approached in Central Park to sifting through the waves of meatheads in my inbox—it pained me to think that anyone might think this. (Or that I somehow schemed to get rid of Wayne, Troy, and Colin, as well as have Matt, Jeffrey, and Martin taken off the market.) I spent far more time than I ever wanted thinking about how to attract straight men that the women in the house would like. If I could somehow find five or six beefcake male models who were considerate and knew how to cook and/or clean, I would sign them all up and then take a seriously long nap. So I began to hope that Dylan, Vanessa's guest, might be unambiguously straight, tall, and single.

When Dylan arrived, what I first noticed about him was that he was probably too short for that beanpole Natasha. Still, he was tall enough, and he played for my team. At the kegerator, he asked about the acoustic guitars hanging on the wall, telling me that he was in a band. During dinner, I learned that he spoke Italian, knew how to cook, and taught art history at

City College, rounding out a solid Renaissance-man resume. He was good-looking, and the women were curious. When I saw him making fast friends with Mandy, he might as well have been wearing a fucking cape (of the Superman—not Liberace—variety).

After dinner, Dani led an exodus to the jacuzzi, and I followed them down.

"The bossman's getting in the hot tub!" Dani called out.

"Yeah, how come you never get in the hot tub?" Maurice asked.

"It's true," Rufus chimed in. "I don't think I've ever seen you in the hot tub."

"What are you talking about?" I said. "I was in the tub just last weekend."

Despite my foray post-nude-swim, it was true that I wasn't much of a weekend hot tubber. Sand, sunscreen, and sunburned skin all came together in an axis of jacuzzi evil, and I cleaned it weekly, since most people coming from the beach didn't bother showering before getting in. Possibly people thought that the jacuzzi had a water line in, not understanding that it was just a sitting tub of water that dozens of people climb in and out of on any given weekend. Aside from the water quality, however, the jacuzzi added up to a sore spot that nudged me one square closer on the Misanthropy Land game board. Generally, people in a jacuzzi are drunk and/or high and trying to get laid. While I believe such goals to be admirable, I wish that their pursuit was not mutually exclusive from common sense and consideration. People frequently left trash around the tub, or they carried down stemware that ended up breaking. Then, upon draining the tub, I was sometimes treated to cigarette filters, lime wedges, and once, most unfortunately, a Coney Island whitefish that I fished out from beneath a grate.

Aside from their maintenance, jacuzzis are overrated. I'm just not into that whole California bourgeois porno sensibility. They make more sense at ski houses, when it's cold outside and people have a legitimate therapeutic reason to be in one. I would never have bought a jacuzzi if it wasn't such a huge selling point. Women like them more than men, and most men know this and come to see the offer of a high-octane fruity cocktail in the jacuzzi as the speediest of social lubricants. Still, such guys are a throwback to when men felt that women had to be tricked into casual sex. These days, most sophisticated, sexually active single women from the City don't need to be cajoled; they are sexually independent and their hang-ups are fading fast. If they want to have sex for the sake of having sex, fewer of them are willing to bother with the expense, trouble, or ruse of a tropical vacation. (Or, for them, Fire Island is far enough out to sea...) When they want to screw, they are going to screw, and the bullshit come-ons that used to be an integral part of that equation were going the way of the cassette deck.

Since I had just changed the water that afternoon, it was a good time for me to join them. As soon as everyone was settled, Dani enlisted Maurice to give her a massage. We were joined by Tracy, Maggie, and Dylan, bringing the body count up to eight and sending the water level over the top. (I would encourage people to refill the tub when they got out, but leaving a running hose in the tub is the absolute easiest thing to forget—even when you're not drunk or high and trying to get laid.) Once there are more than six people, many jacuzzi conversations adhere to a script. Whoo-hoos are tossed about as people begin picking over sex and gossip. I braced myself for people to start talking about Colin, only no one mentioned it. My way of discretely informing them that Colin had left the house to spend more time with his family had been to send out a revised list of e-mails for trading, a list that no longer included Colin. Still, Tracy had told Maggie and a couple of other people, and Mandy (for whom Colin had been—and possibly still was—a friend with benefits) had found out about it, so I was certain that high-school rules would apply, namely that once one person knew, everyone would know. People possibly kept quiet about it for the sake of Tracy (and Mandy) and possibly because most people—despite recognizing that what Colin did was incredibly stupid—still liked him. When you're up against the ruthless dictates of the gossip mill, nothing is more important than being liked.

Rufus began dominating the conversation in a loud voice. Dani tuned him out while Maggie rolled her eyes. Remembering Joe's wisdom about patterns, I could no longer ignore that Rufus was just REALLY FUCKING LOUD. Since he worked odd hours, he was frequently buzzed at times when everyone else was sober. He increasingly reperformed anecdotes when people were watching television or trying to have a conversation about other matters. People had begun to complain, citing his inability to participate in a balanced conversation without putting on The Rufus Show for everyone within earshot. It was as though he were trouncing through the forest blasting a sawed-off shotgun instead of tiptoeing with a rifle and a scope. Aside from his vociferousness, Maggie complained about him leaving copies of *Playboy* lying around the house. (In the list of male house members who the women thought could pass for gay, Rufus was the clear—albeit distant—second after "Gay" Clay, prompting Maggie's deconstruction as to why Rufus felt the need to treat the rest of the house to his smut.) Having commenced dating in earnest, Rufus began spouting off blanket proclamations on the practice. This, more than anything else, is what pushed even some of his admirers over the edge. Many people in the house, like me, had already been dating for years back when Rufus took possession of his own pubic hair. We found the unsolicited advice of a newbie the height of arrogance.

Even though Rufus was starting to get on my nerves, I defended him. He was exuberant, interesting, and certainly different (and his sushi dinner—including his daytrip back to the City to fetch his bamboo rollers—was simply one of the great moments in epicurean sharehouse history). He reminded me of Tobey Maguire in *Spiderman* when he first learned that he had superpowers but didn't know how to use them, resulting in him jizzing all over himself in his bedroom. Rufus had considerably more on the ball than I did at his age, and I held out the hope that the house might help him understand that certain things could only be learned by being an adult for a while. (Eleven years older than he, there were so many things about which I knew I was still an ignoramus.) Ultimately, I defended Rufus because he participated vigorously in the house and because he was different. In this day and age when more and more people look and sound the same and do and buy and talk about all of the same shit, being different went a long way with me.

"I think," Maggie whispered over the jets, "that next year you should enforce your age range."

*   *   *

On Saturday, the surf was huge, and only the most intrepid bathers ventured in for short dips. Unlike parts of the Jersey shore where you have to wade out twenty yards for the water to be up to your waist, in Kismet the beach drops off precipitously and you are soon in over your head. During rough days, this can make for rather treacherous waves that break right onto the beach. I waded into the surf past my knees; feeling the force of the riptide while gaping at a succession of awesome waves, I retreated.

Despite my love of the ocean, when it comes to big surf, I can be a pussy. Once, when I was a share in Bicycle Bill's house, I blithely set out on a boogie board on a similarly rough day. A large wave tossed me head over heels and I landed upside down on my shoulder, feeling a distinct crunch. Still being tossed beneath the wave like a rag doll, I couldn't move and wondered, for a long second, if I hadn't just snapped my spine.

When I washed up on the beach, a bracing pain shot through one side of my chest and back. My relief at being able to move my legs was short-lived as I could barely draw a breath. Staggering to my feet, I clutched my rib cage, feeling as though I had been struck by a sledgehammer. Spotting a woman from my house, I hobbled toward her and dropped to my knees.

"I need...help," I gasped, crashing down on the sand.

"Ohmygod! *Ohmygod!*" she yelled, dashing off toward the lifeguard chair. I tried to lie on my back, but it was too painful, and so I slumped on my side and tried to breathe. By the time the lifeguard crouched down next to me, I was able to draw regular, albeit shallow breaths. Matt rushed over and assessed the situation, and after fifteen minutes or so, my breathing returned to normal—just in time for the EMTs to show up. One of them walked me over to the ambulance where they then strapped me onto a backboard, loaded me inside, and checked my vitals. Everything was fine. Except the entire right side of my chest and back flooded with pain upon every move.

I've been pretty lucky in that the last time I spent a night in a hospital was after badly breaking my arm—in 1975. Whereas Matt (as befits the cowboy-reckless job description of the baby in any family) has always been accident prone. Additionally, Matt was in and out of hospitals during his postgrad years for a persistent, vague medical condition that once left him unable to walk up a single flight of stairs. Since he better understood the body's resilience, he was far more blasé about my situation. Sitting next to me in the ambulance, he advised me not to go to the hospital.

"Your vitals are fine and you're gonna be fine. You just got jacked really hard. Even if you broke a couple of ribs, there's nothing you can do about it. If you take a turn for the worse, we'll call a water taxi and take you to the hospital."

The EMTs, still pushing the hospital, reminded me of electronics salesmen working on commission.

"These guys don't know what they're doing," Matt whispered. "Why did they walk you all the way over here and then strap you down?"

The EMTs got between Matt and me, and when I tried to sit up I was reminded of the fact that I was restrained. They persisted with their hard sell, but I demanded in a rather strident tone that they kindly loosen the straps. They made me sign a bunch of forms, and then Matt walked me back to Bicycle Bill's crew on the beach. Someone set up an umbrella over me, although lying down was too painful and so I reclined sideways on a beach chair, and someone fetched me some codeine. Every cough, laugh, or move was painful, but I reached over to the cooler and grabbed a beer and the church key. While opening a beer was never such an ordeal, it was one of those rare moments when cold beer just tastes heavenly. Staring out at those huge waves that had had their way with me, I developed, from that moment on, a new understanding of and respect for the ocean.

The ocean is the largest most powerful thing on the planet and proof of the interconnectedness of all of humanity. Even if you don't believe in God, you can't not believe in the ocean, which, for me, is a better illustration of God than any of the Catholic-school notions that had been pumped into my head—like the one where God is a nine-foot-tall bearded white male who sits on a throne wielding a joystick that controls wars and disasters and grants favors to all those who pray unto Him. The ocean—unlike this cartoon version of God—is not aware of how we've dishonored it; the ocean cannot be petitioned for help from the free-throw line; the ocean is not on our side. It is the ultimate indiscriminate force that at any time could swallow me, or my house, or all of Fire Island, or all of us.

I'm hardly the only person in Kismet contending with some level of depression or trauma or anxiety who came to the ocean—consciously or unconsciously—in search of calm. Years before I ever came to Kismet (before realizing the ocean's persistent draw in my life), I frequented Coney Island. As with Kismet, Coney was love at first sight. I fell hard for its carnivalesque air and its clams and kebabs and the Latino flavor of its pier where I would buy fried bacala and beer and churros before the Friday night fireworks. During the nineties, my friends grew tired of my constant desire to trek out there, and when I couldn't convince anyone to join me, I would go by myself. One afternoon, I approached a group of people eating and drinking on the beach and asked them to watch my bag while I went for a swim. When I returned, a middle-aged Puerto Rican woman offered to mix me a rum cocktail; another woman offered me some food. A lit joint was passed my way, but I was so thrilled to have been welcomed by these strangers that I hardly wanted to smoke anything. I passed the J to the guy next to me, who took a hit and then pulled off his shirt to go for a swim. Speaking of the water, he began to sound quasi-religious tones, claiming that being immersed in the ocean cleansed him.

"Every time you go in the ocean," he said, "it can be a baptism."

I inwardly scoffed upon hearing that, thinking it so much stoner sentimentalism. In the interim—especially after my boogie-boarding mishap—his proclamation began sounding less far out. I was baptized as a baby on a small carpeted stage where a man in a white robe who had taken a vow to deny his own biology poured a trickle of water over my forehead. Who is to say that that ritual (so far removed from the way Jesus was baptized) is more meaningful than someone immersing themselves in the ocean, of their own accord, with the desire to be spiritually cleansed, to be baptized anew in the most powerful force on the planet? Would a surfside collection plate make it more meaningful?

Every time you go in the ocean, it can be a baptism.

It just doesn't sound so schmaltzy anymore.

On a sunny day like today, staring out at the horizon, the warm sand beneath me and the blue sky above, the beach feels like an embrace. I felt a pang of hunger. Looking to the east, amid the slow train of bikini-clad beauties, I could make out Alexis, casting out her line, topless. Sometimes sunny days on the beach just make me want to eat and have sex with abandon, yet these primordial urges are not raging in a flood of testosterone; rather, my appetites feel as natural as the rhythm of the waves.

I like to anticipate whatever I am going to eat next, whether something I might create, or, more often, something that someone else might make for everyone. Preparing something for someone else to eat is about the most loving, caring thing you can do for that person while keeping your pants on, and there was a lot of love in the Chance house. Watching the parade of women, their natural human bodies with flaws that only rendered them that much more real and desirable, I imagined that this was how Walt Whitman felt when he wrote, "Passing stranger! You don't know how longingly I look upon you..." Or that maybe this is how that modern man of letters Jay-Z felt when he wrote, "I got ninety-nine problems but a bitch aint one."

I regularly lapsed into flights of fancy on the beach, where sex and the prospect of sex felt like picking a piece of fruit from a tree, like something we could do whenever we wanted if we didn't commodify it or bow down to so much fundamentalist horseshit. Eating and having sex are just two things that humans do, that humans have to do, only we hadn't even figured out how to properly eat, let alone have sex. It's a collective work in progress, and while we seemed to be getting closer, we were definitely riding the short bus.

Approaching along the surf was Julianne, a woman who was part of a smaller, less-structured sharehouse. She stopped, and we began to chat. If there is a level of interaction that falls just short of flirtation, we had been going at it all summer long, the two of us arching up on our toes like kids at a carnival who don't clear the red line. She had been coming to Kismet longer than I had, so both of us knew full well the small-town consequences of hooking up. As she wandered off, my thoughts drifted down from the stratosphere and I lamented my utter lack of privacy. Since late May, I hadn't spent a single night alone, putting my entire social and romantic life under a microscope. While Rule Number One and I were not exclusive, I hardly felt free to pursue other women. This social pressure cooker made it easier to continue on with Rule Number One; everyone already knew about us and being with her didn't spawn new rounds of gossip. I had had my fill of gossip, both in my house as well as with the milder level of town gossip. From time to time, Kismetians would crack jokes about me screwing all of the SHMILFs in my house, probably figuring why the hell wouldn't I? The week before, I had met my friend Anne at the dock. Normally slender, Anne was seven months pregnant, and it was my first time seeing her engorged belly. I couldn't believe the sight of her. As she rushed toward me, I made eye contact with a Kismet old-timer who nodded at me from behind Anne on the dock. I stretched out my arms to hug Anne, only she grabbed my wrists and clapped each of my hands over her swollen buttcheeks, laughing as though to say, Can You Believe My Big Fat Ass? So there I was with my rep as a low-grade Hefner squeezing the ass of a very pregnant woman on the dock...

As with the house, however, I tried to remember that you can only ever be who you are, because gossipers are going to think whatever they want to think anyway.

Feeling hot, I got up from my chair to check the waves. They were still huge, so I began walking west along the surf. I spotted Abby in the distance with Jackson, her boxer.

"Jackson!" I called out.

Abby let him off his leash, and he ran toward me. We walked back to Abby, and I took the leash from her to take Jackson for a stroll. Walking eastward, I spotted an approaching Rule-*age*, a curvaceous woman whose dark curls cascaded over her shoulder in the breeze. While Rule Number One

was more svelte, this woman was hardly self-conscious of her body, wearing a high-strapped bikini that only accentuated the curve of her hips. Jackson veered toward her, and she approached him, hinging forward to give him a pat.

We exchanged small, tight smiles, and then she was gone. I went a bit farther and then turned around, following her back toward Abby. I wished that Rule Number One was there with me, poking fun at my quirks while watching the parade of bodies, enjoying the anticipation of rounding out an epicurean day and night together. After dropping off Jackson, I turned toward the ocean.

Every time you go in the ocean, it can be a baptism.

The waves were still huge, but I was hot so I waded in past my knees, feeling the surge of the riptide as I waited for my moment.

*   *   *

On Saturday night, Vanessa stormed the kitchen. After searing scallops in truffle oil, we plated them over grits, along with steamed kale and pears she had baked with gorgonzola and sage. When I was done eating, I picked up my plate and licked it clean.

After dessert, Dylan and I pulled the guitars off the wall and began to play. I'm a hack, but Dylan could play anything and could match my key in just about any song that came to mind. Risa joined us, singing Pat Benatar, The Go-Gos, and when someone called out, "Play 'Ring of Fire'!" I strummed a G chord and Dylan matched it, and we figured the song out on the fly. The house bong (fashioned out of a Philippo Berrio Extra Virgin Olive Oil bottle) circled the couch bank and stopped at me. I like playing the guitar when stoned, as the weed creates a minor disconnect between my hands and brain that makes it feel almost as though someone else is playing. Meanwhile, my voice gets throatier until it almost breaks.

After hanging up the guitars, we moved out to the deck. I stood alone in the corner, watching. It was a warm night, and Dylan began chatting up Tina—he didn't yet realize that she was off-limits. I thought to say something, but figured he'd suss it out for himself. Tracy was talking to Joo-chan, and Joe approached me, gesturing, sloshing beer onto his wrist.

"You know," he licked his forearm, "I've been fucking the same woman for three years now."

Joe had said this to me once before, about six months earlier, at one of Matt's parties. While it's the kind of comment that would have prompted a sit-down with another friend, I never thought Joe was signaling an intention to cheat on Tina; rather I thought he was voicing his apprehension over the inevitable nailing of his single-guy dick to the wall.

"I'm going to tell you something that a wise man once said about the grass."

"I don't smoke weed," Joe said.

"No, not that grass. Actual grass."

"What? Like lawn?" He laughed, spilling beer on his wrist again, only when he tried to lick it off, he spilled a drop on his cheek.

"I think you have a drinking problem," I said. Joe wasn't too wasted to pick up the *Airplane* reference.

"Have you ever seen a grown man naked?" He laughed. Feeling rather stoned, I went with it:

"Why I can make a hat, or a brooch, a pterodactyl..."

"And Leon is getting larger!"

We just stood there, doing lines from *Airplane*, possibly going at it for longer than the actual movie. He laughed in a full-bodied way that seemed to release whatever had been bottled up in him, before cooling down with "Excuse me, but I speak jive."

"So," he said. "What did the wise man once tell you about grass?"

"The wise man said that the grass, on other side, is always greener."

"This is true," he said. "But it would be a lot more fun to be in this house if you were single."

"Sure it would," I said. "And just about every guy here would trade all of that fun in a heartbeat for a girlfriend like the one you've got."

"I know that," Joe said. "I was just stating a fact."

Over his shoulder, I spotted Tina talking to Gay Cl—I mean, Clay.

"Are you going to come up to me next summer and tell me that you've been fucking the same woman for four years?"

He laughed and shook his head, turning toward the federal preserve. We watched the mist rolling in from the beach, getting caught in pockets between the trees.

"Life is good," Joe said, finishing his cup.

Near the railing, Dylan was now chatting with Dani, while Vanessa rolled her eyes at me, laughing. Tracy stood between Maurice and a blushing

Joochan—although his Asian complexion may just have been flushed red from booze. Still, Charlotte wasn't there, and Tracy had a certain gleam in her eye.

Having earlier likened sharehouse sex to grade-school kids completing a test, we were now at that point when the brave kids had handed in their work and a veritable parade was about to begin. It was a muggy night, and sexual tension hung in the air like the mist. Once Mandy and Natasha carried the hula-hoops out to the deck, my little voice stepped up:

"Okay, keep it moving, nothing to see here, folks."

I slipped out of the house and wandered over to The Inn, where through the thick crowd I spotted Julianne at the bar. No sooner did we make eye contact than the stool next to her opened up. I slipped through the crowd and sat down next to her.

"Can I buy you a drink?" I said, trying to catch the eye of Erin, the bartender.

"Are you stoned?" Whenever I smoke, my eyes give me away.

"A little bit," I said, pulling out my billfold. "Are you?"

"Not anymore. Want to go smoke a bowl?"

Erin looked over at me and I shook my head.

"Sure." I stuffed my cash back in my pocket and turned to go.

"Hang on a sec," she said. "I'm just going to run to the ladies room. Umm..."

"Why don't I wait for you outside?" I pointed toward the exit.

"Great," she said. "I'll meet you outside."

I went to the men's room and then walked out of The Inn, meandering a few steps southward on Oak Walk, out of sight of the door. A few minutes later, Julianne walked out.

"Thanks," she said. "It's good that you waited outside. If people saw us leaving together, they might talk."

"They might," I said.

"I love this place," she said, "but you can't scratch yourself without the whole town knowing about it."

"Tell me about it."

"That's true," she said. "You're here all summer, aren't you?"

"Yes."

"So you must really be feeling it."

"I don't know what privacy is anymore."

"That's what's so great about the City," she said. "You can go out with someone and no one else has to know. Not in Kismet, though. There are no secrets in this town."

Sometimes I wondered if I even knew half of what was going on in the house. I was a gossip dead-end and people knew this about me, which made me privy to a couple of items that were otherwise confidential. So I was all but certain that secrets were being kept between people who were mature enough and smart enough to keep them under cover.

"I'll bet there are tons of secrets," I said. "It just takes two people smart enough to keep it to themselves."

We arrived at her house, and the lights were on. Music and voices emanated from the deck behind the house.

"It's such a nice night," Julianne said, smiling. "Let's go have a look at the beach."

After our stealth exit from The Inn, followed by that speedy little negotiation to keep anything confidential, the two of us were now, quite clearly, Tall Enough For This Ride.

"That would be great," I said.

*   *   *

On Sunday morning, I went upstairs to make an espresso. Out on the deck, Joo-chan lay passed out on the hammock. I sat down on the porch swing and watched the waves as I sipped my coffee. I then went downstairs and was about to pedal down to the market to pay our bill and pick up the Sunday papers, when Clay approached me clutching his packed bag.

"Hey, John, what do I owe you for the weekend?" He wore an almost distressed look, and there was no trace of flamingness in his voice.

"Twenty-seven bucks."

He pulled out a wad of cash. "Here's thirty." He uncrumpled a ten and a twenty.

"Okay. Thanks." I reached for my billfold to peel off three bucks.

"That's fine," he said. "I gotta run."

There was something cagey about his demeanor—only I couldn't put my finger on it.

"Cut the guy some slack," My little voice chided me. *"He took the time to settle up in cash even though he was running late."*

Listening to the high-pitched whir-clack of his suitcase rolling over the boards of the ramp down to the sidewalk, I concurred with my little voice, chalking up Clay's discomfort to running late for the boat. Outside, upon passing Joo-chan's window, I spotted, lying on the sill behind the blinds, Exhibit A: a spent condom stuffed back into its wrapper. What was he doing on the hammock? Maybe whoever he had hooked up with had started to snore? Having taken such pains to cover my own tracks the night before, I thought that he had just fucked up big-time, that his in-house procurement of horizontal refreshment was bound to get back to Charlotte.

I returned from the store with the newspapers. Upstairs, Joo-chan was just getting up from the hammock.

"I'd like to explain something to you," I said, approaching him on the deck.

"What's that?"

"When you drop a used condom behind the blinds, it's in full view of whoever walks past the window."

"I don't know what you're talking about."

"Look, I'm not going to break this to Charlotte, but if you want to keep your night under wraps, don't leave your DNA lying around."

He shook his head. "I don't know what you're talking about. I slept out here last night."

"In the hammock?"

"Yeah. Last night I went down to my room, and someone was sleeping in my bed."

For a split second, I pictured Joo-chan as a six-foot-three hungover Asian Goldie Locks.

"Who?" I asked. "Who was sleeping in your bed?"

"I don't know. It was dark and I was fucked up."

"Huh," I said. "Because last night it looked like something was maybe brewing between you and Tracy."

"Well, we did kind of start making out—"

"You and Tracy?"

"Yeah, but I didn't want to screw things up with Charlotte so I gave her the Heisman."

"How hard was that?"

"Pretty fucking hard. So maybe afterward she went down to my room looking for me and found someone else in there?"

"You think someone was the beneficiary of mistaken-identity sex with Tracy?"

"All I know is that whoever had sex in that room wasn't me."

I went downstairs. The door to Penn was ajar. A set of the red queen-sized sheets lay on the full-sized mattress. People in the house knew the bedding code: White sheets are full; blue sheets are twin; red sheets are for the queen-sized mattress in Baltic. That's when I suspected Dylan. He probably thought it was like any other sharehouse, where people just grab whatever bed is open. He must have crashed in Joo-chan's bed, only to be woken up by Tracy wandering in for a second go at Joo-chan.

If that was really the case, I was glad to see that Colin's behavior hadn't discouraged Tracy—although I found it a wee bit ironic that she had adopted his technique of unauthorized entry. I guess I'm going to have to kick her out, I joked to myself, but of course this was one of many ways in which men and women were different. If guys in the house were regularly waking up to find sexy, drunk librarians lying in bed next to them, my male recruiting challenge would be over.

Turtle Soup

Rule Number One next returned to the house for the August 6 weekend, only I missed it to attend my college roommate, Dave's wedding. After a plane, a car, and then the ferry, I returned to Kismet just before sunset on Sunday evening, not expecting to see Rule Number One (as she often left earlier), so I was all the more pleasantly surprised to find her still there. I chilled two cocktail glasses and shook a Christo for her and a Manhattan for myself, dropping in an extra cherry for good luck. I carried the drinks out to the deck and joined Rule Number One on the porch swing.

"Is that a Manhattan?" she asked.

"Yes."

"My father would love you," she said. "He can drink those all night long."

She frequently mentioned her father in the context of letting me know that something I did would or would not meet his approval.

Sipping our cocktails, we watched the sun go down. I fished the good-luck cherry out of my glass.

"Could I convince you to stay over tonight?"

"That depends, Mister."

"What does it depend upon?" Holding the cherry by its stem, I sank my incisors into that bourbon-soaked treat. Rule Number One agreed to stay the night and take the "death boat" at 6:20 in the morning.

Dani came upstairs wearing one of the green rugby staff shirts from The Out, the breast emblazoned with their whale logo.

"Why is Dani wearing an Out shirt?"

This was when Rule Number One's gossiping came in handy. It turned out to have been a rather social weekend in my absence. Now that it was August, the water felt *just...fine.* I learned that Alan had hooked up with Mandy's guest, while Mandy made out with two different guys on the dance floor at The Out, before screwing one of them on the tennis court. Apparently Joo-chan was just warming up the previous weekend with Tracy, as he ended up scoring horizontal refreshment with—get ready for this one—Uptalking Nancy. I began to laugh, picturing Nancy pinned down beneath Joo-chan:

Oh my *God?* That feels so like, *good?* Fuck me, like...*hard*er?

Dani, however, took the crown. A number of the women in the house had been ogling a tall, model-esque guy who worked the door at The Out. Rule Number One informed me that, after closing time, Dani dragged him back to the house and did him in the hall.

"In the hall?"

"Yeah," she said. "Oh, and by the way—he's nineteen."

"Nineteen, huh?"

There was only one thing that I wanted to know: Where were these women when I was nineteen? The difference between nineteen now and nineteen back then was tectonic. Back then—in the age before Al Gore invented the Internet—it was practically the Mesozoic Era. Women weren't trying to compete with porn stars; they still had pubic hair, weren't taking pole-dancing classes, and weren't making out with each other in bars to draw attention to themselves. When I was nineteen, I was not being approached by hot twenty-six-year-olds for hallway sex. I've still never had hallway sex (although I'm willing to let that one go). I could almost picture Dani, bleary-eyed downstairs at four a.m., thinking, *Well, this looks like a perfectly good hallway to me...*

Once I stopped laughing over the image of Dani on her knees while this kid gave it to her over the pile of dirty laundry, her tryst started to gnaw at me. (Hadn't she ever heard of Sex On The Beach? It's an act so lovely they even named a drink after it.) Aside from the cheesiness of spreading her legs in a place where anyone could have happened upon her, it pissed me off that Dani brought a nineteen-year-old into the house. I would have to change my policy of "No Kids" to read "No Kids/Minors," because if that guy were to have drunk anything at the house and later gotten into an accident or drowned, I'd be liable. Yes, of course it's unlikely. My house getting swept away by a flood is also unlikely, but if I were to let my flood insurance lapse, you'd think I was nuts. Nightmare scenarios aside, I maintained an age range that began at twenty-eight because that's when I believe that people become adults. I was thirty-fucking-four and I wanted the other people coming into the house to be full-fledged adults—not kids who rode out the Reagan Administration on a tricycle.

I remembered what Maggie had said about Rufus: "You should just enforce your age range." At twenty-six, Dani was still of a postgrad mindset—something I knew full well when I invited her back. While she didn't have an epicurean bone in her body, she was attractive and that helped recruit guys. Beyond the occasional torturing of the speakers with her teenybopper iPod, Dani never did anything that was so bad. Although she had developed a wicked sense of entitlement, as though she were above pitching in. So far as I could tell, it was all Paris Hilton's fault. That second-rate porn star lowered the bar for millions of girls until they wanted nothing more than to be worshipped. And not for being in a movie or singing in a band or even something so simple as strutting down a catwalk—they wanted to be adored solely for having won the genetic lottery, not caring a whit about contributing anything worthwhile, nor worrying their pretty little heads about anything save their access. Every night is prom night for these chicks, and they're the fucking queens.

And why should they feel the need to accomplish anything, now that meritocracy was dead and accomplishment relegated to extra credit? Maybe Dani was part of a genius avant-garde, the first group to fully grasp that it was all about access. (And she didn't have to look further than our lightweight of a president.)

While other people had complained—as they always put it—that Dani "never lifted a finger," just as many people had complained about Rufus. But Rufus was always doing stuff for others, while Dani possessed the participatory initiative of Marie Antoinette. Still, I really had no right to be upset with Dani. Being a postgrad party girl was hardly a crime, but... Whatever, I thought, borrowing the one-word mission statement of the Paris Hilton Generation.

Whatever.

I chomped my last cherry and decided that next summer, Dani would have to find a different house in which to acquire carpet burns the color of her row in my spreadsheet.

Dani was toast.

I set down my glass and sat sideways on the swing, facing Rule Number One, the lighthouse behind her shoulder. The setting sun lit up her dark curls until they almost looked red, and I thought about my walk on the beach with Julianne. Even though Rule Number One and I never had The Talk, and having The Talk seemed to be the last thing she wanted to do, and even though she might have been advancing her own extracurricular life back in the City, I felt bad about what I had done. I felt as though I had cheated on her.

* * *

The next morning, I picked up an e-mail from a guy who was interested in a midweek visit. He described himself in a few clear, economical sentences that any writer would admire. He seemed like pure Chance material—until he closed his e-mail with "it's too bad that you hate Republicans."

Ever since launching my website in March 2004 (when a majority of Americans still believed that George Bush was both competent and honest) I included the following line in my bio:

I'm an artistic cross-trainer, a hard-core eater, and a patriot committed to the collective goal of preventing the Town Drunk from Texas from driving our country further into the ditch.

Nowhere on the site does it say that I hate Republicans. If this were 1991, I would not be professing my commitment to help gird the country against further damage by Bush 41. Plenty of intelligent people could argue that administration's worldview, and if they appreciated the epicurean life, I would welcome them into the house. Still, I could see how someone might interpret that line in my bio as hostility toward all Republicans, so I e-mailed the guy back. "Despite my feelings for George Bush, I do not hate Republicans. If I were to tell you that I despised O.J. Simpson, would you then conclude that I hated all football players?"

He sent back a snippy little e-mail insisting that George Bush was the leader of the Republican Party, and therefore I was expressing my hatred toward all Republicans.

I didn't think it was worth trying to further convince the guy that I didn't hate Republicans, or that if our country managed to survive the Cheney/Bush Administration, we would probably end up thanking some courageous Republican who grew tired of having true conservatism pissed all over by an apocalyptic extremist with a trillion-dollar hole in his pocket.

(This was the worst part of the damage Karl Rove did to our country. Fifteen years ago, this guy and I might have become friends.)

Conversely, I received the occasional e-mail from prospects who felt compelled to list their credentials as Democrats. I especially remember one woman who touted her extensive volunteer work for Hillary Clinton's senatorial campaign. She wrongly assumed that my passionate distaste for the Cheney/Bush Administration meant that I was a card-carrying Democrat.

I'm not. If I were robbed at knifepoint while a pair of cops stood around and watched, I'd have a lot more venom for those cops than for the robber. I wouldn't brag to be a member of the Democratic Party any more than I'd brag to be an admirer of Neville Chamberlain. Still, I was surrounded by urbane New Yorkers who vehemently hated Bush while giving a free pass to Hillary and the rest of those namby-pamby Democrats who didn't stand up to him. So I had a hard time seeing Hillary's ardent supporters as something more than appeasers of the Cheney/Bush Administration.

When Nicky Mack said *Politics have no relation to morals,* that fabulous Florentine couldn't have been more right. Karl Rove had forced American common sense so far up our ass that we couldn't call a spade a spade. Card-carrying party members who cared more about their candidates than the health of our country were not people that I particularly wanted in the house, and I preferred to avoid anyone who bought their values—political or otherwise—in bulk.

*　　*　　*

Upstairs, Risa was pulling what remained of a carton of eggs from the fridge.

"What are you making?" I asked her.

"*Huevos rancheros.* Do you want some?"

"Absolutely." I opened the fridge.

"Are there more eggs downstairs?" she asked.

"Plenty of eggs downstairs. Are you making bacon?"

She set the eggs down on the counter and faced me. "Well, *I'm* not making bacon."

"How come? Do you want me to make it?"

"That would be great."

"Fine. I'll make bacon. When you're downstairs, can you grab one of those four-pound boxes?"

"I really can't." A funny look came over her face.

"Why not?"

"In case you haven't noticed, we eat quite a bit out here, and we eat an awful lot of bacon. I just can't keep eating the way that you and Matt do."

"Okay."

"You know, I actually considered not doing the house this year."

"Why?"

"Because it's hard not to eat all the great stuff that people cook. Still, I couldn't imagine not being in the house, so I made a deal with myself that I had to run every day and that I couldn't cook any bacon."

I laughed. "So you can eat it, but you just can't cook it?"

"Or carry it upstairs. Or do anything else to encourage the cooking of bacon."

"Well it was my idea to cook bacon."

"Exactly."

"So if I were to go downstairs, get bacon and cook it, you'd eat some?"

"No comment."

"Okay," I said. "I'm going down to the fridge to get eggs and bacon."

"If you want to." She smiled and grabbed a bowl to begin breaking eggs.

*   *   *

That afternoon, I was sitting at my desk when Chris knocked on my door.

"Hey, John?"

"Yeah?"

"There's a turtle on the walkway."

"Really?"

"Yeah. There's a black-and-orange turtle sitting on the walkway."

I got up from my desk and stepped out of the house onto the walkway, where, sure enough, a black-and-orange turtle the size of a pie plate had managed to crawl all the way up the ramp, turning two corners on the walkway. I picked it up, and its head retracted into its shell.

"Well," I said, carrying it over to the tall grass, "it's hardly the strangest creature that ever made its way to our door."

*   *   *

Later that night, I was on the phone with my parents when my mother asked me the following question:

"So. Are there any interesting women in the house?"

"Sure," I said. "Lots of interesting women. There's Natasha, who's a choreographer, there's this other woman Vanessa, who brews beer..."

I can't believe I'm being such a douche to my own mom.

"Is there any romance brewing in the house?"

"Maybe," I said. "There's a couple of people who seem like they might be into each other, but—"

"She wants to know," my father cut in, "if there are any women of interest to you."

When your youngest child is thirty-two, and two of your three children remain unmarried, this subject sops up a fair amount of parents' mental capacity.

With Rule Number One and I hardly conducting ourselves in a way I wanted to describe to my parents, I felt a twinge when I said, "No. Maybe next summer…"

While brushing my teeth, I thought that I should have told my parents that I was "dating" Rule Number One, although the closest we ever came to a "date" consisted of eight ounces of ground beef and sixteen ounces of beer. I could have said that I was "seeing" her, but that didn't sound great, either. Watching the toothpaste foam wash down the drain, I thought how it was always a bad sign whenever I hid something from my parents.

*　　*　　*

On Thursday afternoon, I was sitting at my desk when Chris once again knocked on my door.

"John, you gotta see this." He pointed toward the front door.

"What's that?"

"There's an old guy out on the sidewalk wearing nothing but a jockstrap.
"Come on!"

"I am not shitting you."

Skeptical, I rose from my desk and stepped out onto the walkway. Sure enough, there was a sixtyish bald guy standing on the other side of Pine Walk, his full ass hanging out of a black jockstrap.

"Maybe he wandered in from the nude beach?" Chris said.

"Maybe he works for the national weather service," I said.

Who the hell knew? It was Kismet, and you were bound to see anything in this town. If Chris were to come into my room the following day and insist that a Great Dane was giving it to Condoleezza Rice over the garbage cans, I would have believed him.

*　　*　　*

Stoner Jeffrey e-mailed me, wanting to reserve a guest spot for his friend that weekend. I replied to him that the August 13 weekend had been full since late May and that the guest waitlist was already three people deep. On Friday morning, while waiting on line at Costco, I picked up a rather huffy voice mail from Jeffrey:

"It seems like there's an awful lot of last-minute guests coming out so...uhh...I don't see why my friend can't come out this weekend."

He was referring to the weekend when Lizzie's last-minute cancellations created last-minute openings. I scrolled through my phone to call him and tell him no a second time, but then flipped my phone shut. Normal people understood that one weekend was different from another. I had already told him no, that guest spots were guaranteed to people who reserved them, and still I was treated to a spoiled ten-year-old throwing a tantrum because his wittle fwiend couldn't come out. I pulled out my phone again. I was going to call Jeffrey and tell him that I didn't show up at his place of business and tell him how to give hand jobs and to please spare me his stoner fucking wisdom about how to run the house. Once again, however, I flipped my phone shut. Enough, I thought. *Basta. No mas. Auf Wiedersehen,* bee-yotch.

Jeffrey was toast.

*   *   *

Grace, the first weekender to arrive that Friday afternoon, was sitting on the porch swing working a pair of knitting needles.

"Hey, John? Do you have a four-foot piece of rope?"

"Sure. What for?"

"I want to tie a rope to the railing so that I can rock myself in the hammock."

"That's a good idea. What are you knitting over there?"

"Oh, I don't know."

"How can you not know what you're knitting?"

"I'll figure it out."

I went downstairs just as Martin, PI and Sonia came through the door. Martin's face was red as though he were angry; Sonia's was expressionless. I could only guess that they had been arguing.

"Hey, Johnny, nice to see ya," Martin said, putting on a happy face and shaking my hand. I then greeted Sonia before winding around to the shed and finding a piece of rope for Grace. Having tended to the house since returning from Costco, I went to the beach and walked down to Saltaire, turning around and watching the sunset as I returned. As I walked up the ramp to the house, Martin dashed around the walkway, a distressed look on his face.

"Johnny, what's the combo for the bikes?"

I gave him the combination, and he hurried past me.

"Is everything okay?"

"Sonia just took off."

"Where?"

"I have no fucking idea." He shook his head and tapped his temple with four fingers. "It's all *fakakte*," he muttered, pronouncing that old Yiddish word "fah*cocked*," using it as an adverb.

Watching our private eye pedal toward the bay reminded me of the proverbial plumber for whom the last thing he wanted to do upon arriving home was fix his own sink. Nevertheless, that Martin was still hanging in with Sonia was his choice and not for me to feel bad about. Part of me wished that she was already on a ferry back to the mainland, because I just didn't want that kind of thing playing out in the house, but I doubted that would happen. She'd be at the dock or in the bars or some other obvious place where you hardly had to be a private investigator to find her. She didn't need to run off the island; she just needed to take Martin down a peg in the ongoing negotiation of their contract.

Upstairs, a new wave of house members had arrived, including Jeffrey and Rosemarie. I greeted them and stepped out onto the deck. Grace lay in the hammock, rocking herself with the length of rope. She had tied a large, symmetrical knot that I had never seen.

"Nice knot," I said. "Did you have to blow a Boy Scout to learn how to tie that?"

"I was in the *Girl* Scouts," she said, mock offended at my bad joke.

"They don't teach you how to tie knots in the Girl Scouts."

"I know." She displayed that Cheshire-cat grin. "I learned how to tie knots in the Navy."

I was dumbfounded to learn that Grace had enlisted straight out of high school, served four years, and then went to college. I pulled up a chair next to her and rocked the hammock, peppering her with questions. She described growing up in an economically depressed southern town where high school grads didn't have many options. She was one of those people who actually enlisted to reach for her own bootstraps. Everything about her initial guardedness began to make sense. She had clawed her way up and out on her own, and I could only guess that someone in that situation had to be all the more focused to steer clear of the snags. I liked that cooking was what first drew Grace out of her shell—she had started out sous-cheffing and then wowed us with her watermelon chicken.

"Would you like a blue margarita?" I asked her.

"That would be great."

I got up to go inside and Grace grabbed her pull rope and resumed rocking herself.

*   *   *

For dessert that night, Grace pulled two chocolate peanut butter pies from the freezer. I grabbed the bottle of 151 rum and a lighter.

"What are doing with that?" Grace asked.

"I'm gonna flambé it," I said.

"You're going to light it on *fire?*"

"Absolutely."

"Well...why would you do that?"

It was, I suppose, a reasonable question. Why would I set on fire the dessert she had prepared for all of us? Well, I didn't really have a great answer other than setting food on fire is fun and makes for a great presentation.

"If a dessert can be lit on fire—" I twisted the cap off the 151. "—let the motherfucker burn."

"Isn't it going to melt?"

"Those things are bricks," I pointed at her pies. "If anything, it might soften them up a bit."

She made a squeaking noise. I put an arm around her.

"Grace, I promise it will be fine."

I doused the top of one of the pies with 151 and set it ablaze. A blue flame formed a minaret over the pie to a chorus of oohs and ahs until the rum cooked off and the flame burned out. Grace stuck a tentative finger toward the pie. It was still quite hard.

"What do you think?" I said.

She grabbed the bottle of rum. "Can I do the next one?"

After dessert, I wandered out to the deck. A thick mist hung in the air and I thought it would be a good night to check out the beach. I went back inside where Jeffrey sat on the couch, firing up his bowl. He took a hit and, holding in the smoke, held up his bowl, offering it to me. Taking a toke would hardly be the worst thing to do before a foggy-night walk on the beach—only I didn't want to smoke Jeffrey's weed, not after how annoying he had been.

"Wrap hands around stick," my little voice said, *"and remove from ass."*

Watching Jeffrey expel the smoke with a baby cough, I laughed and approached the couch. It's one thing to become angry with someone, but it's another thing altogether to nurse anger—especially with someone like Jeffrey. It would be like trying to stay mad at a puppy that had chewed your couch. And that's exactly what Jeffrey was like: a panting, eager creature who always wanted to play. To stay mad at a guy like that would require soul-crushing work. And so while he'd still have to find another house (hopefully a sushi-free zone with plenty of shot glasses), I accepted his peace pipe with thanks.

*   *   *

I was eating breakfast on Saturday morning when Vanessa asked me if there was an open guest spot for Dylan that coming weekend.

"E-mail me."

"You want me to e-mail you even though I'm standing right in front of you?"

"Yes," I said. "Yes, I do."

This happens all the time. People think I'm being a dick when I send them back to their computers, but unless I'm in front of my spreadsheets, I'm helpless. And even if I did happen to know the answer, there is no way to guarantee that I'd remember to enter the request. Nicky Mack posed this question: *Do we try to make things easy on ourselves or do we try to make things easy on our customers?*

The answer, of course, is that it's a balance that involves plenty of other instances when people think I'm being a category-five dick for no reason at all. They could all point to a rule or a guideline that seems to them like so much anal, overly officious nonsense. They repeated the joke about breaking Rule Number 637, Section 2a, only they didn't get that I *hated* rules. I would love nothing better than to run a house with no rules, where everything was governed by common sense. But whenever I relied on common sense, it has never failed to bite me in the ass, advancing me one square further in the game of Misanthropy Land. This was one of those times when I just had to be a dick—only those small investments in dickishness paid off considerable returns in the larger picture of my emotional health.

*   *   *

On Saturday afternoon, a loud, drunken mob wearing costumes and hoisting plastic cups advanced southward on Pine Walk toward my house. This was the Kismet House Krawl, a roaming party that unfolded every summer, organized by Punk Rock Pete. Seven or eight houses volunteered to host, decorating their houses and creating costumes to go along with their themes. The Krawl dropped by each house for an hour, loaded up on drinks, and then moved on to the next house. This roving, costumed mob snowballed after each stop, absorbing stragglers who, like mutating, regenerating mammals, improvised costumes with items removed from other partiers or adopted from previous houses.

They crossed the Main Road and turned up the ramp of Bananas, the house next door. I watched the parade from my kitchen. There were pirates and chain-gang jailbirds wearing black-and-white striped prison outfits. There were women dressed up as sexy cops; a guy that I recognized as an actual cop was dressed in drag. The entire Bananas crew was decked out in whites with epaulettes, approximating the characters from *The Love Boat*.

Andrea Wikso, an old-school Kismet stalwart who works for the water taxis, had tried to coax me into being one of the houses on the Krawl. Back in May, participating in the Krawl felt like a great idea and I began tossing around themes, but by mid-August, my season had been going on for three months and I was starting to burn out. At this point, I didn't want to organize anything I didn't have to. The people who do the Krawl are pretty creative, and I didn't want to just phone in a theme. Aside from the work involved, a lot of the houses on the Krawl are the way my house was when I bought it—rudimentary shacks thrown up thirty-odd years ago before anyone imagined that they might be worth anything. Most of them could be cleaned out with a hose, which is great in that people can party hard in them with negligible wear-and-tear. These were houses where people were first and foremost drinking, with most of what they drank consumed directly from a can or bottle. I remembered the massive loss of stemware during the pig roast, and aside from the house taking a beating, it was always a buzzkill when I was reminded that I was in charge, that I had to be responsible. Sometimes, I regretted my renovations; I could have spared myself six figures worth of trouble and then wouldn't have to sweat the wear and tear. I wouldn't feel like Felix Unger dealing with a drunken horde of Oscar Madisons. (I was an Oscar for most of my life, and it's much more fun than being a Felix.) When I really started to think about it—recalling my crappy kitchen, or the doors and windows that didn't properly open, or my living room floor that consisted of gray-painted plywood that was impossible to clean, or the foul shower stalls that I had spray-painted white—I didn't regret my renovations at all. Still, Lovers & Other Strangers, a house owned by Dennis Waldman (who sold me my house) was a regular stopover on the Krawl, and Dennis had recently renovated that house. All I'd really have to do is put away the stemware and drag the kegerator out to the deck next to a stack of plastic cups. Still, while it feels almost blasphemous to admit this, I'm just not that into huge parties. Matt loves hosting huge parties. A couple of times a year, he allows more than a hundred people to invade and occupy his lush apartment, including his ever-popular pajama party, where everyone dons nightwear and a good number of women show up in lingerie. If Matt owned Chance, he'd be all over the Kismet House Krawl. I just never understood the desire that he and other people have to throw large parties. I'd really rather just eat.

*   *   *

Dylan, as you can imagine, expressed an interest in coming back to the house. He returned that Sunday afternoon for a full midweek, this time bringing his own guitar. Late on Monday night, I took a walk on the beach and found him sitting on the sand next to Sharon, another short-stay midweeker. I tried to imagine going to another beach house where each visit resulted in horizontal refreshment with a different woman. Not surprisingly, Dylan asked if he could extend his stay to guest that following weekend. Considering our virility shortfall, I took Colin's remaining weekend and cobbled together a small share, signing Dylan up as a new house member.

Raw Oysters and Steak Tartare

After composing the August 20 weekend update, I scheduled Rule Number One in my room. It felt good to do so. We had spoken earlier that week, and I got her to cough up which ferry she was taking so that I could meet her at the dock with a cocktail, an idea planted in my head by Jeannie, who had inspired one of the tenets of "Belief & Technique for Epicurean Sharehouse Management":

"Surprise someone arriving at dock on sunny day with icy sunset cocktail not too potent but strong in Spirit."

Despite having prescribed this to other people, I had never actually done it myself. So on Friday afternoon, I put a chilled bottle of prosecco into my knapsack and grabbed the crème de cassis from the wet bar, along with two champagne flutes, before walking down to the dock. I chose a secluded spot behind a stack of freight pallets and uncorked the prosecco. The first passengers disembarked just as I dropped twists into my knockoff Kir Royales. Craning my head around the stack of pallets, I spotted Rule Number One lugging her bag. I watched her from between the slats, and when she arrived at the pallets, I leaned back, clutching the flutes. She dropped her bag and bit her lower lip. The look on her face was precious: there was no devil grin; no trace of her tough-girl posturing. It was as though there were a crack in her countenance emitting light that rendered her beautiful in a way I had never seen. The warm feeling in my gut branched into my chest as I sprang up and pulled her against me.

"This is so nice," she said, shaking her head.

We sat down on the dock facing the lighthouse, and I put my arm around her. Our feet dangled over the water as we talked and drank. Another boat came and went, and I fixed Kir Royales until the prosecco was kicked.

"This is so nice," she kept repeating, clutching my arm. Watching the sun break apart behind the lighthouse, I recalled the one line I remembered from Baudelaire's *Flowers of Evil*:

Le soleil s'est noyé dans son sang qui se fige.

In English, this means, "The sun has drowned in its blood that coagulates around it."

While a beautiful image, it sounds a hell of a lot more poetic in French. Once you learn a second language, you begin to appreciate the full extent of what gets lost in translation. Such disconnects were all too frequent between Rule Number One and me, as we shared a knack for the clunkiest communication. Now, drinking in the sight of her and this expression I had never seen, this look of surrender and light, I felt as though we were speaking the same language for the very first time. While hardly drunk, I indeed felt strong in Spirit. A balmy breeze blew across the bay as we watched another boat come and go. With the sun now fully coagulated in its blood, we rose up from the dock, and I clutched Rule Number One's hand as we walked back to the house. I'm glad that I didn't know then that this would be the nicest moment we would ever share together.

*   *   *

On the morning of October 31, 1991, I woke up before the sun rose in Normandy—where I had just begun "studying" abroad—to attempt hitchhiking for the first time. I was twenty, and my French was still a work in progress, but I was challenging myself in all sorts of ways back then. I wanted to see if I could make it all the way to Maastricht, Holland, where my friend Stan was studying. I was soon picked up by a truck driver who spoke a guttural, countryside French that I could barely understand. At the Belgian border, he offered to buy me lunch at a truck stop. A regular there, he didn't look at the menu, and when the waitress approached, I couldn't understand what he had just ordered. She glanced at me and I said, *"Je prends la même chose,"* or, I'll have what he's having.

A few minutes later, the waitress set down a half-pint of lager and a large plate of fries circling a mound of raw, red meat garnished with capers. On top of the meat sat half an egg shell containing a raw yolk. It was 11:30 a.m. I watched the truck driver mix the egg yolk and the capers into that pile of ground meat. I did the same, bracing myself for the worst as I raised that first bite to my mouth...

I have never tasted anything so unexpectedly sublime.

It was as though I were tasting meat for the first time. Forking up bite after bite of that tartare and fries while draining my lager, I decided that my first attempt at hitchhiking was going extremely well. Halfway to my destination before noon, I felt all-powerful, as though I could go anywhere and eat anything and figure out how to communicate in any language. I felt like a cougar charging across the plains, like a rock star on a European tour. Whenever I taste tartare now, a flashback calls up that first bite, and I once again feel the buzz from the megawatts of power that I felt in that moment when I was twenty and green and saw the world as one big playground.

So many house members had stepped up to cook that I hadn't done much group cooking beyond sous-cheffing. So, I decided to prepare steak tartare for the house on Friday night. To my surprise, Rule Number One was also a raw steak lover. (She once again informed me that her father would approve.) Together we sliced up the lovely pink Kirkland sirloin, and after mixing in the onions, capers, spices, oil, vinegar, Worcestershire sauce, and egg yolks, I grabbed the Jason-league blade I had used to slice up the sirloin and stabbed it through a sixteen-ounce plastic cup, slicing off the bottom two-thirds.

"Whatcha doin' there, Mister?" Rule Number One scoffed.

"I'm making a mold so that we can plate this. Look." I held the cup rim side down in the center of a plate and then filled it with tartare, tamping it down so that when I pulled up the cup, the plate bore a perfect cylinder of meat. I angled two thick-cut potato chips into the top and gave it a pinch of parsley and a few more capers. I then finished the plate by adding two slices of crostini toasted with olive oil, as well as a mound of chips.

"I want to do one," she said, taking the mold. The look of wonder that came over her face was precious. Having never cooked in the house, Rule Number One began plating the tartare with glee. A few people in the house had never eaten tartare, and Matt was balling up some of it for cheeseburgers. But when we sat down to eat, and the raw diners began moaning their approval, curiosity got the better of Chris, himself a tartare virgin. A few other people left half-eaten cheeseburgers on their plates to come to the raw side. I liked watching the look on their faces as they tasted those first bites, wondering if they were having a moment like I had at that Belgian truckstop.

Rule Number One plated seconds for both of us, beaming again with that look of surrender. I began to wonder what it would be like to have her as my girlfriend.

In terms of maintenance, she was practically bipolar. While her extreme flirting, hard-core jealousy, and persistent gossiping rendered her rather high maintenance, this was cut by the many ways in which she was so easy. I never had to sell her on anything. She was always game, and my enthusiasm to do something was reason enough for her to become enthusiastic as well. She always went with the flow, and in the end this may have been what didn't add up between us. I always had to have a plan. Having a plan is how I ended up with a condo in West Harlem and a house on the beach despite having never cleared forty grand in a single year. Still, there were times when I could have stood to loosen up, and in the measure that I took Having A Plan too far, Rule Number One discounted it. She got married, got divorced; she went to law school, worked at a firm, then became an executive assistant without any thought of what came next. While my own career path hardly made sense, I was always looking down the line. (The funk that I fell into after losing my nannying job and shelving *Killing Mercutio* was primarily triggered by the fact that I No Longer Had A Plan.) In this way, Rule Number One and I couldn't have been more different. Maybe that's why we liked one another. Maybe she admired my drive and focus as much as I admired her irreverent spontaneity, her sense that fun could always be had, her insistence that the torpedoes be perpetually damned. Maybe in this way we were perfect for one another.

While we all have our significant-other wish lists, most of us who find ourselves still single in our thirties begin scaling back our expectations, hoping to just check off a couple of the items we consider important. Only with Rule Number One, I really couldn't check off much at all. Of course there was a big, fat check mark next to Sense of Humor. You'd never believe it but I can, on occasion, be a grumpy, cantankerous bastard; that Rule Number One could make me laugh was no small thing. Certainly it didn't hurt that I found her wildly attractive, that whenever I saw her, I just wanted to grab her, to have her in my arms, and now, once again, there was that look on her face, that look of vulnerability, apprehension, and maybe even a touch of fear. I thought that I was glimpsing her true self conquering all that posturing, her expression glowing in a way that damn near set my checklist on fire.

*   *   *

I was pouring a snifter of calvados at the wet bar when Dylan approached me.

"Is there any place where we could buy oysters tomorrow?"

"Well," I said, "Maggie's cooking paella for dinner."

"I meant for brunch."

"Oysters for brunch?"

"Yeah. With bacon, eggs, rosemary home fries, and Bloody Marys."

"I'll order ten dozen to be delivered on one of the passenger ferries tomorrow morning."

"Nice. What time should I cook brunch?"

"Eleven-thirty," I said, thinking that Dylan was working out very well.

Dani and Rule Number One sat together on the couches. I could tell, just from the expressive look on their faces, that they were gossiping. Their animated chat dropped to a whisper as I approached, sitting down adjacent to them. Rule Number One shot me that devil grin, and I thought how everything was so much better between us when no one else was around. Wondering if we could learn to be that way around other people, I thought of something Nicky Mack once said:

Where the willingness is great, the difficulties cannot be great.

Only Nicky Mack never met Rule Number One. I finished my calvados, and Rule Number One shot me her smoldering glance; she wanted to go downstairs. We had yet to consummate our weekend, and as was usually the case, she was more in a hurry to do this than I was. I liked to wait until the dance party had started, when everyone was upstairs being loud. Besides, I relished the exchanges that led up to our finally being alone. It was almost like foreplay to the foreplay. Only Rule Number One frequently lacked the patience for actual foreplay. She wanted to fast-forward to the good part, while I wanted to draw it out. It was as if I were the woman and she were the man. Then I realized that my notion of working through our challenging differences—as well as her behavior—was just one more gender role reversal. I was like one of those women who, after taming the Bad Boy for a short spell, mistook her own powers, believing that she could change him forever.

*   *   *

On Saturday morning, I pedaled down to the dock to pick up the oysters and it dawned on me that we didn't have an oyster knife. The last time I had shucked oysters, I had improvised with an old screwdriver and a bent butter knife, and it left chips of shell in the liquor. After picking up my styrofoam container from Dean's Seafood at the dock, I stepped into The Inn, where Larry, the Cole family patriarch, stood near the service bar.

"Hey, Larry? Do you have an oyster knife that I could borrow?"

"Hang on a second." He disappeared into the kitchen and returned with a well-worn oyster knife, a dull, double-edged blade with a bent tip. I thanked him and began pedaling back to the house. Kismetians are great about lending all sorts of stuff—tools, cooking equipment...wives. We had to, because we were all on an island together. People regularly borrowed stuff from me as well, and I liked being able to give someone what they needed—especially when it was something obscure. In Kismet, it is a point of pride to drop what you're doing to help someone out. Everyone does this because we are literally all in the same boat. As I rode back to my house, I was thinking how this was a very different mentality from that other island where I live. Then, while parking my bike, I was approached by a guy that I barely knew from another sharehouse further south on Pine Walk—who explained that their propane tank had run out in the middle of their barbecue. I took him up to the deck and lent him one of my spare tanks.

Out on the deck, Maggie was leading an informal yoga class. It was pretty funny to watch Maurice sandwiched among five woman, all of their butts sticking up in the air in Downward Dog. On the other side of them, Dylan began teaching people how to properly shuck an oyster and they assembled half-shells on trays of ice. In the kitchen, Tracy began mixing up a mignonette sauce with champagne vinegar. I made Bloody Mary mix at the wet bar and then steamed two dozen jumbo shrimp.

Bloody Marys are a curious drink. If I were to tap a beer in the morning, even in my house, people would crack hair-of-the-dog jokes about starting early, but Bloody Marys—even though they are made with hard liquor— enjoy a popular status of alcoholic immunity. I rimmed the tall beer glasses with Old Bay seasoning, gave them a scoop of ice, filled the glasses half with vodka, half with the mix, and then curled a jumbo shrimp over the rim (a touch I stole from the Mermaid Inn in the East Village) right next to a slitted lime wheel. Before making my own, I remembered another variation from Jefferson, the restaurant in the Village where I had tended bar. I poured some of the mix into a shaker and added a pinch of wasabi, shaking it up before pouring it over tequila and ice.

Eggs and bacon and rosemary home fries were carried out to the deck and placed next to the raw oysters and mignonette sauce.

Maurice sipped his Bloody Mary. "Yoga and then Bloodies. This is a pretty nice way to start the day."

Back in the kitchen, I spotted the plastic container that bore what remained of the steak tartare from the night before and decided to have an all-raw brunch. Rule Number One approached the kitchen.

"Would you like some steak tartare?"

"Sure," she said.

I began plating a serving for us to share and Rule Number One grabbed the bag of thick-cut chips.

"I'm feeling a bit decadent," I said. In place of chips, I angled two strips of crispy bacon into that mound of raw meat.

*   *   *

Saturday was one of those great August beach days, with a steady breeze blowing beneath a cloudless sky. Joe and I interspersed round after round of bocce with dips in the surf. Further east, Alexis, the topless fisherman, was casting out her clam bellies with both nipples blazing. More than once I followed Rule Number One into the water, swimming out to meet her in the surf. Later that afternoon, after most of the families had gone home and the crests of the waves began turning silver, I returned to the house, where Vanessa was preparing snacks to accompany our homebrew. Downstairs, I stuck our pony keg of blackberry wheat ale into our deep-fry pot and poured ice around it. Dylan helped me carry this and the CO2 tank down to the beach. Vanessa and Mandy carried platters of almond-stuffed dates that had been wrapped in prosciutto and then baked.

We were joined by people from Bicycle Bill's and Abby and Sabrina's house, as well as a few random stragglers, all of us reaching for the dates that were soft and crispy and salty and sweet, washing them down with blackberry wheat ale until the pony keg was kicked.

*   *   *

Later that night, we sat down to two huge trays of paella and pitchers of sangria prepared by Maggie. Forking up a bite of chorizo and shrimp covered in that saffron-infused rice, I thought that this had been the most epicurean weekend, starting with the tartare on Friday night and just continuing with great things to eat and drink all weekend long. After dinner, Dylan brought up his guitar. I pulled one off the wall, and we got in tune.

"Play a chord," he said to me.

"What chord?"

"It doesn't matter. Play a G."

I played a G and he matched it, and then we just started strumming, synching up in a rhythm that sounded vaguely familiar.

"What is that?" he asked.

"I don't know."

We kept strumming and then the song came to me. I stepped up to an A and Dylan followed. We both began singing at the same time:

"Wasting away again in Margaritaville..."

People began to laugh, pointing a finger at me and exclaiming that "Margaritaville" was banned.

Matt sat down with us and began keeping time on an African drum. After "Margaritaville," we began playing all of the banned songs, doing "Brown-Eyed Girl" and then "You Shook Me All Night Long," which segued into "Hotel California." The handy thing about the banned songs was that people knew the words and could sing along.

Mandy, who had knocked back more than a few glasses of sangria, grabbed one of the hula hoops and set it in motion around her hips, keeping time to the song. "Hotel California" is not the fastest song in the world, and I almost couldn't believe how slow Mandy could move while still keeping the hoop aloft. If hula hooping is sexy, slow hula hooping is like porn. Wearing only a jean miniskirt, halter top, and flip-flops, Mandy just stood there, writhing, her taut belly undulating with the slow knock of her hips as she mouthed the words with her eyes closed, turning in a slow circle as her hands clutched the air above her head. It was damn-near hypnotic and when we arrived at the part of the song where the lyrics ended, I stopped strumming. Dylan nodded insistently at me to continue playing rhythm while he soloed, and we kept Mandy in motion for another time around on the guitar.

Afterward, people began calling out obscure songs, and we gave them the college try. From "Puff the Magic Dragon" to the theme song from *Diff'rent Strokes,* we banged them all out. Then someone yelled out, "Play Kumbaya!"

Everyone laughed.

"Try it in A," Dylan said.

Five seconds later, they were all singing the chorus:

"Kumbaya my Lord, Kumbaya..."

Everyone was in stitches—only they were laughing in a way that our performance didn't quite seem to merit. I looked around, and Maggie, covering her mouth with a hand, pointed toward the loveseats near the stairwell to Baltic. I stood and saw what held their attention: Mandy and Chris were making out in full view. I cranked a fist in the air and began cracking up.

"*Kumbaya my Lord.*" We all sang even louder. "*Kum-ba-ya...*"

Natasha rose up from the couch. "I'm going to bed," she said. "Goodnight." She walked downstairs. (In the way that Stoner Jeffrey was the person most disturbed by Wayne, I wondered if superflirt Natasha thought that Mandy had gone too far.)

Maggie grabbed the folder containing lyric and chord sheets and began rifling through the pages.

"Can you play this one?" She handed me the sheet. It was Tom Petty's "American Girl," a song she regularly punched up on the jukebox at The Inn.

"Sure," Dylan said.

"*Well, she was an American girl, raised on promises...*"

Like the girl in the song, Maggie had also been raised on promises, expected to have every opportunity afforded men while replicating the domestic home life with which she grew up. I wondered if this overload of expectations fueled the Paris Hilton Generation—if girls like Dani didn't look at women like Maggie and feel overwhelmed by the prospect of Having It All, if being shoulder candy armed with credit cards didn't seem more manageable.

I've gone out on enough dates with women like Maggie—attractive career women in their early thirties. Sometimes, looking into their eyes was like beholding rising floodwaters. I used to think that these women were falling hard for me until I realized that I was merely Good Enough. These women didn't have time to fall in love. As soon as they met a guy who was Good Enough, they pushed a little button somewhere and were imbued with InstaLove. So long as the guy was Good Enough, whomever he was mattered about as much as whomever the guy was in a porno, mattered about as much as Joseph did to Mary. The Good Enough Guy was just a stand-in with certain responsibilities, walking across the stage of these busy women's lives. These women made their own love because it was all about them; it was all about them because how could it possibly be about anyone else when they had been saddled with so many promises to keep? Promises made by a previous generation of women who didn't have to contend with CrackBerrys and sixty-hour workweeks. I only hoped that Maggie actually wanted all of these things, that she wasn't trying in vain to live out someone else's excessive expectations. I thought that the girl in Tom Petty's song was someone who had lost her naiveté. I wondered if Maggie—despite being caught in the throes of this all-consuming competition—wasn't also someone who *"couldn't help thinking that there was a little more to life—somewhere else."*

I looked right at her when I sang:

"God, it's so painful
When something that's so close
Is still so far out of reach."

While Maggie could hardly hold a tune, she sang along with verve and I admired how she belted out the song in the best way that she knew how.

"She was an American girl..."

*   *   *

After we hung up the guitars, Maggie approached me.

"Can I talk to you for a minute?"

"Sure." I followed her downstairs into Penn, the smallest room in the house, normally reserved for couples.

"Is there any way that I could have a private room tonight?"

Whenever a room was empty on a Friday or Sunday night, I would first give a heads-up to Maggie and let her have a room to herself—a thank you for having helped me set up the house back in 2004. But this was Saturday.

"There's no way. We're jam-packed."

"Well..." She blushed. "I would be sharing it with someone else."

"Who?!"

"Maurice."

"No shit." I began to laugh. "Has this been going on for a while?"

"Not really," she said. "Maybe a couple of weeks. It's totally confidential."

"Not for long." I hugged her. "Is this serious?"

"I'm not sure," she said. "We'll see."

"Have you met up in the City?"

"Uh-huh."

In Kismet, many hookups never go beyond the beach; meeting up in the City was a stamp of validation.

"So it's serious," I said.

"I don't think it's *that* serious," she said. "I just want to see what happens."

The year before, Maggie had starting dating a guy and was soon cruising upon a plane of expectations that rose up to a point of hyperventilation, whereupon she lost all contact with the situation on the ground. Now, she looked happy in a more modest, grounded way, and I realized that I had her all wrong.

"Why don't you take this room," I said. "It's the coziest."

"Thanks."

"The Lovely Miss Margaret is gonna get her freak on."

"That's right." A look of focus came over her face as she stepped into the hall to fetch a set of full-sized sheets.

Back upstairs, Dani was plugging her iPod into the stereo. She cued up the song "Milkshake" by Kelis, a hesitant look coming over her face when she saw me. She didn't know that I happen to love that song.

"Crank it up," I said.

"You *like* that song?" Matt asked me.

"It's a catchy tune," I said, grooving to those Middle Eastern tones. Rule Number One shot me that coy look that I found irresistible: She wanted to go downstairs. I thought about her near insatiable drive—but she was in her late thirties, that age when a lot of women find their sex drives red-lining. Still, that I was the brakes and she was the gas was just another dimension of our role reversals—only when she sidled up to me...well...let's just say that her milkshake brought this boy to the yard.

"Let's go," I said, slipping discreetly down the stairs. Or so I thought.

"Goodnight, John!" Dani called out. "Goodnight, Rule!"

The rest of them joined in. "Goodnight, John! Goodnight, Rule!"

"Goodnight!" I called out to them, laughing.

Downstairs, I crawled into bed and watched Rule Number One undress. She covered the delicate lip of her belly as she approached the bed.

"Go stand in the corner," I said.

She let off a nervous laugh.

"Just do it." I got out of bed and sat down at my desk. "Go stand over there." I pointed toward my closet. She backed into the corner and folded her arms in front of her breasts. "Drop your hands."

"Why?"

"Because I asked you to."

She dropped her hands at her sides, and her face flushed red. "What are you doing?"

"I just want to look at you."

"You look at me all the time."

"Not like this."

She started to approach the bed.

"Wait," I said. "Just stand still."

"Why?"

"Just stand there for a minute. You're not coming out of that corner until I feel you've matured."

She laughed and returned to the corner, dropping her hands. Had all of those gossip rags convinced her that she didn't stack up to anorexic celebrities? Maybe she thought she wasn't tall enough or thin enough, and despite the number of times I had told her how much I liked her body, she shook it off. It was tough to curb her jokiness when we were alone. She was always whipping up drama and excitement, grooving in her drive as though she needed to constantly distract herself. I thought of how easily she allowed herself to get carried away with other people, how unself-conscious she could be (like when I came across her performing a mock striptease in the jacuzzi). Yet when we were alone, she resisted getting carried away with me.

"What?" She fidgeted. "What?"

"You're a fine looking woman," I said, "and I just want to get a good look at you."

Her cheeks and the skin over her collarbones flushed red, and I watched her chest rise and fall.

*   *   *

On Sunday morning, a breeze blew against the blinds, letting in the sun. Rule Number One began to stir.

"How did you sleep?" I asked her.

"Really good." She rubbed the sleep from her eyes.

It pleased me in no small way that Rule Number One had never experienced one of her night terrors when we slept together.

Curling against me, she revealed that a few house members had begun lobbying her to put in a good word for them with me, hoping that I would invite them back in 2006. I laughed. It was funny to me how some people could forget that their behavior had consequences, until late August when they suddenly realized that in 2006 there would actually be—get ready for this one—another summer.

Men are so simple and yield so readily to the desires of the moment.

Of all these people, I was most puzzled that Mandy had petitioned Rule Number One. While Mandy was hardly the most epicurean house member, I had never painted her row red. Apparently, Mandy was concerned about her standing because of her—for lack of a better term—involved sociability, especially on the dance floor at The Out, which on at least one occasion culminated with tennis-court sex. Mandy didn't understand that I only cared about two things: that people are considerate and that they are good with money. And Mandy—despite having twice reminded her—had blown off paying me for Uptalking Nancy's Labor Day spot. A line in my spreadsheet would show a balance of $265 until she settled up, but as Nicky Mack said:

The wise man does at once what the fool does finally.

Mandy didn't get that I couldn't care if she made out with the entire dishwashing staff at The Out; I didn't care if she had tennis-court sex with Andre Agassi. People's romantic or sexual desires are their own business and do not necessarily determine how they stack up as human beings. (If you doubt even for a second that that is true, ask yourself if we were better off under Bill Clinton or George Bush and then consider their respective sex lives.)

I explained this to Rule Number One, confident that it would make its way back to Mandy and spare me from having to ask her a third time for her balance. Still, I wished the level of gossip, hadn't become toxic. Even house members like Maggie fell victim to anything remotely juicy and then began trucking in it themselves. It was starting to get to me, only I had no idea that I was two seconds away from becoming a party to the worst of it.

"Guess who Gay Clay made out with?"

"Was it a person of the female persuasion?"

"Uh-huh."

"That doesn't really surprise me. I don't know. Who?"

"Tina."

"What?!"

Rule Number One was beaming. "One night, Joe got wasted and passed out and Tina ended up on the loveseat next to Gay Clay and they had themselves a little drunken makeout session."

Joe and I had been friends for ten years, and he and Tina had been dating for more than three. Everyone who knew them assumed that they had paid their toll on the marriage turnpike and were now cruising down the left lane.

"When did this happen?"

An exuberant look came over Rule Number One's face. "Was there some weekend when Clay took off really early on Sunday morning?"

It was the weekend when I had hooked up with Julianne, when Tracy supposedly walked in on Dylan, when the level of sexual energy in the house was almost crackling.

"Yeah. He was running late for a boat, but he actually took the time to pay me what he owed for the weekend."

"That's when it happened," she said. "He was all freaked out and so on Sunday morning he just took off."

"That's why he was so cagey." I shook my head. "Goddamnit."

It hardly surprised me that "Gay Clay" wasn't really gay. I thought about all the closeted gays who are in no way effeminate but are rainbow striped through and through—from sheep-herding cowboys who don't prefer separate tents to blustery NeoCons working out their sexual frustration on the world stage. For every one of those alpha-male closeted cocksuckers there probably exists a sissified *Star*-magazine reading, E! Channel-watching, touchy-feely, femmy guy like Gay

Clay who is very much in the vagina business.

"I *knew* he wasn't gay," I said.

"Yeah, he's got his own little MO working there."

Was that what it was? Was Clay's *modus operandi* to get women to let down their guards with the sense of security they feel around gay men who, under Section 2c of the Gay Male Girlfriend Guidelines, are permitted to paw and kiss their female friends with abandon.

"Oh, fuck," I said.

Rule Number One didn't get that Joe had been dating Tina for three years, that they were on track to get married, that Joe was my friend, my good friend, and that for me to now be carrying around this information was a moral quandary. She didn't get it, because revelation is the best part of gossip and Rule Number One was still cruising on the buzz.

I climbed out of bed, pulled on my Bermuda shorts, and stepped into my Crocs.

"I'm going to get the papers." I grabbed my billfold to settle up at the Kismet Market, only it felt thin, so I grabbed my wallet. I wasn't sure what kind of tab we had racked up that week, and I wanted to make sure I could cover the damage.

Baked Alaska

I was sitting at my desk on Friday when Chris knocked on my door.

"Hey, John?"

"Yeah?"

"I'd like to make Baked Alaska this weekend."

"Baked Alaska?"

"Yeah, I was wondering if maybe I could make it for dessert on Saturday night."

His request caught me off guard. While I had heard of Baked Alaska, I had vaguely thought that it involved salmon, not having known that it was a dessert.

"Let's see." I checked the cooking schedule. "Tracy's grilling rack of lamb. She doesn't have a dessert penciled in. Sure, that would be great. What do you need?"

"I think we have everything. I'm going to need a shitload of eggs."

"We've always got a shitload of eggs," I said.

"Great." His face lit up.

I turned back toward my screen, but I couldn't stop thinking about the strangeness of Chris's request. Then I realized that it wasn't strange at all. The man stepped up to make Baked Alaska for all of us. This was exactly what I had set out to accomplish from the very beginning.

*   *   *

Later that afternoon, Mandy knocked on my door. She paid her food and booze balance as well as the $265 that she owed for the Labor Day spot. While it could have been a coincidence, I could only guess that word of how to help her standing had filtered down from Rule Number One.

During the cocktail hour, the sun began to fall behind shredded layers of clouds, the kind that make for the most spectacular sunsets. We were visited by a married couple who were friends of Mandy's. The previous

213

winter, she had brought them to Matt's pajama party; now they were staying in Saltaire, where the woman's parents owned a house. Both of them were a bit buttoned up for Kismet—he wore khakis and a pressed linen shirt, while a conservative-looking maternity dress hung over her engorged belly. She wore an uncomfortable expression—as though everything around her was icky—casting a horrific glance at the drip tray on the kegerator. Both of them were attorneys, and the guy made a point of explaining that they wanted to buy a house on Fire Island, but right now, with their baby on the way, they just didn't have time to look around. They wandered around the house like appraisers, asking a number of informed questions about the renovations and finishes. When they saw the bathroom covered with money, the woman's jaw dropped. Most people, upon first taking in the pennies, let out a holy-shit laugh and tell me how cool they think it is. This woman was just plain confused, and the guy laughed nervously, visibly rubbed the wrong way by something they found subversive. I think I liked that reaction even more.

"What do you charge for a share?" he asked.

"$1775."

"So," he cocked his head to the side. "How much money are you making doing this?"

While it wasn't the first time I had been asked that question, it never ceased to shock me that certain people were so brazen as to ask it. (There is only one question concerning money that socially acceptable New Yorkers can ask one another, and that question is How Much Do You Pay in Rent? That's it.)

"I'm cleaning up," I said. "I'm easily clearing a hundred a summer because I only paid fifty grand for this house and a team of fairy-fucking-elves did my renovations for free. And while we're asking personal questions, I couldn't help but wonder if the wifey here takes it up the Hershey Highway?"

(As politesse is a two-way street, my not having actually said this had less to do with respect than the icky look on his wife's face that made me doubt if even oral sex was on the menu.)

Aside from the rudeness of such a question, I resented it because my financial situation—solely with respect to Chance—is something I tried not to think about. Contrary to our contemporary notion most succinctly expressed by Snoop Doggy Dogg, I did everything in my power to *not* have my mind on my money and my money on my mind. My two properties and all my debts were interwoven parts of my portfolio. While all the costs associated with my renovations exist in my spreadsheet as cost basis and expenses, I purposely never totaled those costs, because part of me was afraid that I'd find that number too staggering, and that it might compromise my enjoyment of the house, or cause me to slouch toward chintzy-ness. I've willfully avoiding calculating a concrete bottom line with respect to the house, focusing instead on my overall debt, of which my West Harlem condo is a considerable factor.

Now this pressed-linen punk began asking about Matt's apartment in the City. (Matt had gutted and redesigned his apartment into the kind of pad that you see on TV shows set in Manhattan.) He then proceeded to ask some rather personal questions about my brother's real-estate development, which I also deflected.

"Man," he said, looking out at the ocean from the deck. "You guys are set up."

People frequently, inappropriately, grouped Matt and me together. Matt was a wildly successful real-estate developer with a team of employees doing cutting-edge condo conversions; I was a struggling writer who happened into owning a beach house. If Matt was Tiger Woods, I was Bill Murray in *Caddyshack*. Other misconceptions abounded—like the one where Matt bought Chance and gave it to me to run, or that well-heeled parents gave us property.

My father is a civil engineer who used to perform home inspections after work and during the weekends to send us to a private school outside of Paterson's substandard school district. For almost forty years now, he has worked for the City of Paterson's Department of Redevelopment. My parents still live in the same house in Paterson where we grew up, the last of the Caucasians on their tree-lined block on the other side of town from the Red, White and Blue Thrift Store where our millionaire mother purchased our school clothes secondhand.

In 1995, shortly after I had returned from France, and Matt had just graduated from college, we found a dumpy apartment to rent in Hoboken. Our parents took us to dinner at Margherita's, a local Italian restaurant, where, seated in one of the bay windows, my father said the following:

"You guys should look into buying something here."

I had just begun working at the Authors Guild at an entry-level salary, so the prospect of buying real estate made me feel like a six-year-old stepping into FAO Schwarz with five bucks in my pocket. (Also, I harbored this stupid notion that buying real estate was somehow antithetical to becoming a writer or an artist.) I do remember, however, seeing Matt's wheels begin to turn. The following year, he bought a two-bedroom apartment, and I began paying him rent. After living with Matt for a couple of years, I got religion once I ran the numbers and learned that I could own my own place for less than I was shelling out to my landlord brother in rent. My family consulted me through my purchase of a beat-up one-bedroom railroad apartment on Willow Avenue in Hoboken for which I paid $78,000. (While this happened as recently as 1998, I now feel like an old codger reminiscing about gas that cost a buck-twenty-five a gallon.)

Matt then purchased a second apartment in Hoboken and was working as a real-estate banker. He eventually quit that job and started his own business to train credit analysts. That business didn't work out quite the way he had hoped, but instead of tucking his tail between his legs, he cashed out of Hoboken and rolled the proceeds into a run-down brownstone in Manhattan, where he began plowing through the red tape of a condo conversion. After construction began, he lined up a string of investors and purchased a second building to convert to condos. He then quit his banking job and established Blesso Properties.

Meanwhile, gentrification had swept though Hoboken, and the one-bedroom I had fixed up had almost tripled in value. I cashed out and purchased my one-bedroom condo in West Harlem, renovating it myself. I had benefited from my access to the best resources imaginable: my brother's understanding of the New York City marketplace; my father's structural knowledge and lifelong pursuit of urban renewal; my parents' excellent taste and suggestions for fixtures and renovations (not to mention my mother's enthusiasm to swing a paint brush and my father's continued willingness to serve as my de facto electrician, architect, and construction manager).

Once Blesso Properties took off and Matt began hiring employees, a lot of people began to liken Matt to Donald Trump. He is absolutely not Donald Trump. Aside from the fact that he doesn't date women a third his age, or wrap around his head a single strand of hair that is nineteen feet long, our parents—unlike Trump's father—were hardly rich. I don't care if people wrongly think this about me, or if they remain convinced that my brother is the real owner of Chance, but it's ugly that some people feel the need to undercut Matt, who achieved his success through hard work, a persistent willingness to roll the dice following setbacks, and by possessing an industrial-sized set of rocks.

For these people—who pissed away tens of thousands of dollars on rent during a booming real-estate market instead of building up equity—it's probably easier to reconcile their own lack of testicular fortitude with the notion that Matt had some kind of advantage, that like Trump, we had a father who set us up. In fact, what our parents provided in abundance was encouragement, information, and excellent advice. They put in the time looking at countless properties (especially with Matt), helping us sort through potential purchases to see if they made sense.

So anyone who thinks that I was somehow "set up" is absolutely right. I was lucky enough to be surrounded by people who were smart, savvy, and who—despite being put by me through rigors that other families would have never stood for—also happened to love me unconditionally. This was how we were set up and it was a *huge* advantage. It was like stepping up to the plate with an assfull of steroids. This is something that Pressed Linen and his prego wife will probably never understand.

Recently, the National Merit Scholarship Corporation tried to find common hobbies or habits shared by whiz kids. They wanted to see if playing the violin or studying Mandarin or practicing Norwegian yodeling somehow bolstered academic performance. It turned out that the interests and fascinations of smart kids were as varied as they were for the rest of us. Nevertheless, they did find one common thread: These kids came from families that regularly ate dinner together. Meanwhile, an overwhelming majority of American kids no longer eat regular meals with their families. For me, this was like learning that large quantities of gin prevented Alzheimer's, or that a diet rich in pork fat lowers your cholesterol. Think of it: All those kids being shuttled from fencing class to their Japanese tutors will never be able to compete with your kids so long as you get home from work in time to eat dinner with them.

Even if Pressed Linen and his wife were to learn about that study, they'd probably dismiss the results, preferring to put in seventy-hour workweeks to adorn themselves in overpriced baubles, making sure that their kids Have All Of The Best Things, discounting their absenteeism, and doping up their overscheduled superachiever children on a bunch of pharmaceutical drugs, never understanding that being there trumps being rich.

"So," he said, "if you don't mind me asking—"

"I'm sorry," I said. "I have to go take care of something."

I went downstairs and outside, where I unlocked one of the rusted beach cruisers and coasted down the ramp. I pedaled over to West Lighthouse Walk and turned right, riding down to its secluded slip to the bay, where I could get a good look at the garish pink and blue patchwork of the sunset in peace.

Afterward, I stopped in front of a dilapidated single-story house on the eastern side of West Lighthouse. Its posts badly needed to be replaced, the house literally sinking into the ground. Before buying Chance, I had almost bought this house. It had four bedrooms and an efficiency in back. I had planned on running it as-is for a summer and then adding a second story and a roof deck. It was owned by a rather emotionally troubled old lady who apparently didn't have any friends or family. Ali Beqaj, my broker, put in an incredible amount of time trying to make the deal happen, but the seller was being difficult. Two months after she had accepted my offer, after Ali and I had bent over backward for her, she decided that she wanted ten thousand dollars more. (I later heard a rumor that another broker—clueless as to how difficult this woman was—had whispered in her ear that he could get her more money for her house.) I told Ali to tell her in whatever way he thought appropriate to go piss up a tree. Still, it felt like a huge setback. There weren't many houses on the market, and I wondered if I would find another suitable one in time for the 2004 season.

"What about that two-story house you told me about on the ocean block?" Matt had said to me.

"Echo Beach? There's no way I can afford that."

"How do you know?"

"Because it costs almost twice as much."

"Sure," Matt said. "But it would probably cost a lot less to renovate. And with a bigger house you can fit more shares. Money's cheap right now, and when money is cheap—"

"Debt is your friend," I said, repeating his mantra.

"Exactly. So if you're willing to take on that debt, your carrying costs might not be that much more."

We plugged in conservative numbers, and the number at the bottom was better than I had imagined. I landed on Echo Beach, the house that ultimately became Chance.

Now, staring at this shit-heap on rotting posts that was almost mine, I shook my head. The collapse of that deal was the luckiest thing that had ever happened to me. Having a house on the ocean block is just a different experience. Aside from the beach being that much closer to the food and the bathrooms, that I can see and hear the waves from inside my house and from my deck is something that, for me, cannot be calculated in a spreadsheet.

If the rumor about that other broker was true, my good fortune came to me by the grace of another man's treachery. For me, that is just a mindfuck. Although, I could think of other instances when what seemed like the worst turn of events ended up working out for the better—like when my inability to land an interview in 2002 led me to begin working for myself. I remembered a line from some forgotten Mickey Rourke movie, when, in the middle of a botched heist, his partner whined that everything was going wrong.

"Nothing goes wrong," Mickey Rourke responded. *"It just goes."*

After closing on the house, I understood more than ever that life was just a gamble, and that the only secret was to keep playing, because so much of life came down to Chance.

"Nothing goes wrong," I said, pedaling away. "It just goes."

*   *   *

Back at the house, Mandy's friends had left, while Matt, Martin, PI, and Sonia had arrived. Martin was out on the deck, grilling ribeyes. I approached the wet bar to mix up a Manhattan, bracing myself for more drama, but Sonia sat on the couch, away from Martin, chatting with Charlotte. (Remember that Martin had dated Charlotte the previous winter...) It was the first time I had seen Sonia appear truly relaxed and comfortable in the house. When she saw me, she stood and gave me a warm hug hello.

Martin carried his platter of ambrosia inside, and we sat around the table, scarfing down those fatty strips along with fried spinach and garlic bread. Amazingly, Martin sat at the far end of the table, while Sonia sat across from me. Watching Sonia and Martin now, sitting apart from one another and conversing with other people, I wondered if they were finally through with the contract negotiation phase, if maybe they finally understood each other. Looking at the two of them now, I thought they might even be perfect for one another.

No one had made dessert, and so people began pouring crème de cassis over scoops of vanilla ice cream. I experienced a sensation that I remember from childhood, where, after dessert (especially after ice cream), I want to eat more of what I just had for dinner. All that remained of the ribeye platter, however, was a red-black pool of congealing fat and blood. I sliced a ciabatta roll in half and dropped the cut side into the platter, then coated it with salt and slid it in the toaster. Impatient, I grabbed a piece of garlic bread to mop up some of the juice.

"I dare you to do a tray lick," Matt said.

I've always been a sucker for a good dare, and of course Matt knew this. I reached for the twenty-four-inch platter and gave it an extra sprinkle of salt.

"Oh, no, John, that is foul," Tracy said.

"John, do *not* do that," Grace said.

I looked across the table at Sonia, this new-and-improved Sonia, and decided to leave it up to her.

"Do it," she said.

The rest of them groaned as I raised the corner to my mouth, drinking it all down and then licking the platter clean.

"Nice," Sonia said.

*   *   *

On Saturday, Tracy and I were sprawled out on the beach, lost in the throes of a trash-talking Scrabble match when, to the left of the dune crossing, I spotted Joochan pitching to Martin, PI. While hardly throwing heat, Joo-chan's pitches made a distinct thwack in Martin's mitt. Despite his relaxed windup, I admired the grace of his form and tried to picture him on the mound, that moment of concentration before firing off his best stuff.

In 1996, eight years before meeting Joo-chan, I created Joe D., one of the main characters in *Killing Mercutio*. Joe D. was an All-American quarterback who, during his junior year of college, suffered a career-ending injury. He ended up going to law school, converting all his muscle mass to fat, and then drinking to stave off the reality that his life was not going to unfold the way he had originally planned. Essentially, I had wanted to create a character who occupied the loftiest perch in popular American culture, a golden boy who hit his apex at twenty, only to lose it all and then have to figure out his second act in life. After a couple of messy years, Joe D. ultimately learned (years before I was forced to do the same after shelving *Killing Mercutio*) to find happiness elsewhere and to move on. It was sometimes strange to behold Joo-chan, a guy that practically sprang from the pages of my novel.

Watching our unemployed pitcher, I remembered how I felt after having stalled out on *Killing Mercutio*; but writing—most unlike pitching—hardly required peak physical health and performance, nor were writers limited to publishing something during their twenties. Even during those dark days, I still held out hope that I would eventually start writing again, whereas Joo-chan, after having come within striking distance of every boy's dream, had to then swallow that he was never going to pitch in the majors. I just had no idea what it might be like to—

"Hey, John?" Tracy said. "You do know it's your turn, right?"

"Oh, yeah, I'm sorry."

"Take your time," she said, lighting a cigarette. "I just wanted to make sure that you knew it was your turn."

"Thanks." I shook my head. "I know, I've got to get cracking here." I began jockeying my tiles and surveying the situation, trying to find my words.

*   *   *

Reason #237 that I'm thankful to no longer work in an office is that I no longer have to shave every day. Doing it every day inflamed my neck, but the business-casual dress code dictated that a red, scraped neck trumped a day of stubble. At the beach, I settled into shaving on a weekly basis. Since there weren't many occasions that called for a clean face in Kismet, I took to shaving on Saturday before dinner. As this was the only time that the whole house was regularly assembled, sitting down to eat our largest, most elaborate meal with a smooth face felt almost like putting on my Sunday best before going off to church.

I was Tracy's grillman for rack of lamb, which she served with fig chutney. During the salad course that followed, Chris began beating egg whites and sugar for the meringue that would coat his Baked Alaska. I removed the entire cheese drawer from the fridge and began assembling a plate, while Chris pulled the pound cake he had baked from scratch and then inlaid with vanilla ice cream from the freezer. After coating it with meringue, he slid that cinder block of goodness into the oven. When he pulled it out a few minutes later, the crests of the meringue were golden brown. I doused it with 151 rum, and Chris set it ablaze. He sliced it up and served us. It was warm and light on the outside, while still cold and dense in the middle, and for a little while the table was quiet.

After dessert, Natasha led the cleaning brigade. I poured a snifter of brandy and sat down at the table next to Joo-chan. Having begun his cocktail hour early, Joo-chan was faced, his complexion flushed red from the booze.

He started to blab about having hooked up with Uptalking Nancy.

"I mean, Charlotte's pretty good, but she doesn't hold a can-dle to Nancy."

Mandy, who was friends with Charlotte, rose from the table, disgusted.

Watching Joo-chan, I remembered how I had only been out of work for a number of weeks before being unemployed started to fuck with me; Joo-chan had stopped playing baseball a couple of years ago. Besides, I had never nursed any dreams of fetching children at school in the Nanny Major League. Losing that job didn't screw with my identity (although having to shelve my novel certainly did). Like Joe D., Joo-chan had a lot on the ball, only his exceptional intelligence didn't seem to be helping him. I hoped that Joo-chan would get a job, any job, and that, like Joe D., he might climb out of his hole. I got up from the table and left Joo-chan sitting by himself, red-faced, shaking his head.

*   *   *

When we walked in to The Out, the DJ was playing a hip-hop track and Natasha made a beeline for the dance floor, probably figuring that she had to get while the getting was good. She was followed by Risa, Martin, and Sonia. Near the bar, I spotted the Rule-*age* I had once seen at The Inn. From behind she was a dead ringer for Rule Number One, only the face framed in those dark curls was jarringly different. When I turned around, Natasha was dancing with Johnny Thunder, who was wearing a glo-stick necklace. Some guy approached Risa, who perked up upon being chatted up. It felt like one of those nights when a collective mood was in the air—as though someone had slipped the whole town a mickey. In the maddening way that I sometimes check for a lost item a second time in the same place, I stole another glance at the Rule-age, only to once again experience the anticlimax of her not being as comely as Rule Number One.

I was shaken from my reverie when the DJ cued up "Your Love" by The Outfield, a track that I happened to love, but one that left Natasha sighing. We left The Out for The Inn, where Huge Hefner—a local band ostensibly named for its rotund lead singer—was setting up a bongo station next to the mic. I walked out to the deck, where I joined a group of house members sitting around one of the outdoor tables. Rufus, dominating the conversation, referred to the *New York Times* as a left-wing paper.

"Why do you think the *New York Times* is a left-wing paper?" I asked.

"Because it is," he said. "*The New York Times* is a left-wing newspaper."

"Is it the job of left-wing newspapers to help the Bush Administration lie its way into Iraq?"

"Well, that's just one—"

"Look," I said, cutting him off, "I don't care that you work for Fox News, I really don't. But don't give me that liberal-news-media bullshit when you work for a network that has become a propaganda arm for the Bush Administration."

"First of all, the news media *does* have a liberal bias, and second of all, Fox News is not propaganda."

"That's horseshit!" I pointed a finger at him. "Where was this 'liberal news media' when we rushed off half-cocked into Iraq?! Look, Rufus, I don't begrudge you your paycheck, but your network is a fucking joke."

"Oh. And CNN isn't a joke?"

"They're not disseminating lies the way you guys do, but they're a journalistic joke, too."

"We're not *disseminating lies*," he said, mockingly. "Besides, the fact of the matter is that our country *wanted* to go to war and we *wanted* to be lied to."

"The war was sold to us. And I don't want to be lied to. Do you want to be lied to?"

"People want to be lied to."

"Answer the fucking question. Do you, Rufus, want to be lied to?"

From the uncomfortable expression on Tracy's face, I realized that I was lacing into Rufus. Only he wore this smug little grin that made me wonder if he was baiting me and maybe even taking deviant pleasure in my reaction (the way Wayne did when he blasted the stereo at three a.m.). I remembered the weekend back in June when Uptalking Nancy returned to the house with her guest, Rory, and the glee with which Rufus went along with my ploy to kill Nancy with kindness, and how he got just a bit too into it.

I wondered if I was now feeling something that I had witnessed among so many other house members: people bothered by people who were like them but in a more extreme way. (Stoner Jeffrey being freaked out by Wayne; Mandy's public make-out session putting a bug up the ass of überflirt Natasha...) Rufus was an opinionated generalist. Just like me. Only he was quite a bit louder. And quite a bit—No, fuck that. Rufus was nothing like me. He had no understanding of measured doses. This was something he would either figure out on his own or he wouldn't—only I decided that I was through defending him. Huge Hefner launched into their set, and I got up from the table.

Walking toward the bar, I was thinking that I had deteriorated into a rather testy bastard. It was as though my nerves had worn thin, and I realized that, in fact, they had. A touch of sexual frustration wasn't helping matters, either, though it had only been six days since I had last seen Rule Number One, and six days is not a long time. I turned to approach the bar when I spotted Matt walking into The Inn wearing a *lucha libre* wrestling mask laced up behind his head. You might wonder how I knew it was him; well, he's my brother and I can pick out his idiosyncrasies a mile away. Also, who else would walk into The Inn wearing a *lucha libre* mask? (Then again, it would hardly surprise me if Doctor Stern had such a mask in her arsenal of costumes. Besides, people in Kismet wear the strangest shit out to the bars all the time.)

The sight of Matt shaking hands with people made me laugh. At the bar, I caught the eye of Kevin the bartender and ordered a beer. The people grouped behind me began to laugh hysterically, crowding back against me. I spun around and saw what was cracking them up: Matt was playing the bongos along with Huge Hefner. The lead singer sidled up to Matt and faced him, pumping his fist while Matt's hands skittered across the drums. I've witnessed many ill-fated attempts by uninvited crowd members joining in with a live band, but Matt worked it. I don't think he could have pulled it off without the mask. It was just really funny, and the crowd was grooving to the sight of this masked man keeping time on the bongos.

After the song, the lead singer pulled Matt against him for a one-armed hug and congratulated the "masked man."

When I walked back outside, Rufus had taken off. The only people left at the table were Alan and Tracy. They both wore that odd look that I knew too well—a mix of apprehension, enthusiasm, and bashfulness. Like I said, it was just one of those nights in Kismet. I finished my beer and then left the two of them sitting alone at The Inn.

*   *   *

Early on Sunday morning, I found Rufus puttering around the kitchen. No one else was up.

"Oh, hey, John," he said. "I made waffles and bacon for everyone. Do you want some before I put these in the oven to keep warm?"

"Sure." Still pre-coffee, I shook my head, trying to wake up. "That would be great." I took two waffles and some bacon, and then Rufus covered the platter with a sheet of foil and put it in the oven, along with a plate of bacon. I placed a mug beneath the spout of the cappuccino machine and pressed the button.

"I've gotta work today," Rufus said, unplugging the waffle iron. "I wish I didn't have to rush out on such a nice day." He set down the gravy boat next to me.

"What's this?" I said.

"The blueberries were on their last legs, so I made blueberry syrup."

Risa wandered upstairs, rubbing her eyes. "Wow," she said. "Who made breakfast?"

"Rufus," I said.

"Guys, I've gotta run," Rufus said, shaking my hand. "John, always a pleasure. See you later." He grabbed his bag and walked out.

"Oh, wow," Risa said, opening the oven. "Look at all these waffles."

I poured Rufus's blueberry syrup over my waffles and forked up a bite.

"How are they?" Risa asked.

Rufus had put just enough butter in the mix to give his waffles crispy, golden edges. "They're delicious," I said, taking another bite.

Natasha and Tracy wandered upstairs, followed by Alan. "Who made breakfast?" Natasha asked.

Risa explained how Rufus had cooked us all breakfast before leaving for work.

"That was nice of him," Tracy said.

I chomped on a strip of bacon, thinking, That little fucker...

*   *   *

It was quite hot on Sunday afternoon, and there wasn't much of a breeze down on the beach where Jackson, Abby's boxer, got into a tussle with another dog. Panting heavily in the heat, Jackson collapsed onto his side. Abby called out his name. Then she screamed it. When she tried to rouse him, she discovered that his heart had stopped.

Jackson had been given to Abby as a Christmas present by Larry, her boyfriend, a couple of years before Larry became one of the 343 firefighters killed on 9/11. They had been living together for many years and had talked about marriage just before the attack. Despite Abby having paid the property taxes and half the mortgage on Larry's house, Larry didn't have a will, so the house went to Larry's mother, who slapped Abby with a ten-day notice to vacate the premises. (Whenever I dwelled on the pervasive shittiness of these post-9/11 years, I tried to remember how peripheral it was for me, and I didn't need to look any further than Abby to put my own crappy mood into perspective.) Jackson was Abby's last link to Larry and the years they had spent together before that terrible day.

A crowd of people circled Abby, yelling out all kinds of dog wisdom, until Pete, a Kismetian who owned boxers, broke through the crowd and crashed down next to Jackson, grabbing the dog's head and performing mouth-to-snout. Abby screamed at Jackson, trying to break through his unconsciousness as the minutes passed with Jackson lying in the sand, immobile, showing no sign of life. Jackson was eight, which, for the breed, apparently, was a bit long in the tooth. Still, Pete continued to pump the dog's rib cage and inflate its lungs, his cheeks covered with sand and Jackson's saliva. Abby took a step back, consumed with an almost dissociated dread.

That Abby and I both turned up in Kismet and fell into managing share-houses was probably not a coincidence. Her tragedy, of course, dwarfed mine. Aside from having shelved *Killing Mercutio*, I was sad for what felt like the loss of the soul of our country. What Abby lost was hardly abstract. Nevertheless, Abby also sought refuge in epicurean living, going so far as to spend eight months in Paris honing her cooking skills at the Cordon Bleu Institute. On the house web-site, I joke how the chefs at Chance were "classically untrained." Well, Abby was classically trained and her cooking showed it—even in such simple dishes as crêpes suzette that left me licking the Grand Marnier and butter from my plate.

For me, September 11, 2001, began when I bolted up in bed and saw the time on my clock—9:03. As I normally woke before eight, I jumped out of bed and pulled on my boots without socks, rushing downstairs. (I had probably been roused by the crash of the second plane into the south tower of the World Trade Center, just a mile or two south of my apartment on the top floor of Matt's building.) I was already three minutes late to park my motorcycle on the other side of West 20th Street for street cleaning restrictions and was hoping to get to my bike before the meter maid. The rest, of course, is overdocumented history. What I remember most from that day is trying to fall asleep that night. Even with my windows closed, I could still smell that appalling toxic stench. Lying awake in my stuffy room, I wished that I hadn't learned on the news that there were people trapped alive beneath the twisted, burning rubble, calling their family members from cell phones. I didn't sleep very well that night.

Still, I was one of the many New Yorkers who did not lose anyone close to me. This was lucky in more ways than one, because once the smoke cleared, there were no terrorists more significant than the American ones who begin fueling our hysteria, wielding color-coded fear to bypass the checks and balances that once protected us. If on top of all that I had also been saddled with the loss of a loved one, I would have fucking cracked. I would have landed on that square in Misanthropy Land where you take the express route to the terminus.

Or maybe I wouldn't have.

Maybe my self-preservation instincts would have kicked in and led me to do what Abby did, which was to stop watching and reading the news altogether (the way I did after shelving *Killing Mercutio*). It's a good thing I didn't know then that this massive loss of life was just the beginning, that this tragedy would be exploited to steal our country out from under us. Only this too would become apparent soon enough. Our state of affairs had only gotten worse with each passing year, and 2005—with still a third of the year to go—was already the shittiest.

Jackson still lay on his back, immobile. Pete, his sand-covered face now red as a beet from exertion, continued to inflate Jackson's lungs and pump his chest in vain, while Abby resigned herself to finally letting go of the last, best vestige of her life together with Larry—until Jackson's legs kicked and he struggled up to his feet, coughing and sputtering with life.

Labor Day

Low Country Boil

After the weekend, I was hardly surprised to pick up an e-mail from Tracy, asking to be scheduled in a private room with Alan during Labor Day weekend. Having already reconfigured the bed assignments to put Maggie and Maurice in Penn, I had to make a few more switches, but was able to schedule Tracy and Alan in Baltic.

Baltic is far and away the most interesting bedroom, because it didn't exist when I bought the house. On a cold, grim day in March 2004, I was moving around the house, wearing two sweatshirts and a wool cap. A heap of trash sat above the upstairs bathroom, beneath the peak of the house's open cathedral ceiling. I climbed up there, stepping carefully on the beams between the insulation as I threw down the trash. For the first time in that cold, drafty house, I began to sweat. My light bulb popped and I nailed down a couple sheets of plywood over those beams. Then I threw up a mattress, so that I could sleep in the highest (and hottest) point in the house. I then tacked up three dollar-store plastic tablecloths, both for privacy and to better trap the heat. Once the season started, I needed a place to store my tools, so I ran two-by-sixes from the edge of the "loft" over to the beam on the eastern wall, laying down more plywood and extending "Baltic," which, during that first season, became a guest bed. The following winter, Jim Wikso, my contractor, walled it off and added a window, giving the house its only bay view. I then built a ladder up to its hatch, closing it off with a trap door for privacy.

Only four feet high in the middle, Baltic is obviously the least desirable room in the house. Nevertheless, it does have its advantages. As there are normally only two people scheduled there, privacy is easier to arrange. Also, it is the only room in the house with a queen-sized mattress. In a further effort to compensate for its low ceiling, I painted the interior with the red paint left over from the house's exterior and added a floor-to-ceiling mirror on one of the walls. (All it lacked was a porno soundtrack.) So while Baltic lacked verticality, a few house members had appreciated what it offered horizontally. Now Tracy and Alan were going to become members of that club.

231

*   *   *

Upstairs, I fried some peppers and eggs for breakfast, then grabbed the OJ from the fridge. When I shook the container, the cap flew off, sending a stream of juice splattering over the floor.

"Who are these people?" I asked out loud to no one.

There are a couple of people in the house who, upon putting the caps back on containers and bottles, can't seem to trouble their wrists to twist the fuckers all the way back on. They do this with everything—with vodka and vinegar, with soda and soy sauce. It would be better if they just left the caps off, because some more responsible person would come along, see that the caps were missing, and replace them properly.

I mopped up the juice and then sat down to eat my cooling breakfast. Only the half-cappers began to eat away at me. I tried to stop thinking about them. Being careless was a part of being human, but if I thought about the half-cappers long enough, I'd begin to equate them with that dipshit Donald Rumsfeld and the rest of those chicken-hawk civilian planners who sent too small of a force off to Iraq without the proper body armor and without a plan to fight.

I knew that I needed to think less about our incompetent leaders, but I thought about them every day. Five years of ham-fisted shit-for-brains futility. Why couldn't I just tune them out? Slap a magnet on my tailgate stating my support for our troops and then put their state of affairs out of my mind? I wanted to forget about Iraq and George Bush (that's why I came to Kismet in the first place), but it was like trying to forget about the four-year-old seated behind you on a plane, crying and screaming as he worked all four of his limbs against the back of your seat.

In the way that I despised the appeasement Democrats far more than George Bush, I had the most trouble relating to people who *knew* the war was a shitstorm, who *knew* Bush was a wrong-headed incompetent, but were just not fazed by grand-scale death and destruction waged in their name. Most of these people came from the upper classes, and without a draft, they didn't have to worry about their younger brothers receiving an all-expenses-paid vacation to Fallujah. That nineteen-year-old who got sawed in half by an IED outside of Mosul? He was someone else's brother. (Besides, *he volunteered*...) These people never stopped shopping or poring over celebrities or blowing off their electoral steam on "American Idol." They were behaving just the way Karl Rove wanted 'em to.

This made me feel as though I were at a huge party where everyone was cruising on the coolest drug except me. Somehow I had been left out, and this created in me a low-simmering testiness. Whenever someone in the house got worked up over whatever it was that Tom Cruise said to Matt Lauer, I would think of Guantanamo Bay; I'd want to shake that person and demand to know how they could become so offended by a single Hollywood jackass when Dick Cheney was climbing out of bed every morning to take a great big dump on our Constitution.

Why did my mind work this way? Why couldn't I get that people were free to ignore whatever they wanted? That they were free to be offended by whatever they wanted? Why, for me, did all roads of stupidity lead to Iraq? Whoever half-capped the OJ was not responsible for marching our troops off into a meat grinder, and my stewing over that stupid war was not going to prevent a single soldier from returning to this country as a quadriplegic.

This was when I realized that my way of processing the news about Iraq and our country was staggeringly dysfunctional and that I needed to work on it.

I began loading dishes into the dishwasher when Maurice came upstairs carrying a five-gallon paint bucket. "Look what I got." His bucket bore two bluefish. "I'll clean 'em if you cook 'em," he said.

"You got it," I said. "Let's make fish cakes."

"Do you know how to do that?"

"I'll figure it out."

I had recently eaten fried fish cakes that my neighbor Nick had made from blues he had reeled in, and they were delicious. Cooking was still the best way to take my mind off unpleasantness, and it felt good to focus on something as mundane as figuring out fish cakes.

That afternoon, Gwen—the midweeker whom Rule Number One had asked if I was screwing back in July—returned with her husband, Tim. Later that night, we all sat down to a dinner of fish cakes and grilled asparagus, and I really wasn't thinking about anything beyond the kitchen and the house— until we went to The Inn to catch the last performance of the season by the Empire State Stompers, the Dixieland jazz band. Outside The Inn, an old-timer stood near the door, smoking a cigarette. He wore one of those FDNY-NYPD 9/11 shirts with the towers and a flag and an eagle beneath the words

NEVER FORGET. Whenever I see any of that "Never Forget" regalia, it only makes me think of how we fucked up nailing Osama bin Laden when we had him pinned down at Tora Bora. With Osama still on the loose and the Taliban having reconstituted itself in Afghanistan after we got distracted in Iraq, I wondered how we could possibly forget who did 9/11 more than we already had.

Justin, the bartender, took my drink order, and we sat down at one of the empty tables in front as the Empire State Stompers began their last set. The banjo player sat on a stool in front of the mike and said, "We've got a war going on right now, and I don't care what your politics are, but we're going to play this song to show our support for our troops over in Iraq. Here it is. 'The Battle Hymn of the Republic.'"

Great, I thought. That's just great. Only the trumpeter began the intro, slowly, patiently, until it sounded almost like "Taps." Then the banjo and the other players joined in, drawing out the first verse and turning that rah-rah thumper into a dirge. Their elegiac rendition gave me the chills. Staring at that American flag on the back wall beneath the word LIBERTY, I finished my cognac.

"Hey, John?" Tim pointed at my empty snifter as he rose from the table. "You want another one?"

"No, thanks," I said. "I'm good."

* * *

A lot of people ditched work early on Friday for the holiday weekend. Once they started to arrive, I began zipping around the house like a lunatic, rocking out the OCD and busying myself with whatever popped into mind until Rule Number One wound around the walkway and I had her in my arms.

"It's really nice to see you," I said.

"Where is everyone?" She looked around.

"They all went to get ice cream at Ocean Beach."

"We're all alone?"

"Uh-huh." I pulled her into my room.

For the very first time, we were alone in the house, and I wasn't about to drag out anything. I began to paw at her, pulling down the back of her curls and kissing her neck.

"Wait a minute," she said.

"What?"

"Can we go up to Baltic?"

I snatched the top sheet off my bed. "Let's go." I led Rule Number One upstairs and up the ladder into Baltic, where I spread out my sheet on that queensized mattress, watching her expression in the mirror on the wall as I pulled off

her clothes.

"I missed you," I said to her reflection in the mirror.

"I missed you, too."

Some time later—really at about the most inopportune time possible— the crew returned from Ocean Beach and walked upstairs into the living room. We stopped moving and I could hear Tina say, "Is someone up in Baltic?" Rule Number One began to laugh, and I cupped a hand over her mouth, dreading our walk of shame. Rule Number One couldn't have cared less. A peal of laughter escaped from beneath my hand. I looked down at her writhing beneath me, her dark curls splayed across the pillow. We picked up our pace, and the voices down in the living room began to fade away. I clamped my hand tighter over her mouth, watching us in the mirror.

*   *   *

After lunch on Saturday, I followed Joe as he carried the knapsack filled with my heirloom bocce balls down to the beach. While we were evenly matched, Joe swept me in our first best-of-three. He followed up by winning our next seven-point game, then taking a six-one lead in game two, on the verge of sweeping me again.

"So," I finally managed to say. "How're things going with Tina?"

"We're going to Disney World." He laughed, twirling a finger in the air. "Whoo-hoo!"

"Seriously," I said. "How are things going?"

"Seriously," he said. "We're going to Disney World. Our whole families are going. Both of us have nieces and nephews who've never been, so they're pretty excited."

"Are your families meeting for the first time?"

"Yeah. That's the whole point of the trip."

This was the first time that Joe had ever mentioned—even obliquely— marriage. In many ways, Joe was the stereotypical guy. (I've never seen anyone look more at peace than Joe lying on the couch next to a bowl of nachos while watching *The Simpsons*.) A true caveman, Joe didn't express himself much, and with the sole addition of basic cable, would have been perfectly happy in the Paleolithic Era. I've had deeper conversations with lesser friends. So while Tina's drunken make-out session still baffled me, it sort of made sense that it unfolded with the overly-emotive Faux-Gay Clay. Still, what was I to do with that information? Didn't I have a responsibility to tell him what Rule Number One had told me now that he was two steps away from marriage?

Joe's last ball was sitting right on top of the *pallino*, or the "pell," as we called it. Unless I could dislodge him, the game would be his. I lined up my shot and landed a direct hit, sending the pell off on its own. Lining up my next shot, I remembered Joe's advice: It's all about patterns. Maybe this was just a sign of Tina's apprehension (like when Joe treated me to his "I've-been-fucking-thesame-woman-for-three-years" comment). Maybe she was nervous about getting married and just made a mistake.

I decided that a single, drunken, above-the-waist infraction didn't outweigh a three-year relationship—especially one that was on its way to Disney World.

With my last ball, I won the round. Come-from-behinds are frequent in beach bocce, and I patiently took the rounds, trash-talking and keeping control of the pell until I came back, crushing Joe.

*   *   *

That night, Bicycle Bill was hosting Kismet's annual BLT, a party where everyone must come dressed in black tie, lingerie, or a toga. (I keep hoping that someone might host a real BLT party, where everyone smears their bodies with mayonnaise and then rolls in bacon, lettuce, tomato, and toast, and everyone just eats off of everyone else...) Abby and Sabrina invited me to join their house for a seafood boil that night. (They scheduled theirs around our Cajun shrimp boil so that they could borrow my jet burner and fifty-quart stockpot.) I had asked Abby if I could also bring Rule Number One, and we decided to put on our togas so that we could then go straight to Bicycle Bill's. Wrapped up in one of the blue top sheets, Rule Number One's curls spilled over her bare shoulder, making her look vaguely nurse-like.

"You look really pretty," I said.

"Thanks, Mister. You're looking rather pretty there yourself."

Remembering the night when I made her stand in the corner and the amount of work required to break her down enough to take a compliment, I hardly expected her to openly receive that one.

Abby and Sabrina had a great house on the ocean block of East Lighthouse Walk. When we stepped inside, Jackson zipped back and forth in front of me, panting as he reared up on his hind legs.

"Relax!" I called out to him, hunching over to pat his neck and chest. "Don't fucking die, okay?"

Abby laughed. We stepped inside and I kissed her hello. Then I led Rule Number One up the stairs to the roof deck where, like Bicycle Bill, they enjoyed a 360-degree bay-to-ocean view. The sun was setting behind the lighthouse, and I clutched Rule Number One's hand.

"Check it out," I said.

"Did you ever have sex with Abby?"

Remembering how angry I had become six weeks earlier when Rule Number One had asked me point-blank if I was fucking Gwen, this just didn't faze me. Sometimes, communicating with Rule Number One was like flying from New York to Boston via Dallas-Fort Worth. Jealousy had no better friend than Insecurity; so even though it was the second time Rule Number One had asked me if I had gotten biblical with Abby, I took it to mean that she cared for me.

"Nope," I said, squeezing her hand. "Look at the sunset. Look at all the pink."

She gave the sunset a cursory glance before turning back to scope out the other people on the deck.

*　*　*

We joined other house members at the BLT. In the corner, I spotted Tracy leaning against Alan. Something about their body language and their attention to one another made me suspect that this was more than just horizontal refreshment. So I went to the source:

"What's going on with Tracy and Alan?" I asked.

"They've met up in the City," Rule Number One said.

I thought they made a nice couple, that Alan's dry wit complemented Tracy's cosmopolitan swagger. Then I spotted Maggie and Maurice, also looking rather couple-y. Although people probably looked at Rule Number

One and me and thought that we were more serious than we were, so who knew?

We climbed the spiral staircase to the roof deck, where I recognized people from different sharehouses. I also saw Jeannie, who wore a sequined bustier and fishnet stockings, and Doctor Stern, who wore an electric blue wig and what looked like a black rubber corset beneath a pink boa. Alexis, the topless fisherman, was clad in a bedsheet and I joked that this was the most dressed up I had seen her all summer. Next to her stood that heavily pierced and tattooed bi couple from Motel-O (the one that weaseled out of their fifteen-dollar share for group sex). Nearby, Natasha was dancing with Bicycle Bill, who looked to be enjoying himself very much. Watching him, I wondered just how long I might manage Chance. Forty was only six years away; would I still be doing this when I was forty? Or fifty? Would my group age with me or would I gradually end up partying with people decades younger than me? At sixty, would I be sneaking large quantities of fiber into Saturday night dinners? Would five ounces of gin be replaced with a slug of Geritol?

If you can't find a particularly good reason to grow up, Kismet is about the best place to be. It's like a geriatric college where classes are permanently cancelled. And with the whole country working overtime to further enrich billionaire war profiteers, the Peter Pan Complex fit like a glove. Still, I doubted that I would be doing this when I was Bicycle Bill's age—although he certainly looked like he was having fun, and what was more important than that?

The song came to an end, and Bill approached me. "Hey, doctor."

"Hey, Bill. Nice party."

"Are you kidding me?" A look of disbelief and borderline offense came over Bill's face. "It's a fucking GREAT party!"

"Absolutely," Rule Number One said, but Bill was already off, returning to the throng dancing on his roof deck.

Meanwhile, the pierced, tattooed bi couple was openly checking out Rule Number One. The woman sidled up to us.

"Do you want to do shots?" the woman said to Rule Number One.

"Sure," she said.

We stepped over to a folding table, and the woman grabbed four plastic shot glasses and the bottle of tequila. We all threw one back, and then the woman poured another round, treating Rule Number One to a set of fuck-me eyes that couldn't have been more obvious. After our second round, the woman wanted to do a third, but I declined.

"C'mon. We don't need him," the woman joked (or not), nudging Rule Number One. "You look so sexy. Have another one with me."

"I will," she said. "I just need to take a little breather."

We wandered over to the railing.

"So," I said, "I think that woman might be interested in you."

"Ya think?" She shook her head and then a sly, detached look came over her face. "Actually, she's pretty hot."

Rule Number One, so far as I knew, was not into women. She didn't even like pretty boys and complained whenever I shaved. At six feet, 175, I was not exactly petite. (And when you eat the way I do, washboard abs are not part of the picture...) Yet Rule Number One had communicated—in her most indirect style—that if I were a burlier, more bearded, Ultimate-Fighting-Championship kind of grunter, that would have worked out quite well for her. So I wondered if, having exhausted trying to make me jealous with other men, she thought to give it a try with women. I called her on it.

"Do you want to kiss her?" I said.

"I don't know. Kind of."

"If you want to kiss her," I said, "you should kiss her."

She shrugged.

"You really do look very sexy," I said.

She smiled and took the compliment, and I thought about how we had arrived at that point, once again, via Dallas-Fort Worth.

Where the willingness is great, the difficulties cannot be great.

Was that really true? Could Rule Number One and I ever figure each other out? Would our communication improve if our relationship maybe had a wee bit of structure?

"Let's go for a walk," I said.

"Okay."

We left the party and walked out to the beach. It was warm and a thick fog hung in the air, illuminating the swipe of the lighthouse. We walked westward past the slip road and I pulled Rule Number One against me, running my hands down her back.

"You know what the best part of the BLT is?"

"No," she said. "What?"

I pulled off my sheet and spread it out on the sand. "You don't need to go back to the house for a blanket."

*　　*　　*

Early on Sunday morning, when the sun was just coming up and we had only been asleep for a couple of hours, I woke up to find Rule Number One leaning over my chest, staring sleepy-eyed at the window next to my bed.

"Hey," I said.

"Who's that girl?" She pointed at the window, shrinking back as though scared, her lids half-open.

"What are you talking about?"

"That girl outside." She leveled a timid finger toward the crack between the window and the blinds, like a little girl pointing out a bully to the teacher. "She wants you to sneak away and have sex with her."

"Rule, baby, there's no one there." I placed a hand on her cheek, and then her eyes fully opened.

"I'm sorry." She shook her head. "I was having a night terror." She lay back and closed her eyes.

That was a night terror?

I had imagined her being terrorized by knife-wielding psychos, not thong-stretching bimbos. In trying to figure out her supersized jealousy, I never imagined that she might even be jealous in her sleep. Her chest rose and fell, and she promptly drifted off—but I didn't.

*　　*　　*

Rule Number One once quipped that her idea of hell was lying in bed with me while I watched Sunday morning talk shows.

A few days earlier, Hurricane Katrina had struck the Gulf Coast, and we lay in my bed, watching Tim Russert interview Aaron Broussard, the Jefferson Parish President. Broussard, while describing how a coworker's stranded mother died, broke down in the middle of the interview.

I hadn't paid much attention to Katrina. While I knew it was not your average hurricane, I had put my faith in American can-do-ism, figuring we'd repair the damage and move on. Matt and I had had a blast at Jazzfest just a few months earlier and had talked about going back to New Orleans in 2006. That morning, however, I became aware of Katrina's enormity. Watching the devastated, unshaven Broussard sobbing in the throes of exhaustion as he described the failure of FEMA and all other levels of government was the most dramatic moment I had ever witnessed on a Sunday morning talk show, bringing home how a great American city had been left for dead. Rule Number One finished her iced coffee and stared down at her glass, knocking around the melting cubes. During the commercial, I tried to relate to her what was just then sinking in for me—that Katrina had laid bare just how badly our government and institutions had been wormed out.

"When we can't even rescue these people stranded on their roofs, from a natural disaster that arrived with a warning, what's going to happen the next time we're attacked by terrorists?"

A concerned look came over Rule Number One's face, but I knew that she was indulging me, that she would prefer to have the TV tuned in to just about anything else, that—as she had joked—it was her idea of hell.

I pulled her closer and buried my face in her neck, almost disbelieving how good she smelled. I had learned long ago that smell is an integral part of attraction, that when you think someone smells good, it does something to your brain that can cause you to convince yourself of all kinds of things. So even after witnessing her insecurity-fueled night terror a few hours earlier, I still lay there, selling myself on that old cliché that opposites attract. If that was really true, then we were like Tracy and Hepburn. Now that I *knew* that the news was taking a toll on my well-being, didn't it make sense for me to be with someone like Rule Number One? Whenever she made me laugh, I certainly wasn't thinking about Iraq. Had I been dating a fellow news junkie, we would have surely talked a lot more about stuff that is downright depressing.

Still, the Bush Administration's radical takeover of our government was the most monumental course of events in the United States since World War II. If it were 1943, could I have dated someone who was indifferent about whether or not we defeated Hitler? If I were living in occupied France, could I lie next to someone who felt that collaboration with the Germans was better than fighting with the French Resistance?

I could hear Mandy and Dani coming down the stairs, expressing their outrage over Britney Spears' mothering skills and I realized, then and there, that I was the freak. We just didn't care. We were the United States of Apathy, and Rule Number One was just part of the zeitgeist. I was the freak. The hot-and-bothered freak raising a stink. What kind of fucked up Charlie-Brown-charging-the-football masochist was I to set myself up for this misery over and over and over again?

"Come on," I said, squeezing Rule Number One. "It's time for breakfast."

*   *   *

After breakfast, I rode down to the dock to pick up the shrimp I had ordered for our Cajun shrimp boil (our version of a Louisiana low-country boil, in which we substitute shrimp for crawfish and use Italian sausage instead of andouille sausage). Fifteen pounds of shrimp would be boiled in the stockpot with sausages, corn, potatoes, green beans, and Cajun spice, all of it tossed onto a paper-covered table out on the deck.

Eating, like sex, should engage all five senses, only too many people (here I point my freshly licked finger at excess politesse) give short shrift to Touch. Whether it's sushi or the head of a fish, a chicken leg or a rib, I love food that you eat with your hands. The Cajun shrimp boil was my absolute favorite meal, because not only are there no utensils, there aren't even plates. You just reach out with both hands and grab whatever looks good. On the table, that is.

Everyone was down at the beach, enjoying the lush, balmy afternoon when I returned to the house, plugged my iPod into the stereo, and dialed up Metallica's *Load*. While engaging in a bit of low-impact headbanging, I grabbed a cutting board and our cartoon-sized cleaver, making a detour to the bathroom to check that the first aid kit was still under the sink. I have never gone to culinary school, nor do I have any formal training as a cook; no one has ever shown me the proper way to swing a cleaver; I am the equivalent of a drunken yahoo having just rented a turbo-juiced jet ski. (Or a former Texas governor dropped behind the desk in the Oval Office.) Ears of corn can be easily snapped into thirds, but bringing down that cleaver over and over again upon so many helpless vegetables with Metallica pumping from the speakers was, if you can imagine, more gratifying. (I liked to imagine that those furious power chords might somehow exorcise my house of the evil sound-wave demons of Justin Timberlake.) I began swinging the cleaver in time with the music, bringing it down on the sausages, halving them. Then I quartered the onions, sending chunks skittering off the board.

I tossed the sausages and the onions (as well as two packages of Cajun spices I had brought back from New Orleans) into my stockpot and covered everything with water. Out on the deck, I fired up the jet burner and set the pot over the flame. Sitting down to mind the flame, I could already smell the infusion of the spices and I remembered Jazzfest. After two full days, the music had begun to impinge upon my eating and I blew off some of the concerts for long walks, even riding the ferry across the Mississippi for a stroll in the sleepy neighborhood of Algiers.

On the third day, I had rejoined Matt after he returned from the fairgrounds. We met at a restaurant during the cocktail hour, and he ordered a dozen oysters. I had come away from my years in France underwhelmed by oysters. That they are so expensive in New York hardly heightened my interest in a delicacy I had thought overrated—until I tasted one of those Gulf Coast oysters. They were so sweet and succulent and simply head and shoulders above any oyster that I had ever eaten in France. I was beside myself. And at seven bucks a dozen, they cost half of what oysters cost in New York. Instead of ordering entrees, we just ordered more oysters, washing them down with Sancerre until we were satisfied.

Munching unlimited oysters is quite different from staring down at a mere half-dozen, watching them, one by one, disappear. And these just tasted so much better. Sitting across from Matt, I worked some rough calculations: If I were to eat another fifteen dozen Gulf Coast oysters at that price, I would completely absorb the cost of my flight. I had momentarily forgotten that this would only make sense if I actually had a mind to eat fifteen dozen oysters in New York at New York prices. But it wasn't the first flight of fancy that I had experienced while wandering around that lush city. When I think of New Orleans, drunk girls flashing their tits on Bourbon Street do not first come to mind; I think of the people sitting on their porch swings sipping drinks and conversing in the shade of their verandas. I loved their relaxed yet cordial manner. Music (good music) was a part of their day, every day. Eating unhurried meals with their friends and family was a part of their day, every day. Most unlike New York City, time in New Orleans didn't always equal money, and I have never been to an American city that was more epicurean.

Maybe it's not a coincidence that many of those people originally came from France, as I had enjoyed a lifestyle with a similar emphasis in Paris and Normandy. In the way that African rhythms survived generations of slavery and sharecropping to show up in the blues, I wondered if an epicurean sensibility was passed down from these people who disembarked France in the early 1600s. They arrived in Acadia (what is now Nova Scotia) only to get deported to the New England colonies by the English before the French and Indian War. Families were split apart and many of these people ended up in New Orleans. In fact, the word "Cajun" is just a slurred form of the word "Acadian." My mom grew up in the French-speaking part of Northern Maine, and these people were my forebears. When she married my father, a second-generation Italian-American, she was the first person in her line to have broken out from that French gene pool. Maybe that's why I liked the Cajun culture so much; maybe my DNA was just enjoying a 400-year reunion.

Joe came upstairs and grabbed a glass. "So," he said, approaching the kegerator, "people are naked in the hot tub."

"Really?"

He flipped open the tap. "Hey, you mind if I turn off the music and put the TV on?"

"Go right ahead." I crossed the living room and stepped out onto the deck. After not succumbing to Rule Number One's jealousy tactics the night before, I wondered if she was now, quite literally, breaking out the big guns. I braced myself and approached the railing, leaning over to indeed find three sets of bobbing boobies, none of which, thankfully, belonged to Rule Number One. Mandy and two women from Abby and Sabrina's house were joined by Rufus and some guy I didn't know, all of them passing a magnum of white wine. Suddenly, the jets timed off (as they do every fifteen minutes) and the bubbles cleared, revealing that the five of them were indeed quite naked. They pressed the button and powered the jets back on, and I stepped back into the living room.

On the TV, it was still all Katrina all the time, and one of the talking heads blamed local corruption. I stepped out to the deck and pulled the lid off the stockpot. Taking in that divine aroma of sausage and cayenne pepper, I realized that my desire to dine well in large groups had become more fundamental as our country became increasingly corrupt. New Orleans' motto was *"Laissez les bons temps rouler."* Let the good times roll. For the poorer people especially, good times were all they had. All that they ever had. Maybe my evangelical reinforcement of the epicurean life stemmed from some deep-seated fear that, if our country kept getting weaker, good times might one day be all that I would ever have as well, and were therefore something to protect. The lid of the stockpot began to dance on the rim, and I turned down the heat.

Rule Number One returned from the beach to check up on me. We lined up the folding tables out on the deck and were joined by Natasha.

"So there's naked people in the hot tub," Natasha said in a schoolmarmish tone. "Very interesting."

She helped Rule Number One cover the tables with brown paper while I tossed the corn into the pot, followed by the shrimp. Then I began mixing the dough for beignets—New Orleans' famous pastry—that we'd later deep fry, cover with powdered sugar, and then serve with prosecco for dessert. Maurice helped me wheel the kegerator out onto the deck, then I went down to my room and stole my brother Francis's trick: I pulled off my shorts and boxer-briefs and put on a speedo bathing suit. (I *swear* that I own one for exercise purposes only.) Then I pulled my boxer-briefs and shorts back on top of them. In the e-mail update, I had suggested that the Cajun shrimp boil should be eaten while wearing as little as possible. Having a base of naked people in the hot tub, I wanted to see if I could strip the rest of them down.

Upstairs, with everyone gathered around the table, Matt and I drained the boil, mixed in two sticks of butter, and then poured out all that spicy goodness in a fragrant, steaming row on the table. I sat down next to Rule Number One, and as people started to reach for the food, I wanted to say something about Katrina, but a festive mood abounded. After my morning in bed with Rule Number One, I buttoned my lip, deciding that other people might think it a downer. I was reaching for a shrimp when Vanessa stood and raised her glass.

"Since we're eating a Cajun shrimp boil, I think we should think about New Orleans. We're so lucky to be able to share our great lives together out here at the beach, so let's not forget that they're having a really hard time down there right now."

God, I was glad to hear her say that.

We raised our glasses, and then I grabbed a shrimp, tossing it back with a piece of sausage and a slug of beer. Then I remembered my shorts...

"By the way," I broke the silence. "This meal was meant to be enjoyed wearing as few clothes as possible."

I wiggled out of my Bermudas and tossed them to the side. A couple of people laughed. Then I slid off my boxer briefs and twirled them in the air before letting go. I figured someone would look beneath the table to see if I was really naked, but no one did. Then Mandy let out a whoop and pulled off her top. Matt pulled off his shirt and so did the other guys, and then a few other women followed Mandy's lead, stripping down to bras and bikini tops.

It felt good to have the summer winding down. Ever since I was a kid, summer moved too fast for me. Now, running Chance had slowed summer down enough that for the first time in my life I was ready to move on with it. I licked my fingers and then dropped my hand onto Rule Number One's thigh, giving it a squeeze before reaching back to that spicy bounty spilled out before me.

Deep-Fried Oreos

After Labor Day, I hit a wall. Somehow, I had forgotten that two more weeks remained in our season. Two more weekends of meals to executive produce, two more trips to the liquor store and the beer distributor and, of course, two more trips to Costco. What was really starting to wear on me, however, was the lack of downtime. For three-and-a-half months, I had not spent a single night home alone. Upon schlepping my last load back from Costco, I began to question whether being "The Hardest Working Man in Sharehouse Business" was really worth all that glamour. Pulling my garden cart up the ramp to the house, I once again indulged my daydream of running Chance without providing food or coordinating meals. No more taking inventory, no more dodging seniors in Costco, and no more schlepping. Everyone would figure out what to bring and then divide up the receipts, and I could just stay above it all.

While my title had spurred and distracted me at a critical time, now it just sounded silly—like declaring oneself the hardest working dog walker, or the world's best Zamboni driver. While I've never received an e-mail from Bill Gates, I doubted that his signature included the line "Richest Motherfucker on the Planet." He just was and everyone knew it. So I decided that if I did end up providing the same level of service in 2006, I would do so without an outlandish title. After unloading the food, I crashed down at my desk and removed "The Hardest Working Man in Sharehouse Business" first from the website and then from my e-mail. My e-mail signature no longer looked so unwieldy. Just address, telephone, e-mail, and URL. It looked like the signature of a normal person.

Grace was the first weekender to arrive. "Hang on," she called out, dropping off her bag. "I've got something for you."

"Did you bring me a present?" I jokingly rubbed my hands together like an expectant child. Only I couldn't have been more surprised when she did in fact present me with a box bearing a bow. I opened it and pulled out a scarf knitted from the same blue and green yarn I had seen her working with out on the deck.

"I know you're going to be out here by yourself into the fall, so I hope this helps keep you warm once it cools down."

I hugged her. "That was really nice of you." I shook my head.

"What?" she said.

I remembered Grace's first weekend at the house and her attempt to read the *New Yorker* while everyone was partying and how her row had once been painted red in my spreadsheet. I never imagined then that Grace might loosen up enough to contribute to the house, only it was all the epicurean stuff—the sous-cheffing, the cooking, the group swim—that drew her out of her shell. Now I could only hope that she'd come back in 2006.

"Nothing," I said. "Thank you."

*   *   *

Aside from my indecisiveness about Rule Number One, I had begun to notice a delayed emotional response in myself to all sorts of things. (Even when Grace gave me the scarf, it took me a minute to fully grasp the thoughtfulness of her gesture. Maybe spending the entire summer in a sharehouse is the polar opposite of four months in solitary.) This is an overcomplicated way of saying that I was burned out. Despite feeling emotionally spent, I had also noticed a marked uptick in my appetites. I had been eating and drinking more, popping my acid reducers like candy, all while anticipating the return of Rule Number One. With my appetites boxing out my other feelings and reflection in short supply, I abdicated any responsibility to consider what might happen between us after the summer. What made this even easier was the fact that Rule Number One never sweated the future. Far in the outer reaches of my emotional landscape, a tiny warning light began to flash, suggesting that this was not a license for me to blow off the future as well. But when Rule Number One finally arrived, I wasn't thinking about what might become of us after the weekend; I wasn't even thinking about the next five minutes.

Men are so simple and yield so readily to the desires of the moment.

I led her into my room and closed the door behind us.

*   *   *

On Saturday, just before sunset, Vanessa and I tapped our last pony keg of home-brew—a Belgian porter—out on the beach. Maggie and Risa carried down platters of bite-sized slices of cornbread topped with chorizo and goat cheese. Only a couple of days away from the equinox, the sun was now shining at a lower angle, lighting up the turquoise sheets of water sliding over the surf until they almost looked metallic.

Uptalking Nancy had brought out a guest, and after the cocktail hour, the two of them ditched our dinner of lamb couscous with white raisins in favor of cheeseburgers at The Out.

For dessert, Risa and I set up the candy thermometer in a pan of oil to once again deep-fry Oreos. After the flutes of prosecco were passed around, I was about to dig in, when Chris put his spoon to the glass.

"Hang on, John," he said, rising up from the table. "We've got something for you."

Vanessa raised her glass. "Let's make a toast to John." She turned and faced me. "We really appreciate how you stock the house and organize so much of the fun stuff we do and fix everything after we break it and then fix it again. We know it's a lot of work dealing with all of us, and so we wanted to get you a little something to show our thanks."

Chris handed me a small box. I pulled off the lid and unfolded what looked like an official-looking certificate. My eyes fell down to the words "The Hardest Working Man in Sharehouse Business." I inwardly groaned, thinking it a goof, that they had just made up some cheesy certificate proclaiming what I had just deleted from all of my materials—until I saw the word "Cessna." In fact, they had given me a certificate granting me a lesson and a flight in a Cessna over Fire Island. My jaw dropped, and I gaped at Vanessa.

"Once when we were on the beach," Vanessa said, "you mentioned that you'd like to fly over Fire Island. Now you can."

While Grace's gift had caught me off guard, this one floored me. I hadn't been expecting anything of the sort and it couldn't have come at a better time.

"To the Hardest Working Man in Sharehouse Business," Vanessa said, once again raising her glass.

With Nancy and her guest at The Out, I was most pleased to see that no one assembled beneath the dim glow of the chandelier had had their row painted red. I told them that it was about the nicest gift that I had ever received. Part of me wanted to tell them how their help in building something at a time when everything else seemed to be falling apart had saved me, that by participating with such enthusiasm and upping the epicurean ante, they had made it that much better, only I didn't know where to begin. Before I knew it, the following words flew out of my mouth:

"Thank you. I love you all."

*   *   *

Late that night, after Rule Number One and I had fallen asleep, something woke me up. She still lay unconscious next to me, but I could feel something stirring. The house was moving—only it wasn't particularly windy out. Still, I could feel a barely perceptible rocking, and then I knew what it was: Maurice and Maggie in Baltic.

The Lovely Miss Margaret was getting her groove on.

The rocking picked up a bit in intensity, and then in speed, and then, suddenly, it stopped.

Nice, I thought, closing my eyes. While my future with Rule Number One was still up in the air, at least Maggie and Maurice (as well as Tracy and Alan) had come together because of Chance—although maybe it was just Kismet.

*   *   *

After brunch on Sunday, Rule Number One and I walked down to the beach. She put on her iPod earphones and then lay back on her towel, closing her eyes. Gazing at her body, I wondered if that morning was the last time we would ever be together. Would I never again cup her shoulders beneath me? Would I never again—

Suddenly, something bit my left ankle. A large green-and-black fly then moved over to my right ankle for another stinging chomp before flying away. A few minutes later, my ankles began to itch. The itching intensified until I could barely think straight. I went back to the house and coated my ankles with anti-itch cream, but the itching felt as though it were coming from my bones. Then I noticed a lump forming on the side of my heel. Upon planting my feet on the ground, that lump had no feeling—just a swelling numb patch amid all that burning, and it seemed to be getting larger. Fearing that I was experiencing an allergic reaction—the kind that can balloon-swell body parts—I punched up Doctor Furie in Saltaire, who agreed to see me.

(Something I never mention to potential recruits who are doctors or nurses is that unless they are total jackasses, I'd probably offer them a spot. My boogie-boarding accident and a few other accidents around the house only highlighted how hard it can be to get quick medical attention on Fire Island, and having a couple of doctors or nurses in the house would just make me feel better.)

Dylan offered to come with me to Saltaire. I would have preferred to go with Rule Number One, but it seemed like a rather girlfriendy thing to do at a time when our status was uncertain. We pedaled over to Saltaire. The itching, while still intense, had started to subside. I could now form complete sentences, and the swelling patch on my heel was getting smaller. Still, Doctor Furie checked me out, explained that there was probably some kind of venom still running its course, and gave me fifty milligrams of Benadryl. Back at the house, the itching had almost stopped. It was still quite sunny out, so I tapped a beer in a plastic cup to take down to the beach, rejoining Rule Number One.

The surfers were out in full force, enjoying the hurricane-season waves, and I sipped my beer while watching them carving up the surf. I became engrossed by one of them who rode a wave clear across the beach before finally stalling out. While watching him sink back into the water, the strangest feeling came over me. I have little experience with pharmaceutical drugs. I've never taken Valium or Xanax or any of the new kids in that class of Mother's Little Helpers, so I wasn't expecting what came next. That double dose of Benedryl (and a pint of beer) rolled over me like a marshmallow tank, creating an odd dislocation, whereupon my dilemma over what to do with Rule Number One was laid out for me, almost clinically—only it didn't bother me in the least.

I felt *just...fine...*

I floated off on that beer and Benedryl cloud and into a leaden nap. When I woke up, my back ached and I wanted my bed. Badly. Back in my room, I conked out again, never knowing that sleep could feel so heavy, waking up to find Rule Number One lying next to me. When I began to stir, she made it clear that she wanted to do something more than cuddle. But I was still zonked and I felt about as sexy as George F. Will.

I climbed out of bed and trod upstairs, dialing the cappuccino machine to its strongest espresso setting. Only six or seven people were left at the house, and they were all taking the 7:05 ferry. The caffeine kicked in, and I could once again feel the jagged edges of reality.

"*So what are you gonna do?*"

I didn't have an answer for my little voice.

"*She's leaving today. Is it over or what?*"

I don't know, I thought, placing my empty cup back under the spout and punching up a second espresso, trying to jumpstart my mind, trying to put all of the pieces together.

"*If you can't answer that question, then you've already answered it.*"

All that I understood in that moment was that I felt sad. Very sad. My sadness was compounded by everyone's imminent departure. Despite having counted the days since Labor Day until everyone cleared out, it now pained me to think of them all going back to the City and leaving me in my very large house, alone, for another six weeks until my subletter vacated my condo. I had planned on using this time to start writing again, only I felt about as enthusiastic to write as I did about getting a Brazilian body wax. I had no interest in revisiting *Killing Mercutio*. None. So what was I supposed to write about?

Still trying to get my head straight in that state of half-power, my little voice, also struggling, coughed up the following:

"*Divide and conquer.*"

I went down to my bedroom, where Rule Number One was packing her bag.

"Do you want to stay here tonight?"

"I wish that I could."

"You can't take the death boat?"

"There's no more death boat. There's only the 7:25, and I've got a meeting early in the morning."

The other house members began congregating at the door. I considered walking them all down to the dock, but doubted I could bear the finality of watching Rule Number One board the ferry. They lined up to say good-bye to me on their way out the door, leaving Rule Number One and me standing alone in the hall.

"I'm so sad," I said.

"I am too."

I kissed her and then delivered the lamest, most noncommittal utterance that exists:

"I'll talk to you later."

"Okay." She walked out the door. I listened to the rollers of her suitcase clack over the walkway and down the ramp onto the sidewalk. Then I heard nothing.

Upstairs, the house was staggeringly quiet. With nothing needing my immediate attention, I wasn't sure what to do with myself. I flipped on the TV just to drown out the silence and then stepped out onto the deck. With the days getting shorter, the sun had already set. The moon hung low in the blue-black sky over the silver tops of the waves. I had taken in sights like this all summer long. Sunrises and sunsets; cardinals flitting from treetops; bucks meandering along the dune. Only now, without someone else to provide even the most mundane comment, all that natural wonder was almost too much. I knew that I needed to do something. Anything. I thought about trimming the bathroom window, but it was too late to run the table saw, and running a table saw was hardly a safe activity for a romantic basket case coming off a Benadryl bender. Wandering into the bathroom, however, I knew what to do.

The pennies.

I flipped off the TV and cracked open two rolls of pennies on a board, segregating heads and tails. After giving each one a dollop of construction glue, I carried the board into the bathroom and posted them up two at a time. Dumping out another two rolls, I remembered my father repairing that dining room chair after my grandmother died. Working on the house always made me feel better. Considering how much I had done, I wondered if I wasn't more depressed than I had ever acknowledged.

After pasting up a dozen rolls, my lower back began to ache. Standing up, I still felt fuzzy and slow and decided that I needed to get out of the house. Winding down the walkway, I wasn't feeling particularly conversational, so I turned left and began toward the beach. A pair of bucks stood on the dune, their heads turning in unison as they stopped to acknowledge me in the moonlight. I stood and watched them, forcing myself to take in the sight of them, alone. When I stepped onto the beach, the sand felt cool between my toes and I rocked from the left to the right just to make sure that golden, shimmering path that stretched out over the waves still hung perfectly centered between the moon and me. Turning around, I walked backward toward the surf, picking out the North Star. It was right where it always was, where it always would be. When the surf washed over my ankles, I could hear that Coney Island stoner:

Every time you go in the ocean, it can be a baptism.

I retreated onto the beach and pulled off my shirt and unbuttoned my shorts, letting them fall to the ground. Then I turned westward away from the moon and took off on a sprint along the surf. After passing the last houses, I picked up my clip, moving faster, faster, endorphins raging until my mind went blank and I could only feel the molten heat in my quads and my heart pounding against the dry ache in my lungs as I raced toward the glow behind the lighthouse.

Afterword

If you were to ask Michael Bloomberg and a Mexican dishwasher to describe New York City, they would surely focus on disparate aspects, detailing what might sound like two different cities. In this vein, anyone else in Kismet might paint a picture of the town and of Fire Island that bears little resemblance to mine. There are 250 houses in Kismet, and many of these people have been coming for decades.

Kismet, for me, is still a bit like high school, in that I'm swimming among a sea of names and faces that are familiar, but which I've yet to connect. Still, it would require another book altogether just to tell the stories of the many characters in town whom I already do know. Many of the people I've mentioned—like Bicycle Bill, Jeannie, Johnny Thunder, and Doctor Stern—have been given the most bare-bones treatment. Other Kismetians know that the above-mentioned people are far more complex, and that there are facets to their stories and their unique personalities that I haven't touched upon.

Kismetians are invariably going to approach me and say, "How could you write a book that takes place in Kismet and not mention Sam Wood? Or Greg Pecoraro? Or the Schumachers?" Indeed, these people and many others matter in ways that far surpass a few paragraphs. So I focused on the aspects of Kismet and Fire Island that helped tell the story that unfolded at Chance; there are 249 other houses in town and sixteen other communities on the island.

Fire Island and Kismet are wondrous in ways that I can't begin to describe. I'd tell you to come and see for yourself, only it's such a pain getting on and off the ferries with all the screaming children and barking dogs, and then you have to schlep your stuff from the dock and in case you didn't know, the whole island is *gay,* anyway, and all the celebrities and cool people go to the Hamptons, where you can actually, like, *drive.* (Hel*lo?*) Just take 495 to eastbound 27, and you're so totally there.

Recipes

Sherry-Infused Deep-Fried Turkey

First, get a fire extinguisher and enough booze to last two hours.

While many turkey fryers swear by peanut oil, it is not cheap and you need a couple gallons of the stuff. I use canola oil (which is a third of the price), and I cannot taste the difference when turkey frying. You probably want to buy a deep-frying kit, which comes with a tall, thin pot and a jet burner that hooks directly to a propane tank. Fill your pot with enough oil so that the bird will be submerged. Light the flame and drop in a candy thermometer. Get someone who is fairly sober to mind your flame while you prep your bird.

For a twenty-five-pounder, combine nine ounces sherry, nine ounces Worcestershire sauce, and a tablespoon of Dijon mustard. Load your syringe and stab the bird every couple of inches at a forty-five degree angle, inserting the needle a full inch. (If you see the skin ballooning as you depress the plunger, you're not deep enough.) For the rub, combine equal parts Old Bay seasoning, cumin, ground coriander, and salt. Coat entire bird, including the cavity. Cut a two-inch slit in the skin on either side, just beneath where the roundest part of the drumstick meets the thigh, to allow the oil to circulate and drain. Once your oil is at 350 degrees, lower the bird, inch by inch, into the pot. Then turn up the heat until the flames licking up the side of the pot are not too dangerously close to the rim. It will take a while for the temperature to climb back up to 350. Settle down to mind your flame with your fire extinguisher and your booze. If it's cold out, a large snifter of armagnac is superb. During the summer, beer is fine, but a jar filled with ice and bourbon just feels right. Also, if you happen to own a double-barrel thirty-aught-six, it might feel good to lay it across your lap. (If you manage to deter a terrorist attack while deep-frying, you will have truly earned your supper.) Once the thermometer reads 350 again, tweak the flame to keep the temperature pegged. Multiply the weight of the bird by three and check it after that many minutes in the oil. You can judge it pretty well by the skin, which should be golden brown. If it's not done, check it every ten minutes thereafter. Platter bird to thunderous applause, then assign the task of carving it up while you fry up some sweet potato fries, regular fries, turnip or yucca chips, or batter-dipped blooming onions in that meat-infused oil. Toss the vegetarians a hunk of tofu and tell them to figure it out for themselves.

Low-Fat Smoked Salmon Tartine Brunch

Since Pakistan has got nukes and Islamic fundamentalists in that country are regularly gunning for Musharaf's neck, thus putting scores of Crazy Motherfuckers Who Talk To God one bullet away from The Button, let's just say that I am not in the habit of cutting out fat for health reasons. But whenever the Apocalypse does happen upon us, I will die among a fringe group of eaters who never understood why people pummel the delicate creaminess of smoked salmon—one of those gastronomic delights that is never bad—with a shmear of cream cheese. Those of a less apocalyptic mindset might still consider this lower-fat version an improvement on a popular standby.

The next time you crave lox, avoid the badly parented children at your favorite brunch hole and head to the fish store, the bakery, and then the liquor store. In place of a bagel, use a fresh-baked sourdough baguette. (This, too, is lower in fat.) Back at home, don't bother with a knife—just break off a hunk of baguette and pry it open with your fingers for better texture. Moisten one side with fresh lemon juice. Add a generous amount of smoked salmon and pile on enough capers so that when you raise that tartine for your first bite, a couple dozen of them rain down upon your plate like a toxic hail. (A slice of tomato and a ring of Bermuda onion are optional. Also, if you require a shmear, do what you have to do.)

For dessert, spread half of the cream cheese you would have used on another hunk of baguette, add sliced strawberries, a teaspoon of raw brown sugar, a pinch of cinnamon, and a sprinkle of salt. Since you are in the mind frame of standalone items, prosecco is a perfect accompaniment for both of these courses.

For the full experience of an impromptu brunch on the Riviera, enjoy this meal while seated across from a topless French student of your preferred gender. If, after finishing (and hopefully before doing the dishes), the Apocalypse were to happen upon us, you'll die content; at bare minimum, this will recreate the true meaning of the word "brunch."

Christo

This variation of the Cosmo, without its telltale pink color, is a bit more acidic and a lot easier on your image. Shake together the following:

2 oz. vodka

1 oz. triple sec

½ oz. fresh-squeezed lime juice, strained of pulp

½ oz. cranberry juice

½ oz. orange juice

Serve straight-up in a chilled cocktail glass and garnish with a micro-thin orange slice.

After your fourth one, take a walk in Central Park, where you're guaranteed to see Christo and Jeanne-Claude's saffron sheets blowing in the wind once again.

Low-Fat Steak Tartare

Here are the problems with three-quarters of the steak tartare served in New York City restaurants:

1. Too many chefs mask the rawness of the meat with gobs of mayonnaise, serving up a dish for people who like the idea of eating steak tartare better than its actual taste.

2. They demote the dish to the appetizer column.

Steak tartare is not some pathetic little paramour. If you're going to eat tartare, commit to it. Toss out your little black book and embrace tartare. Tartare is now your main squeeze, and once you surrender to this dish, you will understand that having sampled all those cute little dishes on the side was such a waste of your time, that giving yourself over to the worldly character and body of this unique, misunderstood entree is the culinary bliss for which you've been searching all along.

Once again, so long as George Bush is president and Mahmoud Ahmadinejad is leading Iran, I'm not going to bother avoiding fat for health reasons. This recipe—that better embraces and accentuates the rawness of the meat—just happens to be healthier. Sirloin is already quite lean, and the only other fat in this dish comes from a small amount of olive oil and egg yolk. Here's what you'll need:

2 lbs. sirloin
1 red onion
3 tbs. capers
2 egg yolks
2 tbs. olive oil
1 tbs. apple cider vinegar
1 tsp. Dijon mustard
¼ cup chopped parsley
1 tsp. salt
1 tsp. cumin
1 tsp. ground coriander
2 tsp. black pepper
2 tbs. Worcestershire sauce
1 tsp. Tabasco

While you can run the sirloin through a meat grinder, I prefer to cut it into thin chunks that actually require a bit of mastication, as opposed to grinding it into mushy hamburger. Get a decent knife and just slice it as thin as you can and then cut those slices longways. Mix all of this with your hands in a plastic container. (It's best to prepare this dish beforehand. Cover and let it chill and macerate in the refrigerator for at least two hours before eating.) I like to plate tartare with any kind of a mold. Make columns or squares or trapezoids, as any geometric shape provides an elegant touch to this delicacy. Garnish with chips and a sprinkle of extra capers and parsley. Serve with either an arugula salad, or green beans cooked just enough so that they're still crisp, as well as chips or fries and crostini.

I will never understand people who refuse to try steak tartare due to fears of mad cow disease or other bacteria. I've been eating steak tartare for fifteen years, and it has never once made me sick. What a lot of people don't realize is that Atlantic salmon (the most overrated fish) contains incredibly high levels of mercury; in other words, Atlantic salmon, no matter how thoroughly cooked, is always bad for you. Besides, the idea of not eating something because it might be bad for you—at a time when our health and safety are regularly compromised to fluff billionaires—makes no sense to me. So even if it were dangerous to eat steak tartare, at least we would be getting great taste in return for our exposure to that risk. And in this day and age, that feels like empowerment.

When I make this for myself, I also add finely chopped jalapeno peppers and a lot more salt, so tweak it as you like. I can't tell you how much I love this dish. Beyond its great taste and presentation, it fills you with an all-over fullness that feels primal. I have no scientific evidence to support the following, but all that raw protein does something to you. If, for instance, you happen to be a man of a certain age who sometimes requires a certain blue pill to perform certain activities, let's just say that a big plate of tartare might leave more than a smile on the face of your companion, while leaving Pfizer standing out in the cold.

Chance House Breeze

While Dale De Groff's Belmont Breeze calls for simple syrup and 7-Up, that cocktail—like too many things served up to the masses—is too damn sweet. Corrupt government subsidies to agribusiness have already funneled enough high-fructose corn syrup down our throats. So this Chance house variation on Dale's great recipe is a little less sweet, a little more crisp, and a little less corrupt. Combine the following:

1½ oz. whiskey
¾ oz. cream sherry
¾ oz. fresh lemon juice
1½ oz. orange juice
1½ oz. cranberry juice

Mix and pour over ice in a collins glass and then top it off with two ounces of seltzer. (Add a bit of simple syrup or top with 7-Up, if you'd like it sweeter.) Garnish with a lemon twist, a strawberry, and a sprig of mint. When it comes to booze, you don't get much more underrated than whiskey and sherry, yet they join forces in this most crisp and refreshing cocktail. This is a lovely late-day cocktail, and even people who claim not to like whiskey will love it, resulting in them drinking so many of them that they will wake up feeling wretched and swearing off whiskey forever—or at least until next year's Belmont Stakes.

Deep-Fried Oreos

We must band together to defeat all that is middlebrow, to let the highbrow and the lowbrow live in harmony like lesbian lovers, transcending the bounds of traditional marriage until those virtues are embodied in their purest form: coexisting purely for true love. The heavy goodness of a deep-fried Oreo is perfectly complemented by the crisp lightness of a flute of prosecco, forming a NASCAR ballet in the mouth.

Bring a saucepan of canola oil to 350 degrees. While the oil heats up, follow the directions on the back of a box of Bisquik for pancakes, but use only two-thirds of the milk to create a sludge that will cling to those cookies like a bad date. Float them in the oil until the underside is golden brown. Flip 'em over and fry the other side. Drain over paper towels and then platter. Cover with a blizzard of powdered sugar, followed by a sprinkle of cinnamon.

Prosecco, the Italian take on Champagne, is as underrated as Champagne is overrated. As a person of half-French and half-Italian descent, I defer to my lower half in this area. You can purchase an excellent bottle for less than half of the cost of Champagne. People who have never tried it will forever remember you as the person-in-the-know who introduced them to this exquisite bubbly that can accompany just about any dish and has been known to result in horizontal refreshment.

Belief & Technique for Epicurean Sharehouse Management

Share and share and like.

Open always to Love and in meantime Horizontal Refreshment.

No hierarchy and sharehouse manager is necessary function, like septic tank only he smells better.

Sharehouse does not suck and is holy microcosm of Divine Universal Enlightenment and members go forth and bring Divine Universal Enlightenment to all they encounter except for people at DMV. Those fuckers are hopeless.

Be open and open-minded to receive Divine Universal Enlightenment only ask for it and you shall receive it immediately. Maybe give it a few minutes...

Money is not evil but enables fun and all transactions automatic.

To present cash upon arrival is divine act and doing so makes one radiate with inner light, never wanting for Love or Horizontal Refreshment.

Guests are extension and expression of house member and should never suck.

Guests are holy additions to house rendering all weekends equal.

Free-flow conversation always listening when not talking is verbal oral Krispy Kreme ecstasy and learn to avoid small talk.

To cook and eat and drink are godlike but in sharehouse caste system those who clean are Brahmins.

In sharehouse village all are parents/children responsible at play and looking out for all, especially during drunkenness.

Bitching is what dog do.

Never cook for one person but prepare ambrosia and pour nectar for all who have hunger and thirst.

Pork is not evil but holy pig is intelligent and dignified revered consumed with joy thanks and much Spirit.

Like Saint Julia Child fear not food nor drink but consume with passion and then stop at perfection. Or not too long thereafter...

Never too much garlic or too many onions only ginger use sparingly.

What you eat is eating you.

What you drink is drinking you.

What you smoke is smoking you.

Never have a third martini.

As ferryboat pulls away from mainland dock all stress/anxiety is gathered up and visually deposited onto random mainland house that grows smaller until house turns into speck and disappears along with stress/anxiety. Sucks to be people in that house.

To clean drip tray of kegerator and coffeemaker or any part of sharehouse is to purify soul.

Fire is life-giving and requires sober oversight when handled by mischievous brother.

Love is opposite of money and spending it freely makes one richer.

Love is like riding a bike coasting along in bliss only to suddenly take pole to nuts.

Do something unasked for other house member once per day. Do this for person with whom you are least acquainted and no matter what happens upon that day you will have performed this act that cleanses soul, combats despair, and brings unexpected Horizontal Refreshment.

Time is elastic and hurrynot going from A to B but stop at C and perform small house task when needed expressing faith in abundant sharehouse always open welcome thank you the management.

Sharehouse like campsite always left in better condition.

The Indian movie is always playing.

Smoke to get high, not to die and always mindful of nonsmokers.

Septic tank is not wastebasket, but holy natural processor and must never receive garbage or unnecessary paper or Hoffa.

Mindful of weather and storms and shut all windows and closed screen door is temple in two dimensions.

City can be cruel inhuman hamsterwheel and Higher Island is holy respite/ example/pathway/E-ZPass Lane to Paradise.

There are no rules only spirit of rules to be understood and interpreted always in flux modified for situation only no cokeheroin or cigarettesmoking indoors.

Jacuzzi is holy place of community sharing water life with all.

Cleansing oneself before entering Jacuzzi is direct expression of respect, love, and desire for continuity of all that is good.

Sharehouse like circus thrives on idiosyncrasies and all contribute through individuality.

Sharehouse like circus is pure fun and adults like children once again eternally.

Sharehouse like summercamp only not doing anything for first time.

If doing anything for first time, include sharehouse owner.

When making trip to house from beach bring back all that everyone needs that you can carry easy.

All cooking for others is divine and indulge like Saint Julia Child fearing neither fat nor consequences.

Hot dogs on beach are health food that warm soul and outweigh composition of processed lips and assholes.

Manager is carrying burlap sack of stones and members take a stone by itself is not heavy and smooth and cool talisman placed in pocket wards off stress/anxiety and syncs up with Universe like compass magnet locking in its tractor beam Love and Horizontal Refreshment.

Sharehouse exists on same spectrum but is polar opposite of hotel.

Surprise someone arriving at dock on sunny day with icy sunset cocktail not too potent but strong in Spirit.

Comfort and function are never fashionable but timeless like Ella.

There is no political correctness only no room for criminals or chiselers or Creationist Apocalyptic American Taliban.

There is no sword but rotisserie spit cooking evenly on all sides.

Glass is perfection, blasted and blown from elemental sand organic reused until broken back to sand. Plastic and styrofoam are chemical landfill ozone destroyers oozing with Cheneycinogens only for trips to beach and never indoors.

Never waste anything.

Never drink reflexively but when you want in quantity for relaxation and never punishment as expressed by Party Animal Frederick Douglass.

Either way, aspirin and ibuprofen in every bathroom.

Fear neither broom nor juicer for sand-free surfaces and fresh citrus are beach ecstasy.

Ocean is largest entity and proof of God-Jesus-Buddha-Krishna-Allah-Oprah and interconnectedness of all.

Never go straight from bar to house but stop at beach and give thanks in black and white. This is also a good time/place to puke.

Lounge and loll like infants in crib of present moment.

Quarter share like appetizer with no entree.

Quarter share like foreplay then night-night.

Larger share makes experience ongoing All-U-Can-Eat fluid ecstasy still burning like pilot light in offseason.

There is no offseason.

About the Author

John Blesso was born in Paterson, New Jersey. After receiving a B.A. in English and French from the University of Connecticut, he spent two years in Paris, where he performed The *Un-Hollywood Ending,* a one-man show. From 1995 to 2000, he served as the managing editor of the Authors Guild *Bulletin.* In 2004, he established the Chance beach house in Kismet, Fire Island. In 2005, Chance was featured in *New York Magazine.* In 2006, John Blesso was not awarded the Nobel Prize for Literature. He lives in New York. For more, please visit JohnBlesso.com.

9 780965 445238